S0-CJN-519

Our Legal Heritage

A law-focused education program for young Americans

ALABAMA STATE DEPARTMENT OF EDUCATION

Russell I. Berry
Former Consultant and Chief Specialist in Social Studies,

Marie H. Hendrix
Chief Social Studies Specialist,

W. Arthur Heustess
Coordinator, Basic Sciences Section,

SILVER BURDETT COMPANY **Morristown, New Jersey**
Glenview, Illinois • Palo Alto • Dallas • Atlanta

Program Contributors

END-OF-CHAPTER MATERIAL AUTHOR
Barbara Heenan Fink
Social Studies Teacher, Northern High School,
Dillsburg, Pennsylvania

TEACHER'S MANUAL AUTHOR
David N. Cowden
Social Studies Teacher, Jonathan Dayton High School,
Springfield, New Jersey

CRITIC READERS
Isabel W. Dible
Director of Instruction, Beverly Hills Unified School District,
California

Richard Epstein
Social Studies Teacher, Indian Hills High School,
Oakland, New Jersey

Barbara Heenan Fink
Social Studies Teacher, Northern High School,
Dillsburg, Pennsylvania

Michael S. Froman
Attorney-at-Law
Chicago, Illinois

CREDITS
Cover: *Matt Greene*
Chapter Opener Art: *James Flora*
Illustrations: *Marvin Friedman, Al Fiorento, Robert Barker*

ISBN 0-382-02451-6

Contents

Court Cases

DIAGRAMS

NO
PARKING

Our Legal System 1

Garcia *v.* Allan and Iwasko

TOPIC—Damages for negligent acts

FACTS—Two teen-agers, John Allan and Robert Iwasko, live near each other in Cleveland, Ohio. They both leave their homes at about the same time every day, one to go to work, the other to go to school. Each drives his own car.

One morning Allan and Iwasko meet at a traffic light at the top of a hill near their homes. They decide to have a drag race to the bottom of the hill, which is about a mile long. The speed limit on the hill is 30 mph. The two cars are racing down the hill, moving at about 75 mph. Meanwhile, a car driven by Frank Garcia is nearing an intersection ahead of the two drag racers. Allan is not able to stop in time. He is moving at about 70 mph when he hits Garcia's car. Garcia is hurt in the crash. Iwasko is able to bring his car to a safe stop without hitting anything.

QUESTION—Is a person, such as Robert Iwasko, who takes part in a drag race on a public street responsible under the law for damages that he/she did not directly cause?

OUR LEGAL SYSTEM AT WORK

You're probably wondering what the answer is to the question at the bottom of page 1. You'll have the answer shortly. First, however, you're going to find out how the question came to be decided by a court. You'll find out how a case such as the one on page 1 comes to trial. You will also learn something about what happens at a trial. Later, in Chapter 8, you'll be studying trials and legal procedures in much greater detail.

STEPS IN A LAWSUIT

Person being sued is notified.

Defendant seeks legal advice.

Lawyers for both sides meet with trial judge to try to settle case out of court.

Trial takes place and court decision is made.

If defendant loses case, an appeal may be made.

If appeals court upholds lower court decision, appellant must pay damages.

The case begins As you remember, Frank Garcia was hurt in the automobile accident. He has suffered physical and mental pain as a result. He will not be able to work for some time. He also has medical bills to pay. For those reasons, Garcia believes he should receive damages, or money. He decides to talk to his lawyer.

Garcia's lawyer, Janet Santini, listens carefully to what Garcia has to say. She asks him a great many questions about the accident itself. She may also talk to other people who saw the accident. Santini decides there are grounds for a court action. She must now decide whether Garcia should sue both John Allan and Robert Iwasko, or just Allan since it was his car that hit Garcia's car. After studying similar cases, Santini advises Garcia to sue both Allan and Iwasko.

So a case has begun. It is called *Garcia* v. *Allan and Iwasko.* Garcia is the plaintiff, or the party who is making the complaint. He is asking damages in the amount of $7,131.31. Allan and Iwasko are the defendants. The complaint is being made against them. If the court finds that Allan and Iwasko are responsible for the accident, they will probably have to pay damages to Garcia.

Allan and Iwasko are notified of the lawsuit. They decide they should have a lawyer to represent them. They go to a lawyer, Samuel Arnold, and tell him how the accident happened. Arnold, like Santini, asks a great many questions about the accident. He believes he can successfully defend Allan and Iwasko in court and agrees to handle the case.

---

damages Loss or harm resulting from injury; money awarded by the courts to someone who has suffered loss or harm.

negligent act An action in which there is failure to use reasonable care to avoid injury to oneself or others.

grounds The basis or cause for a legal action.

court action A legal proceeding brought by someone seeking judgment against another for a claimed wrong or injury.

sue To seek judgment against someone by taking legal action against him/her in a court of law.

complaint A formal accusation or charge brought against a person.

lawsuit A case before a court of law in which someone seeks justice for a claimed wrong or injury.

It will probably be several months before the case comes to trial. In the meantime the lawyers for both sides try to find out as much as they can about the accident. They also exchange information about the case. At least once before the trial, the lawyers meet with the trial judge, Arthur Casey. Together they try to settle the case out of court. In such a settlement, the defendant usually pays the plaintiff an agreed-upon amount of money. This saves the time and cost of going through a trial. In this case, the lawyers cannot agree on an out-of-court settlement. So Judge Casey sets a date for the trial.

■ ***The trial*** When the trial begins, the plaintiff, Frank Garcia, is present in court with his lawyer. So are the defendants, John Allan and Robert Iwasko, and their lawyer. The case is going to be tried by a jury, and the jurors, or members of the jury, have already been selected. Judge Casey is presiding. As the trial goes on, he decides any points of law that arise.

During the trial, the jury listens carefully to the testimony of the witnesses for each side. It studies all the evidence that is presented. Then, after the lawyers' arguments for both sides have been heard, the jury must consider all that it has seen and heard in court. It is up to the jury to decide who, if anyone, is at fault for the accident. Judge Casey answers any questions the jury has about the law in this case. The jury decides that Allan and Iwasko are at fault. They caused the accident because they were drag racing. Now the jury must decide if Garcia should receive any damages. It decides that he should, and since Allan and Iwasko were at fault for the

---

jury In a trial, a group of people legally chosen and sworn to inquire into the facts of a case and to give their decision according to the evidence.

testimony Spoken statements made under oath in a legal proceeding. For example, a witness *testifies* under oath.

witness A person called to testify under oath in a legal proceeding.

evidence Anything submitted to a court—testimony of witnesses, documents, objects, etc.—by which the truth of the matter at issue may be determined.

COURT SYSTEM

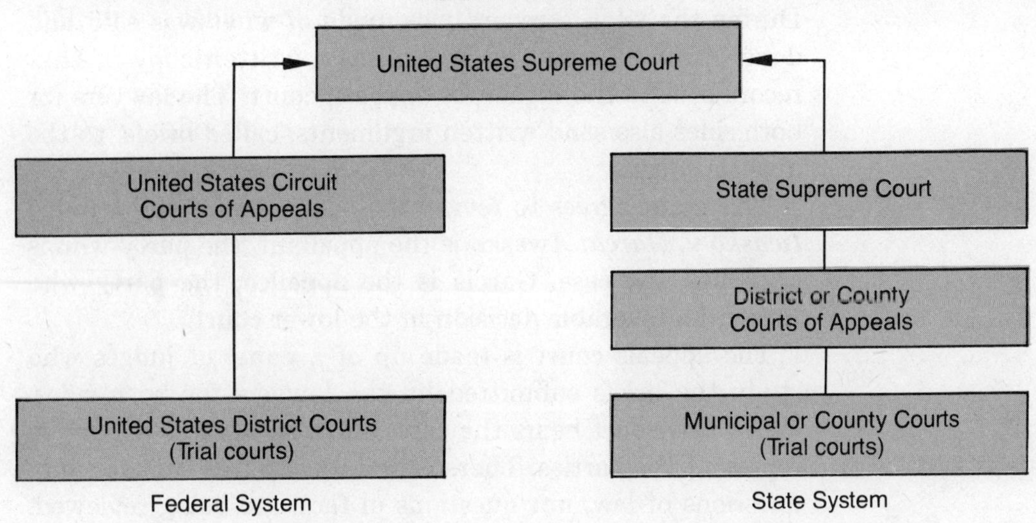

This diagram does not show special federal courts such as customs or claims courts; or local courts such as justice of the peace, juvenile, small claims, or probate courts. Note that state court systems vary from state to state.

accident, they are liable for damages. That means that they must pay damages to Garcia. Judge Casey helps the jury decide what the proper amount of damages should be. It decides that Garcia should receive the full amount he asked for, plus interest on that amount from the time of the accident. Allan and Iwasko also have to pay Garcia's lawyer's fee and the court costs.

■ ***The appeal*** The jury decided that John Allan and Robert Iwasko caused the accident and that they both have to pay damages to Frank Garcia. You will remember that it was Allan's car that hit Garcia's car. Iwasko's car never hit anything. For that reason, Iwasko thinks the jury did not arrive at the proper decision. He feels that he should not have to pay any damages because his car did not hit Garcia's car. His lawyer agrees with him, and they decide to appeal the case.

---

liable Legally responsible.

court costs The amount of money spent by a party to a lawsuit for such things as filing fees or jury fee.

That means they will ask a higher court to review the case. During the trial, a record was made of what was said and done. Arnold, Iwasko's lawyer, has a written copy of that record sent to the higher, or appeals, court. The lawyers for both sides also send written arguments, called briefs, to the appeals court.

This court agrees to review the case, which is now called *Iwasko* v. *Garcia.* Iwasko is the appellant, the party who is appealing the case. Garcia is the appellee, the party who received a favorable decision in the lower court.

The appeals court is made up of a panel of judges who study the briefs submitted by the lawyers for both sides. When this court hears the case, only the lawyers appear to represent the parties. There is no jury. That is because only questions of law, not questions of fact, are being reviewed. Each lawyer is given a certain amount of time, perhaps 15 to 30 minutes, to state his/her views on the case. After each side is presented, the judges discuss the case among themselves. Then they write a decision based upon their findings. The written appeals court decision becomes part of a permanent court record.

The judges often do not agree among themselves as to what the decision should be. In a three-judge court, for example, two judges may agree on a decision, while the third does not. This judge may state her/his views in a dissenting, or minority, opinion.

What did the appeals court decide in the case of *Iwasko* v. *Garcia?* Did it uphold the decision of the lower court, or did it overturn that decision? The decision for that case, as well as for all the other cases in this book, may be found in the section Decision of Court, which begins on page 266. The page number before the name of each case refers to the page on which the case itself appears in this book.

After the state court of appeals hands down its decision, the losing party may ask the state's highest court—the state supreme court—to review the case. In this case, Robert Iwasko decides that he will not appeal. He pays his share of the damages to Frank Garcia.

How Records Are Kept

In our legal system, court decisions made in the past play an important part in the decisions that courts make today. Often a past court decision is cited as a precedent by a lawyer who is arguing a case or by a judge who is handing down a decision. A record of what goes on at a trial and the decision of the court is kept at the courthouse where the trial took place. As a rule, such decisions are not printed unless the case is appealed. Cases that are appealed from a lower to a higher court appear in books called Reporters. There are Reporter systems for each of the states, for the different districts in the federal court system, and for the United States Supreme Court. Each Reporter system is made up of many volumes. Sometimes a case is reported in more than one Reporter system. Now let's look at the citation for a case that was appealed in the state court of appeals in Minnesota.

Lefkowitz *v.* Great Minn. Surplus Store
251 Minn. 188, 86 N.W.2d 689 (1957)

The title of the case, *Lefkowitz* v. *Great Minn. Surplus Store,* tells you who the parties in the case are. Lefkowitz is the appellant, the party who is making the appeal. The Great Minn. Surplus Store is the appellee, the party that received a favorable decision in the lower court. Now look at the second line of the citation. 251 Minn. 188 means that this case is recorded in Volume 251 of the *Minnesota Reporter.* The case begins on page 188 of that volume. The second half of that line of the citation gives another source in which the same case may be found. 86 N.W.2d 689 tells you that the case is recorded in Volume 86 of the *North Western Reporter,* second series, page 689. The decision itself was written in the year 1957.

Now let's look at a citation for a case that was heard in a federal court, rather than a state court.

United States *v.* O'Brien
391 U.S. 367, 88 S. Ct. 1673, 20 L.Ed.2d 672 (1968)

This case is recorded in three publications. 391 U.S. 367 means Volume 391 of *The United States Reporter,* page 367. It is recorded in Volume 88 of *The Supreme Court Reporter,* page 1673. It can also be found in Volume 20 of the *Lawyers' Edition,* second series, page 672. The decision was written in 1968.

citation A reference to a source of legal authority.

SOURCES OF LAW

You have just seen how our legal system works. But where does our legal system come from? What is the source of our legal traditions? Where do our laws come from today?

■ ***Common law*** For the most part, our legal system is based on the common law of England. This is unwritten law that developed over a long period of time. In early English history, judges decided cases according to what they felt were the customs and beliefs of the community. As time went on, judges often made decisions based on what another judge had decided in a similar case. Those earlier rulings were used as guides in deciding cases. The same is still true. Today, when a judge is making a decision or a lawyer is arguing a case, he/she will often cite the decision in an earlier case as a precedent. In Chapter 2 you'll learn more about the common law and how it developed.

■ ***Statutes*** In addition to the common law, which is unwritten, our legal system is also based on written laws. Among these are the laws, or statutes, that are passed by Congress and by state legislatures. These statutes are recorded in code books of laws.

■ ***Administrative law*** Certain government departments and agencies have the power to make regulations that have the effect of laws. On the federal level, for example, the Federal Communications Commission (FCC) regulates radio and television broadcasting. On the state level, a public utility commission decides the rates that may be charged by power and light companies and telephone companies. On the local level, a board of health regulates the standards of purity of drinking water for a community. The body of rules or regulations made by such agencies is called administrative law.

---

cite To refer to, mention, name, or quote.

precedent A court decision that sets an example to be followed in deciding similar cases.

code book of law A book that contains an organized statement of laws, rules, or principles.

■ ***Ordinances*** Laws passed by Congress and by state legislatures are called statutes. Laws passed by a municipal legislature, such as a city council, are called ordinances. Many aspects of our daily life are touched by laws made at the local level. For example, local governments decide tax rates on property, parking and traffic rules, building codes, and zoning laws.

THE CITIZEN LAWMAKER

In a democracy such as the United States, people have a voice in the lawmaking process. They can help decide who their representatives in government will be by voting. They can let their representatives know how they feel about public issues. A citizen can also express his/her voice as a member of a group. There are a number of ways to do that. They include the right to assemble, to petition, and to lobby.

---

building code Laws passed by local legislatures that place restrictions on the way in which a building may be constructed and set standards for the quality of materials used.

zoning laws Laws passed by local legislatures that determine what types of buildings (houses, stores, offices, factories) may be built in certain parts of a town or city.

■ ***Assembly*** Under the Constitution of the United States, citizens have the right to gather together, or assemble, peacefully to make their views known. This is a very effective way for citizens to tell their leaders how they stand on public issues.

■ ***Petition*** Citizens may ask the government to do something by signing a petition. The petition is then sent to a public official, a legislative body, or a court. The officials who receive the petition then decide how to handle the request.

■ ***Lobbying*** People who have the same interest can often have more influence as a group than they could as individuals. A lobby is an interest group that tries to have an influence on the laws that are made. The process by which it tries to influence the lawmakers is called lobbying.

■ ***You and the law*** The younger citizen—the citizen who is not yet old enough to vote—does have power in the lawmaking process. This is especially true in your school and in your neighborhood. Voting in school elections, belonging to the student council, and helping to draw up school regulations are all ways of taking part in the governing of your school.

Young, informed citizens who learn of problems in their neighborhood or community can help bring about change. Many environmental changes, clean-up campaigns, and the like were started by young people who made their local government aware of the problem. Some local governing bodies and boards of education invite student representatives to attend meetings and present their point of view. Youth groups can make their views known to their lawmakers in the local, state, and federal government by writing letters and collecting petitions. They can also express their opinion on issues by taking part in peaceful demonstrations.

In the next chapter you'll learn how our legal system and many of our legal traditions developed.

---

petition A written request for action or relief.

Reviewing the Chapter

Law-Related Terms

Plaintiff *Pp. 3, 307*
Defendant *Pp. 3, 304*
Damages *P. 3*
Liable *P. 5*
Appeal *Pp. 5–6, 302*
Dissenting opinion *Pp. 6, 304*
Appellant *Pp. 6, 302*
Appellee *Pp. 6, 302*
Precedent *Pp. 7, 307*
Common law *Pp. 8, 303*

Review Questions

1. List the steps in a lawsuit. *P. 2*
2. **(a)** In *Garcia* v. *Allan and Iwasko,* who was the plaintiff and who was the defendant? **(b)** When the case was appealed, who was the appellant and who was the appellee? *Pp. 3, 6*
3. What is the role of a judge before and during a trial? *Pp. 4–5*
4. **(a)** What are trial courts in a state court system called? **(b)** To what courts may cases be appealed in a state court system? **(c)** What are trial courts called in the federal court system? **(d)** What are the appeals courts called in the federal court system? **(e)** What is the highest court to which any case may be appealed? *P. 5*
5. Why are past court decisions an important part of our legal system? *P. 7*
6. **(a)** What is the difference between a statute and an ordinance? **(b)** Give four examples of ordinances. *Pp. 8, 9*
7. Explain three ways in which citizens can influence lawmaking. *Pp. 9–10*

Chapter Test

On a separate paper, write the letter of the answer that best completes each statement.

1. Money awarded to someone who has suffered loss or harm is called **(a)** damages, **(b)** citations, **(c)** statutes.
2. In this citation, *Smith* v. *Jones Feed Store,* 139 Pa. 357 (1973), the defendant is **(a)** Smith, **(b)** Jones Feed Store, **(c)** State of Pennsylvania.
3. At a trial, points of law are decided by the **(a)** jury, **(b)** lawyers, **(c)** judge.
4. The party who appeals a case is the **(a)** appellant, **(b)** appellee, **(c)** plaintiff.
5. A request to have a court review a lower court decision is **(a)** a brief, **(b)** a dissenting opinion, **(c)** an appeal.
6. To cite a precedent means to **(a)** refer to a previous court decision, **(b)** object to a court decision, **(c)** overturn or reverse a court decision.
7. An example of an ordinance is **(a)** a regulation of a federal agency, **(b)** a parking regulation passed by a city council, **(c)** a law passed by a state legislature.
8. The system of law in the United States is based mostly on **(a)** Roman law, **(b)** common law, **(c)** Greek law.
9. The sending of signatures to a lawmaker to oppose a highway project is an example of **(a)** an ordinance, **(b)** an assembly, **(c)** a petition.
10. An interest group that tries to have an influence on laws is **(a)** an assembly, **(b)** a lobby, **(c)** joint tortfeasors.

We the People
Article

History of United States Law 2

ORIGIN OF LAW

What would happen if no one needed to pass a driver's test and carry a license in order to drive a car? What would happen if there were no speed limits or traffic lights? How safe would it be to cross a street in Los Angeles or New York City if there were no traffic laws? Or suppose you became ill and needed an operation. Would you feel comfortable if your doctor had not had medical training and passed strict examinations before being allowed to practice? What kind of health problems might you have if the food you bought at the grocery store did not have to meet certain standards?

When did people first begin to think some actions were wrong? How did they first decide to punish someone who acted in one of the ways thought to be wrong? When did the idea of having laws begin?

■ ***Customs*** There was a long, long period of time before people began to have ideas about laws.

Primitive people were ruled by custom. Customs are not laws. They are simply ways of behaving that are accepted by the people. Primitive people had no police officers. Most of them were willing to follow the customs of their tribe. True, no one wanted to risk the anger of the medicine man or of the chief. But the strongest reason for following custom was the fear of falling into disfavor with the group. So it still is today. You might sometimes rather face an angry parent than go against the customs followed by your friends.

The primitive young man began to learn the mysteries of his own tribe in ways that showed him how important it was to follow the customs of the tribe. He might have some of his front teeth knocked out with a club. Or his teeth might be painfully filed down to sharp points. In some tribes, young men had their backs cut open with sharp knives. Something was then rubbed into the wounds to prevent rapid healing. This caused large scars that told everyone how brave the youth was. These experiences were part of the important ceremonies marking the time when a young boy became a grown-up member of the tribe. He took great pride in its customs.

■ ***Customs become law*** Each group of people built up their own set of customs. All of the ideas may not have been original. Sometimes people borrowed an idea and changed it. Sometimes people were conquered and made to accept new ways. Many of these customs developed into *customary law* and then into law.

Which groups developed the customary laws that have become our laws? Our legal institutions can be traced to those peoples who ruled our nation before its independence. These were the French, the Spanish, and the English. Through them, the Greeks, the Romans, and the laws of Moses have also played a part in shaping our legal heritage. Most of our legal traditions, however, are based upon the

---

customary law A body of unwritten, long-standing practices that regulated social life among early peoples.

Hammurabi's Code

The Code of Hammurabi is the oldest known code of written laws. The people of the ancient Middle Eastern civilization of Babylonia believed the laws were given to their king by the sun god. This list of 282 laws, discovered in 1901, was carved on a black stone slab nearly eight feet high. The laws below are numbered as they appear in the Code.

1. If a man charges another with a capital crime, but cannot prove it, he, the accuser, shall be put to death.

3. If a man in a case bears false witness, or does not establish the testimony he has given, if that case be one involving life, that man shall be put to death.

7. If a man buys silver or gold, man slave or woman slave, or ox or sheep from a child or a slave, without witnesses or contracts, that man shall be put to death as a thief.

11. If a man who claims to be the owner of lost property does not produce witnesses to identify his lost property, he has lied and he has stirred up conflict. He shall be put to death.

195. If a son strikes his father, they shall cut off his fingers.

202. If a man strikes someone who is his superior in rank, he shall receive sixty lashes with an ox-tail whip in public.

203. If a man strike another of his own rank, he shall pay one mana of silver.

205. If a slave strikes his superior, they shall cut off his ear.

229. If a builder builds a house for a man, but does not make it strong enough and the house collapses and causes the death of the owner, that builder shall be put to death.

251. If a man's bull has been known to gore and the owner has not protected its horns nor had it tied up, and that bull gores someone and brings about his death, the owner shall pay one-half mana of silver.

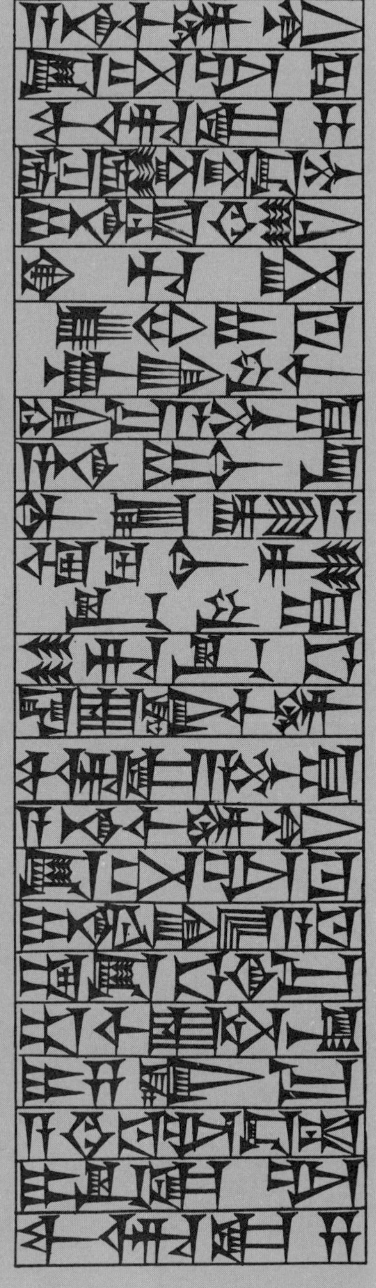

English common law. So it is important for us to learn what the English common law was and how it grew. To do this, we must go back to a period in time just before the birth of Jesus.

LAWS AND CUSTOMS OF ENGLAND

In 58 B.C. Julius Caesar moved the mighty Roman armies across Europe and began his invasion of Gaul, the country now called France. The people who were then living in France were called Franks. They fought back bravely. They were also being sent aid from their island neighbors to the west.

■ ***Overrun by Romans*** To cut off this aid, Caesar took a part of his army, moved across the English Channel, and began to attack Britain. Caesar described the people he met there as being tall, with white skin, light hair, and strong muscles. These brave warriors painted themselves blue before battle to frighten their enemy. They stopped Caesar's

men and forced them back to Gaul. About a hundred years later, however, the Romans returned—this time to stay for four hundred years.

Romans, and people from Roman colonies in Europe, followed the soldiers. They brought with them the Roman talent for organization and government. At once they began to make England a true Roman colony. To do this, they had to try to change the existing laws and customs.

■ ***Druid lawgivers*** Most of the people living in Britain at that time were Celts. The most important of the Celts were their priests, called Druids. These Druids said what the laws were to be and which customs were to be followed. They were very jealous of their power as lawgivers. To protect this power, they wrote the laws in mixed-up words and sentences. No one could read them unless he/she knew the code.

The people were supposed to bring all disputes to a Druid for settlement. If one of the two parties refused to do this, the Celts had an unusual way of handling the problem. For example, if Alan owed Neil some money and would not pay it, Neil would go to Alan's house and sit at his front door. He would also refuse to eat. If Alan allowed Neil to sit there until he starved, the people would condemn Alan. Before Alan would allow this to happen, he would agree to go to a Druid for settlement. If the decision was in favor of Neil and if Alan did not have the money to pay what he owed, Neil could take a part of Alan's property equal to the amount of the debt. If Alan had neither the money nor property, Neil could make Alan and his family his slaves until the obligation was paid off.

To be condemned by the people or to refuse to agree to the decision of a Druid meant that one could not take part in the religious ceremonies. This was thought to be the worst of all punishments. Other Celts would avoid such a person for fear that some evil spirit would possess them.

The Roman army crushed the power of the Druids. The Celts and other English people were forced to accept some of the laws and customs of Rome. With time, however, the

Roman Empire weakened and Rome's control of distant lands broke down. Britain, like other Roman colonies, became open to conquest, and between 417 and 429 a new invasion of the island began. The people who had for hundreds of years depended upon the army for protection were now helpless without it.

■ ***Changes made by the Germanic invaders*** The invaders included tribes of Angles, Saxons, and Jutes from Germany. There were also Danes from the Netherlands, Germany, and Denmark. Today we call these people *Anglo-Saxons.* They brought with them their own customs. And over a period of several hundred years they greatly lessened the Roman influence. Britain slowly became as much a Germanic society as it had been Celtic and Roman.

The different Germanic tribes formed a number of small kingdoms. Each had its own king. To make it easier to enforce the customary laws and the wishes of the king, each kingdom was divided into *shires,* or counties. A shire was governed by an *ealdorman* named by the king. This man was usually a great noble and owned much land in the shire. To aid the ealdorman, the king also appointed a *shire reeve.* This office was the origin of our "sheriff." It was the job of the shire reeve to collect the king's taxes and enforce the laws. He also saw that the ordinary business of government was carried out. The shires were divided into smaller sections known as hundreds. These were so named because, at the time, each hundred contained one hundred families. Both the shire and the hundred were responsible for keeping justice and order in their own areas.

■ ***Anglo-Saxon written laws*** One of the German kings, Ethelbert, wanted to make the customs and laws of his people stronger and more lasting. So he ordered them to be put in writing. There were only about ninety statements in this document. A few of them had to do with property claims. But most of them dealt with how a person was to be punished for doing wrong to another. Such punishments did not

include imprisonment. Jails were used only to hold an accused person until the trial. The guilty really "paid" for their crimes because most punishments were in the form of fines. The fine was paid to the person wronged. Even murder could be paid for with money. In this case, the money went to the victim's family. Part of all fines also went to the king. This was thought to be fair, since the king was the general keeper of the peace that had been broken by the wrongdoer. Anglo-Saxon law, like the law of other ancient peoples, treated different social classes differently. A much higher fine had to be paid for harming or killing a lord or a churchman than for harming a peasant or a serf.

---

lord A man of high rank or position.

churchman Historically, a church official or member of a religious order.

peasant One of an independent class of farmers, farm laborers, or small landowners.

serf In the Middle Ages, a member of a farming or laboring class of servant or slave status subject to the will of a lord.

Some of the recorded offenses and the fines to be paid by the offenders were as follows: For piercing a man's thigh, 30 shillings. If the leg was broken, 30 shillings. If the leg was pierced below the knee, 12 shillings. If the big toe was struck off, 20 shillings. If the second toe was struck off, 15 shillings. If one man struck another with his fist on the nose, 3 shillings. Today the value of the shilling would be about fifteen cents.

■ ***Deciding innocence or guilt*** The Anglo-Saxon ideas about criminal punishment were quite different from ours. Their ways of deciding innocence or guilt also were different. When a person was charged with a crime in a hundred or shire court, there were two usual ways of testing his/her innocence. One way was by oath. The other was by ordeal. If the oath was used, the plaintiff, or the accuser, would swear under oath that his/her claim was true. The defendant, or the accused, would swear that he/she was unjustly charged. It was then up to the court to decide if proof was necessary and which side should give it. The person who had to prove his/her case was told by the court the number of people who could be called as witnesses. These people were not called to give evidence. Their chief duty was to swear that the person they were supporting was telling the truth. The oath of a person of high rank was of more value than the oaths of people in lower positions. The oath of a lord, for example, equaled the oaths of six serfs. After hearing the witnesses, the court decided the verdict. By our standards, no real trial had been held.

The other way of deciding innocence or guilt was by ordeal. Hot iron and water ducking were the two most common forms of trial by ordeal. Three days before the ordeal was to take place, the accused went to the priest to receive the blessing of the church. During the days that followed, he/she was to eat and drink only bread, water, herbs, and

---

 shilling Unit of money long used in England.

salt. The salt was supposed to help clean the blood. Each day the person was to visit the church and pray. On the third day he/she was to give an offering.

In the test by hot iron, a fire was built in the church to heat a piece of iron. The red-hot iron was then carried nine steps by the accused person. As soon as that person was allowed to drop the iron, the hand was bandaged. The hand was not otherwise treated for three days. At the end of this time the priest examined it. If there was no sign of a burn, it was believed God or one of his angels must have protected the accused. Thus, this person must be innocent. If, however, the hand had so much as one blister or the smallest burn, the person was held to be guilty and a fine had to be paid.

In the ordeal of water, the accused was tied hand and foot and thrown into a pond or stream. If the person sank, he/she was said to have been received by the water. That person was then pulled out and freed. That is, if it did not take the court too long to decide that the accused had been truly received by the water. One could be found very innocent, but also very dead from drowning.

If, however, the person on trial was rejected by the water and floated, it was believed he/she must be impure and full of guilt. Again, if the court did not take too long to make its decision, the person was pulled out alive and made to pay a fine.

In trying to understand these strange ways of seeking justice, we must remember that the trials were held in very small communities. Everyone knew everyone else. Also, oaths were very sacred. It would be hard for anyone to swear before God that something was true when he/she knew it was not. The person would be almost sure to hesitate or seem nervous. It was almost a natural lie-detector test. Then, too, God was thought to be watching what went on. It was believed God would surely punish anyone who lied under oath. Both the trial by oath and the trial by ordeal were appeals to God to make the truth known.

■ ***Ruled by custom*** Except for the few written laws stating the penalties for certain crimes, Anglo-Saxon England was ruled by custom. The laws were not made by a legislature and put in a book for everyone to follow. There were no legislatures. Practices that were treated as laws were nothing more than the customary rules of the community. People were expected to do or not do certain things simply because their ancestors had done them or not done them.

This way of making the laws, and of trying and punishing those who broke them, may seem primitive to us. But the legal system that developed from the customary laws of the Anglo-Saxons is considered to have been fairly advanced for that time. The king was head of the government. Under him were the lords. These were men who received land from the king in return for military service. Peasants or serfs were allowed to live on this land and raise crops. They provided the lord with food and other services in return for his protection. As time passed, the administration of justice became the duty of these lords. Many of the lords were churchmen who had inherited large tracts of land. Thus, religious officers were often responsible for handing out justice as well as the word of the church.

REFORMS OF NORMAN CONQUERORS

In 1066 England was again invaded. In that year William, Duke of Normandy, sailed with his army from France to England. The Normans brought a new language and different social manners to Anglo-Saxon England. They did not, however, bring with them a set of new laws. As a matter of fact, Norman laws were not much different from those of the Anglo-Saxons.

---

inherit To receive something by right or legal title from an ancestor at his/her death.

■ ***Trial by battle*** William claimed that he was the true heir to the throne of England. He had no wish to destroy the legal system of his new subjects. He made only a few small changes in the existing laws. One was to add the trial by battle. This was a fight between two armed men, and the winner was said to be the honest one. He would win the case. Old men, women, and children could not be expected to take part in this kind of contest. So they were allowed to hire a champion to fight for them. A champion earned good money, but his was a very dangerous job.

Some people did not think the Norman idea of a trial by battle was any better than their own practice of trial by ordeal. Both were an appeal to God to show who the guilty party was. The people were allowed to keep their own customs so long as they did not become a threat to the king's rules. So hot irons and water ducking were still used over much of England.

REORGANIZATION OF COURTS

The Norman laws were no better than those of the English. But in other ways the government of the Normans was indeed better. One of the changes they made was the setting up of a new kind of court. Under the Anglo-Saxons, officers of the church were in charge of the courts. They did not decide the cases that came before the courts. It was their duty to explain the law to judges who did decide. In this way the church had a great deal of influence upon the courts. Norman kings removed the church officers from these courts and put them in charge of the new kind of court. The new courts tried cases of a religious nature only. For about five hundred years, such courts tried cases that had to do with religion, morals, marriages, and the property of persons who had died. Cases on all other matters were heard in other courts.

During this time, if a churchman was accused of a crime, he was usually tried in a church court. Sometimes, however, he might be convicted of a charge in one of the other courts.

---

heir One who inherits or is entitled to inherit a title or property.

When this happened, he did not receive the same punishment as other people. So a person might "plead the clergy," or claim to be a churchman. He was then asked to read to the court from the Bible. If he was able to do so, his sentence was no more than a simple branding of the thumb, no matter what his crime.

Two other important changes were brought about by the Norman kings. One was the manner in which a person was accused of a wrongdoing. The other was trial by jury.

■ ***Making charges against the accused*** At this time there was much crime in England. Most people had no protection from those who would steal their property or do them harm in other ways. There were no police officers. There was no one who had the regular duty of bringing wrongdoers to trial. To correct this, the Normans tried a new plan. Twice a year each sheriff was to hear *pleas of the Crown.* This meant that four men from each manor, or village, and twelve from each hundred would appear before the sheriff and the court.

---

pleas of the Crown Certain crimes that English kings claimed had to be tried in the royal courts. Some examples would be breaking the king's peace, treason, harboring outlaws, and housebreaking.

Of their own free will they would report any person thought to have broken the law. This may have been our first form of swearing out an arrest warrant. It was considered a public duty. If one of these men was the neighbor of the accused, people were likely to believe that person was guilty. The person would then be arrested. The accused would be sent to the ordeal of water or hot iron, or allowed a trial by battle.

Some years later this way of accusing suspects was changed from a voluntary act to a required one. The group of accusers came to be called a *presenting jury*. This was the beginning of our present grand jury, which hears evidence to decide whether or not a person should stand trial.

■ ***Introduction of trial by jury*** When the church officers were removed from the courts, the judges faced a problem. Who would help them find out the innocence or guilt of the accused? Since there would be a presenting jury in the court, it became natural for the judge to ask the members what they thought. This was not a regular part of the legal process. The accused, therefore, had to agree to be "tried" by a number of neighbors and other people chosen from the presenting jury. No rule stated the exact number to be chosen. It was usually twelve, but the judge might choose more or less. The wishes of the accused were discovered by asking him/her, "Are you willing to put yourself upon the country?" If the answer was No, the judge could order the accused person to be tortured. The idea was to force prisoners to agree to stand trial by a group of people from the presenting jury.

Prisoners who still refused were laid upon the ground and large stones were piled on them. Stones were added until the prisoner either agreed to a trial by jury or died. This was a slow and painful way to die. Yet many were willing to die in this way rather than agree to a jury trial. There were two reasons for this. One was a law that gave to the king all the property of a person convicted of a serious crime. The other

---

arrest warrant A written order, issued by a court or an official having the proper authority, directing the arrest of a person.

was the fact that the jury was made up of some of the very people who had accused the prisoner. A guilty verdict was almost certain. By choosing a painful death, the accused at least saved something for his/her family.

The members of the jury did not have an easy job either. After being named, they were told to go and find out the facts of the case. The jury members had to find the evidence any way they could in a certain number of days. At the end of that time the members of the jury returned to the judge and gave their decision.

People might also have worried about serving on a jury for fear of being wrong. Any jury might make an honest mistake and give a wrong verdict. However, if the judge thought one of these juries had made a mistake, another trial was held. This time, however, the accused was the jury itself. If the judge decided against it, there would be a heavy fine for each member. This may not have been the best of all systems, but it must have made some pretty good detectives out of jurors. It was also the beginning of trial by jury—today one of our most important rights.

COMMON LAW ESTABLISHED

As time passed, English courts came more and more under the rule of judges appointed by the king. These judges were highly trained and experienced. Their decisions were usually logical and consistent. People who had to go to court felt that they had a better chance of getting a fair verdict from these judges than from the courts ruled over by the sheriffs, lords, or even the church. However, many people lived too far away from such a court to be heard by a king's judge. The king solved the problem by naming more judges and having them travel from county to county holding court. The government ordered these judges to record the details of every case as well as the decision given. These written records were stored in books so other judges could study them if they should have similar cases. The king wanted all cases that were alike to have the same judgment. In this way there would be equal justice all over the country.

In William's time and for many years after, there was no national legislature to make laws for all the people. Each part of the country had its own set of customs and customary laws. This made it impossible to have a single code of laws for all of England. Slowly, however, the decisions of the king's judges came to be accepted as the "common law" for all the people. Each decision remained the law until some future judge made a different one. This decision then became the new law. If a judge was not sure about the law and could find no past decision to guide him, he would think up a new solution. Or he might borrow one from some other country. In this way the common law developed–the law that in time ruled all English people.

Before the rights of the common law could be enjoyed by all the people, one great question had to be settled. Was the king above the law or was the law above the king? Could the king say, "No, this law does not apply to that person"? Or could he not?

■ ***Magna Carta*** In 1215 the first step toward answering that question was taken. In that year King John was forced by his nobles to sign a very important paper. It was called the

Magna Carta, or the Great Charter. In this paper John agreed not to raise money by taxes "except by common consent of the realm," meaning the nobles and officers of the church. The king also agreed that no one could be sent to prison or otherwise punished except by the judgment of that person's equals. At that time this simply meant that a lord could not be found guilty without a trial.

At the time it was signed, the Magna Carta protected only the lords and church officers from the power of the king. But as time passed, this protection was given to all English citizens. The law became more mighty than the king.

The signing of the Magna Carta was one of the great events in English history. From this paper comes the American belief that people should not be taxed without their consent. Our belief that any person accused of a crime has the right to a trial by jury also comes from the Magna Carta.

It was with this legal background that a small group of people, early in the seventeenth century, boarded three small ships and sailed for America. Of all the things they brought with them, not one was more important than the English belief that power is limited by law.

ESTABLISHING LAW IN THE UNITED STATES

In early May of 1607, 104 men from the *Susan Constant,* the *Godspeed,* and the *Discovery* landed in Virginia at a spot later to be known as Jamestown. There they began the first permanent English settlement in America. They brought with them their English language, customs, and traditions. They also brought their system of dividing land into "hundreds." They had a charter granted by the king, James I, to the London Company. Later this name was changed to the Virginia Company. The company was owned by a group of London merchants who looked upon the settlement as a business venture.

■ ***English law carried to Virginia*** Their charter promised the Jamestown settlers the right to "enjoy all liberties, franchises and immunities within any of our other dominions to all intents and purposes as if they had been abiding and

---

franchise Freedom, right, or privilege.

immunity Freedom from or protection against penalty.

born within this our realm of England." In other words, it promised them the rights of English citizens. The charter also set forth the form of the local government. There was to be a council to govern the colony according to the laws of England. Further instructions stated that the council could not pass laws affecting life or limb.

While the Jamestown settlers were given all the protection and rights of citizens of England, the charter made several changes in the laws dealing with crime. In England, certain kinds of theft drew the death penalty. So did being friendly with gypsies. Virginia's laws were less cruel. Also, in Virginia, if a person was charged with a crime and refused to plead innocence or guilt, that person was to be judged guilty but the penalty depended on the crime. In England a person who would not plead innocence or guilt was put to death no matter what the crime. England did not change these laws until many years later.

For about two years, the council governed the colony as instructed by the king. But the work of beginning a settlement in a wilderness made it hard for the council to pass laws and see that they were obeyed. Its problems became worse when for some reason vacancies on the council were not filled. At one time Captain John Smith was the only member. This soon led to a change in the structure of the government. A new charter was written that made it possible for the Virginia Company to name a governor with almost absolute authority. The council that had once been the only government of the settlement was now to serve only as an adviser to the governor.

■ ***First legal code*** Lord De La Warr, the first governor, was a powerful noble with many business and political interests. These duties and a fever he caught in Virginia made his stay in America a short one. Since his appointment was for life, De La Warr sent a deputy governor and a marshal to run the affairs of the colony while he was away. From the time he was named governor until his death in 1618, he was in Virginia only a few months.

Before De La Warr left England, he and the Virginia Company made up a list of rules and laws by which the settlement was to be governed. Deputy Governor Thomas Gates and Marshal Thomas Dale added to the list. In 1611 the list was posted in the Jamestown church so that the people could learn about the new laws by which they would have to live.

Since this was the first legal code in English-speaking America, it is important. The colony was ruled like an army trading post. Everything the settlers made or grew went into one common storehouse. The people were in turn fed and clothed from the company's storehouse. Many of the new laws, therefore, had to do with the theft of tools or food, idleness, and the killing of domestic animals owned by the company. The stealing of grapes or ears of corn could be punished by death.

Another part of the code had to do with religion. Any person in England who wanted to come to Virginia had first to take the *Oath of Supremacy.* This was a promise to support the king as head of the Church of England. By making people take this oath, all Roman Catholics would be kept out of the Virginia colony. Laws such as this are a sign of religious intolerance.

The new code came to be known as Dale's Laws. These laws were supposed to be a way of controlling the morals of the settlers. All people newly arrived in the settlement must go to the minister at once and satisfy him that they had the "right" ideas. If they did not do this, they could be whipped every day until they did. Religious services were to be held daily and everyone must attend. The loss of food was the penalty for the first time someone missed a religious service. A whipping was given for the second time. And six months service in the galleys was the punishment for the third. Swearing in God's name might be punished by death. For the use of swear words, the first offense meant a whipping; the second, a needle thrust through the tongue; the third, death. Disrespect for legal or church authority called for the same punishment as the use of swear words. People could also be

punished by being branded, having their ears cut off, or being tied neck and heels together. It was not unusual for a person to lie in this position for forty-eight hours.

Today freedom of religion is one of the most important rights of American citizens. This great idea had no place in early Jamestown. It was first brought to the English colonies by the founders of Maryland in 1634 and the settlers of Pennsylvania in 1681.

The first twelve years of Jamestown's history was a time of harsh rule. The colonists lost many of the rights enjoyed by other English people, even though those rights had been guaranteed by the charter. One reason for this was the size of the job that had to be done. The forest had to be cleared and the settlement made safe. Above all, a profit had to be made for those who were paying the bills.

Jamestown was also in great danger of lack of food. The nearby Indians had nothing to trade but corn. Most of the settlers had come from the English upper classes. They did not know how to work and didn't want to. Most of them wanted to go home. Indeed, the need for workers was so great that the governor wrote to the king about it. He asked that prisoners sentenced to death be sent to Virginia as workers instead.

■ ***First representative government*** By 1619, however, life in the colony was beginning to go well. In that year, the first women landed in Jamestown. Family life, without which the colony could not have survived, could now begin. Also, the settlers had learned to grow tobacco. This crop brought in much-needed cash. The need for military rule came to an end. Soon Virginians were given most of the rights of the people of England. In July of 1619, the new governor, under orders from the Virginia Company, said that every hundred should elect two representatives, or burgesses. These burgesses were to meet in the church and write a new set of laws to govern the people. This assembly became America's first English-speaking representative government.

The members of the assembly divided themselves into two groups. They formed a two-house, or bicameral, legislature. This was something like the English Parliament. The governor and his appointed council acted as the upper house, similar to the English House of Lords. And like the House of Commons, the elected members became the lower body. This form of legislature was used by ten of the American colonies. Later it was used by the Congress of the United States. In Connecticut and Rhode Island the upper and lower houses were both elected. The Pennsylvania assembly had only one house.

■ ***Laws passed by the new government*** The Virginia lawmakers did not have to consider the old legal code as they worked on new laws. Yet the things that had made the old laws necessary were perhaps still in the minds of the members of the assembly. The offenses they named were much the same as those listed by Dale. The punishments, however,

---

English Parliament The lawmaking body of England (the United Kingdom).

were much easier to take. A person who was absent from church, for example, was fined three shillings for each offense. One who often used swear words was no longer in danger of death. Instead, the guilty person could buy a pardon with five shillings.

Before finishing its task of setting up a standard of behavior for the people of Virginia, the assembly wrote a new kind of law into the statute book. "Excess in apparal" was strongly frowned upon. On the way to one of the meetings, a freed servant had been seen wearing a fancy hat with a band of pearls. The burgesses decided to put an end to such wasteful displays. It was written into law that each man in the colony was to be taxed in the church to help pay for public expenses. The amount was to be based upon the appearance of his outer clothing. If he were married, the amount would be based upon either his or his wife's clothes. It seems that dress codes have been with us for a long time.

■ ***Court system created*** Although the duty of the assembly was chiefly to make laws, it also was to serve as a court of justice. The power it was given made it the supreme court of the colony. The burgesses were not too happy about this. Two cases were brought before them soon after the beginning of their first meeting. They sent both cases to the governor and his council for trial. That body became known as the Quarter Court, since it met four times a year. Later, when it met less often, its name was changed to General Court. The assembly sitting as a court, the General Court, and the monthly, or local, courts made up our first judicial system.

During the early years there was no difference between the kinds of cases that could be tried by the assembly or by the General Court. Each court heard both criminal and noncriminal cases. Both courts had the right to hear a case for the first time. Both could also hear a case that had been tried in a lower court and then appealed to a higher court.

The local courts, meeting once a month, also had the right to try both criminal and noncriminal charges. Cases decided in these courts were the ones not important enough to be sent to the burgesses or governor. Justice was not always swift in these courts because they were few in number and not always easy for the people to get to. Things got better when the colony was divided into shires. Then a separate court was set up for each shire. Later the name was changed from monthly court to county court.

The people of the colony thought of themselves as English citizens even though they lived in Virginia. They looked upon their courts as being English courts, trying or settling disputes between English subjects. For this reason their decisions were based on English common law. If a person had his/her case heard in every type of court in Virginia and was still not happy with the verdict, that person had the right to ask a court in England to review the case.

---

judicial system The established and organized process and procedures that deal with the administration of justice.

Until the late fall of 1620 Jamestown was the only English settlement in North America. It was only natural that here was born the English-American code of laws, a representative legislature, and an organized system of courts. This was a great achievement considering the hardship of the settlers and the fact that the colony was less than twenty years old.

BEGINNING OF LAW IN NEW ENGLAND

About the same time that the people of Jamestown were electing the members of their first legislature, other people in England were making plans to form a neighboring colony. Parliament had passed a law making it illegal to be absent from any service of the Anglican Church. This was the established church in England. It was also against the law to attend or take any part in any other kind of religious meeting. People who did not believe in the Anglican Church and who wished to leave it were called Separatists. These people had to decide what to do. They could give up their ideas and do as the law said. They could leave England. Or they could worship their faith in secret. Still another choice was to worship openly as they pleased and risks persecution or arrest.

■ ***Religious laws force people from England*** A group of Separatists made the choice to leave England. They went to Holland because it was not very far away and it allowed freedom of religion. In Holland, they could follow their own faith. But they soon discovered that their choice brought other kinds of problems. Dutch customs were being picked up by their children. The parents feared their English way of life was in danger. Also, it looked as if Holland and Spain were about to go to war. The Separatists decided to look for another home. This time their choice was America.

■ ***Separatists leave Holland for America*** Because Jamestown supported the Anglican Church, the Separatists could not go there. Finally, however, they got permission

from the Virginia Company to start a settlement in the northern part of the Virginia colony. This having been done, a small group of English Separatists left Holland for Southampton, England. Here they were to buy supplies and hire a ship. They were also to be joined by fellow Separatists from London. After a long wait and several disappointments, a little over one hundred passengers set sail for Virginia. When the *Mayflower* arrived off the coast of America, the passengers discovered that they were far off course. Instead of being near Jamestown, they were at Cape Cod, hundreds of miles to the north. The Pilgrims, as this group were called, decided to stay there and take the chance that they might be allowed to remain. Of the more than one hundred people on board the ship, only thirty-five were of the original group that had left Holland. Those who had joined them were of the same faith but had shown very early in the voyage that they did not agree in many matters. William Bradford, the leader of the whole group, wrote during the voyage that some of the London people had made "discontented and mutinous speeches." "When they came ashore," he said, "they would use their own libertie." He also gives us several accounts of the mischief of two London boys, John and Francis Billington. These boys at one time even set fire to the *Mayflower* and almost blew it apart.

■ ***Mayflower Compact*** These religious people at first thought the only law needed for their new settlement was the Bible. But before landing they seemed to have decided that they would also need a civil government. On November 11, 1620, forty-one men signed a paper that history has named the *Mayflower Compact.* It contains only three sentences. The second sentence, however, has 150 words. The form the new government was to take is not outlined in this paper. The men simply agreed to "covenant and combine our selves togeather into a civill body politick, for our better ordering and preservation," which was to "enacte, constitute, and frame . . . lawes, ordinances, acts, constitutions, and offices" to which they did "promise all due submission and obedience." In other words, they agreed to set up a civil government for the colony and promised to obey its laws.

■ ***Pilgrims set trend in government*** At the beginning of the Compact and again at the end, the men pledged their loyalty to the king of England. They did this to place themselves under the rule of English laws. Ten years later this "civill body politick" had to decide how much of the English law could be carried out by the settlers themselves. It also had to decide what cases would have to be sent back to English courts. A case that bothered them a great deal was that of John Billington, Sr. He was accused of murdering a man.

The question was not just Billington's guilt or innocence. The more important question was, Did these people have the legal right to try him? There was real doubt in the minds of the settlers. William Bradford's journal tells how they went

---

civil government A political body formed with the power to make laws and regulations to ensure the orderly function of society.

to a neighboring colony that had recently been settled and asked "the advice of Mr. Winthrop and other ablest gentlemen." These men all agreed that they did have the right to try him. John Billington was found guilty by the Plymouth court and was sentenced to die by hanging. This is the first recorded execution in English America.

As in any matter so important, there were some who did not agree that local officers had the right to take on this kind of authority. The case was reported to England. After looking into the matter, the English officers who were responsible for overseeing the colonies said that what Plymouth had done was right. In this way a custom began. Each colony would take on more and more control over its local affairs so long as it did not go against the common law of England.

Other small groups of Pilgrims came to Cape Cod. Other settlements were made near Plymouth. However, there was no real growth in the population of New England until the founding of the Massachusetts Bay colony.

PURITAN RULE

■ ***Puritans settle Massachusetts Bay*** This colony was begun by a religious group called Puritans. Like the Separatists, the Puritans had belonged to the Anglican Church in England. Like the Separatists, they had become unhappy with the beliefs and practices of their church. The Puritans, however, did not want to leave the church. They wanted to change and purify some of the church's policies. They could not do this in England, so they decided to come to America. They became a much larger and more important group than the Pilgrims.

■ ***Church dictates law*** John Cotton was perhaps the most important religious leader of the Puritans. He came to America to follow his dream of living in a place governed by the laws of Moses. Everyone looked up to the Reverend John Cotton. His ideas about government and law were as important as was his place in the religious life of the settlement. His ideas were quickly accepted. One of these ideas was that the church and the state were one and the same. To vote or hold office, a person had to be a member of the church. Cotton also believed the making and enforcing of the laws should be in the hands of a select few, God's chosen ones.

John Winthrop, the first governor of the Massachusetts Bay colony, worked closely with the officers of the church. Because of his position, he thought he knew best what the laws of God meant. If someone broke the law, Winthrop held that it was also an offense against God. He once stated that "whatsoever sentence the magistrate gives, the judgment is the Lord's." In a system of this kind, the idea of trial by jury found hard going.

Puritan leaders believed the church must decide how people should act as well as how they should worship. As they saw it, one of the most important jobs of the government was to punish anyone who did not act as the church had decided. A church committee was set up to decide what the rules should be. It found 82 "errors and heresies" being practiced in the colony. Persons guilty of these misdeeds were punished with whippings, fines, and imprisonment.

Perhaps the best-known example of Puritan justice based upon primitive beliefs was the wave of witch-hunting that took place in Salem. A group of bored young girls accused some people they did not like of casting witches spells on them. Many people were badly frightened. A special court was named to look into the matter. Hundreds of people were accused. Many were led into a confession of guilt. That seemed to be the easiest and often the only way to escape the death sentence. If the accused confessed to being a witch and repented of evil ways, that person was punished and set free. Those who refused to plead guilty were condemned and "delivered up to Satan."

When the court was done, nineteen persons had been hanged. One old man had been pressed to death. A few had died from the harsh prison conditions under which they were forced to live while waiting trial. About 150 persons were still in confinement.

■ ***Puritan law challenged*** Many more ships bringing people from England were now arriving in Massachusetts. Among those seeking religious freedom were a number whose beliefs differed from those of the established church of the colony. A law was quickly passed that directed whipping and banishment for anyone who spoke against the Puritan teachings. Other laws called for attendance at all Puritan services. Tax laws were passed to pay the salaries of Puritan ministers.

Anne Hutchinson, a well-known religious leader, was one of those who spoke out against the teachings of the colony's church. She did not believe the church was very important. She thought a person could be close to God just by leading a good life. And she said so in public. She was brought to trial and charged with breaking the fifth commandment in that she did not honor her father and mother. When she questioned this, the court told her that her father and mother were the officers of Massachusetts Bay. Anne Hutchinson was ordered to leave the colony. When she asked why, the judge told her to ask no questions because the court knew why. That was all that was necessary.

Two churchmen, Roger Williams and Thomas Hooker, also angered the Massachusetts Bay authorities. They preached other "newe and dangerous opinions." One of these "dangerous" ideas was that government officers did not have the right to interfere in matters of religion. They believed government officials did not have the right to enforce the religious part of the Ten Commandments. They felt that disputes between people should be settled by a fair and impartial third person. They said that slavery was wrong.

impartial Not showing favor of one above another.

And they held the very important belief that people should have the right to change their laws as needed. Thomas Hooker said that government offices should be filled by elections. He believed no one should have to belong to a church in order to vote.

These two men left Massachusetts Bay and founded two new settlements. Hooker settled in Connecticut. Williams founded Rhode Island. When the laws for those two colonies were written, they contained the democratic ideas of their founders. Connecticut's Fundamental Orders was the first written constitution of modern democracy.

ENGLISH LAW BECOMES AMERICANIZED

The lands along the Atlantic coast were not settled in just a few years. Georgia, the last of the English colonies in America, was settled in 1733. The Virginia colony was then 126 years old. None of the first settlers began their work with the idea of founding a new country. They came to America for many reasons, but not with the thought of new citizenship. Those who left the old country because they were not happy with conditions there came to make a new and better England. The British flag came with the settlers. With the flag came the basic English way of life.

■ ***Circumstances determine law*** England, however, was thousands of miles away. There was little chance for contact. Life in America was hard and primitive. The people could not call for help from England every time they had a problem. Things could not always be done exactly as people did them in the old country. All the colonies, however, agreed on one thing—the need for rule by law. And they all wanted the rights of English citizens.

Most of the people who came to the colonies were English, but neither the lands nor the people were really alike. Some land was good for farming. Some was not, and the people had to make a living in other ways. The people had different English backgrounds and different goals to work for. The king had given the people in some colonies the right to settle and a few instructions about their form of government. In other colonies he had given the land to a trading company or to one or more important people who had the major voice in the government. There were people like Roger Williams and Thomas Hooker, who had founded their own settlements without permission from anyone.

As a result, the American colonies for many years served as a laboratory for testing different kinds of government. Almost every form of rule was tried. It was a question of try this, and if it doesn't work, try something else. Governments made the laws that they thought would answer the special needs of the particular place and time. Selling guns to the Indians, for example, might mean added danger to the settlers. So it was made a crime punishable by death. In early Virginia there was little food, so many of the laws dealt severely with anyone stealing it. Pork was much prized because many different kinds of dishes could be made from it and the hogs needed little care. Each hog was branded on an ear and allowed to run loose. People could tell who owned every hog. A person could get the death penalty if caught pig rustling or if found with a pig without a branded ear.

Punishments for breaking the law also depended on the needs and circumstances of the time. There was too little money to spend much of it on wrongdoers. Also, the offender was in most cases needed as a worker. A long jail sentence would cost the government a lot of money. It would also deprive the family or the settlement of a needed pair of hands. In general, therefore, the punishments were designed to be harsh, humiliating, and fast.

This is not to say that colonial judges never gave long sentences. A person could receive a sentence of several years at hard labor, working for the colony or the community. In cases of burglary or robbery the guilty person also had to return the stolen goods. If the person could not return them or pay what they were worth, he/she was made to work for the victim until the debt was paid off. The same was true if the guilty person owned no property that could be taken by the court to pay for the debts. On the other hand, England was at this time sending people to prison for such crimes.

When questions of law arose, colonial judges and lawyers studied the decisions of English judges on like cases. Often those rulings could be followed without change. However, colonial needs and circumstances were not like those in England. So colonial judges sometimes had to make their own law. This also happened when no similar cases could be found in English law. There slowly came into being an American body of law, based on English common law but clearly different and new.

Knowledge of law becomes necessary Many of the colonists were interested in law. The problems of building a new civilization from a very small beginning made some people eager to understand the law. Others were becoming well-to-do farmers, merchants, or owners of small factories. These people felt a need to know something about law in order to protect themselves in their business dealings. There was yet another need for knowing at least a little law. People too poor to pay for a lawyer were not given legal counsel at public expense. Even those who were not so poor found it hard to find legal aid. As a result, most people who came before a court on a criminal charge had to defend themselves as best they could.

Just before the American Revolution there were so many people in the colonies who knew a little law that a well-known Englishman said that everyone in America who reads "endeavors to obtain some smattering in law." General Gage, who had been sent to govern Massachusetts, said that "all his people were lawyers or smatters in law." It is not surprising, then, that the voice of the people became stronger and used many legal terms as it began to express its unhappiness with England. The colonies had had nearly 170 years to give their own style to the growing body of law and to learn its principles.

■ ***Court establishes freedom of the press*** During most of this period, England had been busy with major problems of its own. When some of these had been taken care of, there was time to look into the affairs of the colonies. England was running short of money. It seemed only fair that the colonies should help. To get this money, England passed new tax laws. Trade controls were set up and other new laws were passed. The colonists thought some of those laws were illegal and said so. England simply passed new laws to make the old ones stronger. From America the cry of "violation of rights" grew louder. Thus the conflict began, and it was aided by a famous court case in New York.

John Peter Zenger was a newspaper publisher in New York. He had printed a number of articles saying that the royal governor was wrong in some of his acts. The governor charged him with seditious libel and had him arrested. Seditious libel is a written statement stirring up ill will against the government. Zenger spent ten months behind bars before his case came to trial. Andrew Hamilton, one of the best-known lawyers in the colonies, agreed to handle Zenger's

---

smattering Superficial, or shallow, knowledge.

seditious libel In English law, the publishing of statements with the intent of causing antigovernment feeling.

defense. Hamilton departed from all English precedent. He argued that if what Zenger had printed was true, he had not committed a crime. The court agreed with Hamilton. Freedom of the press was made a reality by this New York court in colonial America.

■ ***England violates legal rights of colonies*** The colonists were greatly angered by the new *writs of assistance.* These were papers that gave a government official the power to enter and search a person's home or place of business. The writs did not have to name either the place to be searched or the things for which the officer was looking. This, the people said, was most certainly illegal.

English soldiers stationed in the colonies were lodged in private homes. Family habits and comfort were disturbed. People viewed this as a bold case of invasion of privacy.

Perhaps the thing that made the colonists more angry than anything else was the Stamp Act. This law, passed in 1765, said that tax stamps had to be placed on all newspapers and on many kinds of legal documents. The people had to pay for these stamps. This was, they said, taxation without representation.

Disagreements over these and other legal matters became more heated. Tempers flared. In Boston, on an evening in March 1770, some men and boys shouted insults at a group of British soldiers. This was followed by a hail of rocks, snowballs, and bricks. Shots were fired and five colonists died. In spite of the fact that British soldiers had killed colonists, many people said the soldiers had the right to a trial by jury. John Adams, one of the leading patriots, was one of these people. He served as the lawyer for the defense of the soldiers. Adams won acquittals for all except two. One of these two "pled the clergy." He was given a brand on the thumb and freed.

---

violate To break a law, an oath, or an agreement; to badly offend or outrage.

acquittal The setting free by court decision of someone from a charge or an accusation of an offense.

THE METROPOLITAN MUSEUM OF ART, GIFT OF MRS. RUSSELL SAGE, 1910

■ ***Colonies organize a policy-making body*** Many people believed the quarrel between England and the colonies called for united action. Virginia asked each colony to send representatives to a congress. This body would stand for all the colonies together. The congress would review the needs and problems of the colonies and suggest ways to solve them. On September 5, 1774, the First Continental Congress met in Philadelphia. From that moment there was a legal body to stand up for the common interests of all. The English colonies of North America were acting together for the first time. This Continental Congress was the foundation of the American federal union.

One of the first acts of this body was to write a paper stating the colonies' rights and grievances. In this paper the congress said that "the respective colonies are entitled to the common law of England." It stated that the colonies were promised by the English constitution and colonial charters the rights of life, liberty, and property. It claimed that the colonies never had given anyone the authority to take these rights away without their consent.

■ *Declaration of Independence* In April of the next year, words gave way to arms in the struggle for rights under the English common law. War had begun. Then in 1776, the reason for fighting changed. Most Americans had come to believe the rights they were fighting for could better be obtained under their own flag. They decided to seek independence.

A committee was named to write a declaration of independence. Thomas Jefferson was asked to do the first copy. He began it by stating why the colonies were fighting. He set forth their idea as to why governments are established and what the people have a right to do if a government does not carry out its duties. Following this was a list of the things done by the English king that the colonists believed illegal and cruel. The declaration closed with the announcement that, since England had remained deaf to the voice of justice, the people declare "That these United Colonies are, and of Right ought to be, Free and Independent States."

Running through the declaration are such phrases as these: all men are created equal; inalienable rights; life, liberty, and the pursuit of happiness; trial by jury; judiciary powers; quartering of troops; laws necessary for the public good; trade with all parts of the world.

The declaration also lists many ideals of democracy that had been stated earlier by English writers. These ideals became more firmly rooted in America. The Declaration of Independence is one of the cornerstones of our constitutional law. It sets forth the ideas of equality and human rights as the basis of our government and legal system.

FROM CONFEDERATION TO FEDERATION

Soon after the signing of the Declaration of Independence, the Continental Congress asked each state to set up its own government. By the end of the war all the states had written constitutions. At the same time the congress had a committee busy at work writing a plan of government for the new country.

■ ***Confederate government established and tested*** In 1777 the congress asked the states to vote on certain Articles of Confederation and Perpetual Union. These articles set up a very weak union. Most of the power to govern was to be kept by the states. The country was to have no president and no national courts–only a congress. In this congress each state, big or small, had only one vote. Laws could be passed only with the approval of nine of the states. To change the articles themselves, all the states must agree. The states were afraid to give up much of their power to the central government. So the United States once more became a testing ground for an experiment in government. It was another time of let's try this and see if it works. It took ten years of problems and near disaster for the people to see that this plan of government was not working. The new congress had so little power that it had to depend upon the local government to protect its members. Once some angry Pennsylvanians marched toward the building where the congress was meeting. The members had to hurry across the Pennsylvania state line for safety.

Could English common law remain the basis of our law? That also was being tested. Many people wanted to declare independence from anything and everything English. Some American lawyers tried to get other lawyers and judges to accept the French legal system. English common law, however, was too firmly rooted to be thrown out. And it has lived on through the years. Today an American lawyer may still call the court's attention to an English case when he/she cannot find an American case that backs up a point. The judge does not have to allow this. But if the case is very much to the point, she/he may consider it.

■ ***Convention called to revise the new government*** It became clear that the government under the Articles of Confederation was not working. A convention was called to change the articles. It was to begin in Philadelphia, on the second Monday in May 1787. Meetings were to be held in the State House in Philadelphia. This was the same building where the Declaration of Independence was adopted. Later this building was to become known as Independence Hall.

When the date arrived, only two delegates—one from Pennsylvania and one from Virginia—were present. For more than ten days the arriving delegates would meet, count the number present, and decide that was not enough to hold the meeting. Then they would go home until the next day. However, by May 25 most of the states were represented. The delegates decided to begin the work. It was hoped that the other delegates would arrive later. George Washington was elected the chief officer. The meeting then started. At the end of June, only delegates from New Hampshire and Rhode Island were absent. New Hampshire's delegate arrived in July. Rhode Island never did send anyone. The twelve states had selected seventy-four delegates in all. Only sixty-five made the trip, and ten of those did not attend any of the meetings. The average age of those attending was forty-two, with Benjamin Franklin the oldest at eighty-one.

The representatives were men of wide knowledge and public service. They were important men in their own states. Many were very wealthy. Thirty-nine were or had been members of the congress. Thirty-one had attended college. Two were college presidents, and three were college teachers. Eight had signed the Declaration of Independence, but nearly all had served the cause of independence in some way. Eight had helped to write their states' constitutions. Seven had served their own states as governor. Two were later to become President of the United States and one would serve as Vice President. Twenty-eight would later be elected to the new congress they had helped form. Four were to be named to the Supreme Court. More than two thirds of the members were lawyers. Of these, ten had been state judges.

As you can see, these men represented many kinds of experience and knowledge. All were leaders. They had tried hard to build national and state governments that would work. They had studied the different forms of government and the ideas of the world's best-known political writers.

■ ***Work of the convention*** It was not strange that most people would be interested in a meeting charged with the task of making changes in their government. But the delegates had to be able to talk openly and frankly. To do this, they must be free of people who wanted their own ideas to be heard. So it was decided not to allow visitors at any of the meetings. The delegates also agreed not to talk about the work of the convention with anyone except other members. They wanted to be sure that their work would be carried on in secret. So guards were posted at the doors, and the windows were kept closed. To work in Philadelphia on a hot summer's day in an upstairs room with all the windows and doors closed was far from pleasant. It is not surprising that the daily attendance was usually no more than thirty-five. There was one good thing, however, about keeping the windows closed. It did keep out some of the horseflies from the nearby stable.

The people of Philadelphia tried hard to make the task of the delegates as pleasant as possible. In the evenings many social events were planned. This city was the home of Benjamin Franklin. He enjoyed the company of many old friends. A few of the delegates were asked to stay close to the old man at evening parties. It was feared that Franklin might, without thinking, begin to talk about the work of the convention. If this happened, he was politely stopped.

Much of what we know about the convention we owe to the work of James Madison. A man had been named to keep a record of what happened, but his account contains few useful facts. Madison, however, took careful notes at the meetings and at night wrote a more complete account.

As the delegates began to recommend changes in the articles, they soon came to see that they were doing more than they had set out to do. They were writing out a new form of government. The men had different political ideas and came from states that had different interests and needs. Some were from farm states. Others were from business and trading centers. Because of their different interests and needs, different plans of government were presented. At times the members became so angry that the convention was in danger of breaking up.

There were many questions to be settled, but the delegates did agree on one point. They believed the best form of government was that already used by the states. Each state government was divided into three different branches—one to make the laws *(legislative)*, another to see that the laws were obeyed *(executive)*, and the third to say what the laws meant *(judicial)*. This was the way the delegates decided the national government should be set up. The three branches were to work together. At the same time, each branch could check the work of the others. In this way no one branch could become too powerful.

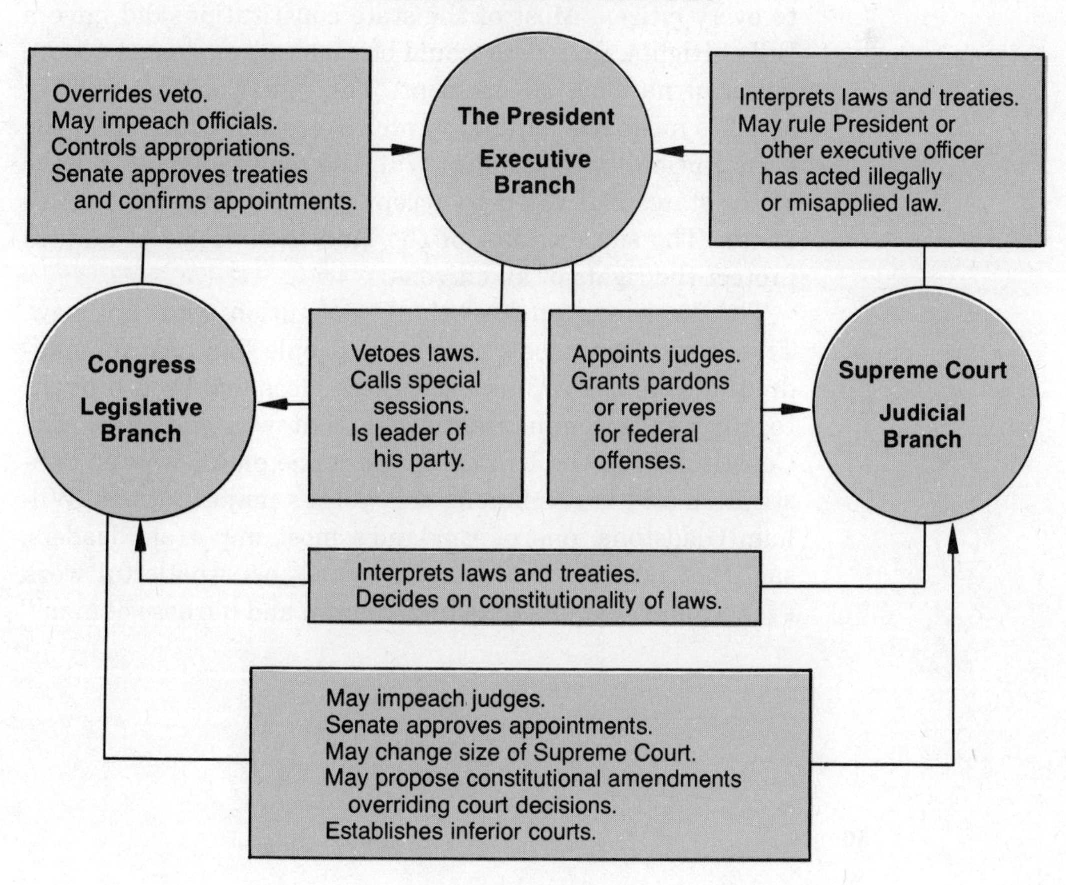

All through the summer the men worked out the many other details of the government. On September 17, 1787, when the work of the convention was over, only forty-two of the original fifty-five delegates were present. Of this number, only thirty-nine wished to sign the new document drawn up at the meeting.

■ ***A new constitutional government established*** The Constitution of the United States went into effect in June 1788. The people now had a new government that put the power into their own hands. There was a two-house legislature called Congress. There was a chief executive, or President. And there was a Supreme Court.

Many people were worried, however, because the Constitution did not have a list of the rights that were guaranteed to every citizen. Most of the state constitutions did have a Bill of Rights. But these would be of no use against the more powerful national government. The new Congress quickly acted to meet this need. It wrote twelve amendments to the Constitution. By December 1791, the required three fourths of the states had voted to accept ten of the twelve amendments. The supreme law of the land then included laws to protect the rights of all citizens.

The ideas written into the Constitution were not new. They came from ideals that some people had held for hundreds of years. Now, however, these ideas had been brought together in a commonsense way that was workable. The Constitution of the United States is the oldest written constitution still in use among the world's major nations. William Gladstone, one of England's most important leaders, said that our Constitution was "the most wonderful work ever struck off at one time by the brain and purpose of man."

Reviewing the Chapter

Law-Related Terms

Warrant *P. 26*
Grand jury *Pp. 26, 305*
Immunity *P. 30*
Acquittal *P. 48*

Review Questions

1. **(a)** How did the Anglo-Saxons decide whether someone was innocent or guilty of having wronged another person? **(b)** How did they punish someone for having committed a wrong? *Pp. 18–23*
2. **(a)** How did the Normans change the English court system? **(b)** Explain the jury system under the Normans. *Pp. 24–27*
3. **(a)** How was common law established in England? **(b)** Why was the Magna Carta important? *Pp. 28–29*
4. **(a)** Who were the Pilgrims? **(b)** Under what agreement did they set up the government for their colony? *Pp. 37–39*
5. **(a)** What colony did the Puritans establish? **(b)** What Puritan teachings did Anne Hutchinson, Roger Williams, and Thomas Hooker challenge? *Pp. 41, 43–44*
6. Explain this statement: "The American colonies for many years served as a laboratory for testing different kinds of government." *Pp. 45–46*
7. Why was the decision in the John Peter Zenger case so important? *Pp. 47–48*
8. Why is the Declaration of Independence a cornerstone of our law? *P. 51*
9. Why was the Bill of Rights added to the Constitution? *P. 56*

Chapter Test

On a separate paper, write T *if the statement is true, and* F *if the statement is false.*

1. Two methods the Anglo-Saxons used to decide whether a person was guilty or innocent of having committed a wrong were trial by oath and trial by ordeal.
2. According to Anglo-Saxon law, a much higher fine had to be paid for harming a lord or a churchman than for harming a peasant or a serf.
3. A written order, issued by a court or an official having the proper authority, is called an acquittal.
4. An important contribution the Normans made to the English system of law was trial by jury.
5. The common law of England developed as a result of judges' making decisions that were based on how similar cases had been decided in the past.
6. The agreement in which the Pilgrims set up the government for their colony is called the Magna Carta.
7. The colony founded by the Puritans was the Massachusetts Bay Colony.
8. Roger Williams and Thomas Hooker believed government officers should not interfere in matters of religion.
9. The trial of John Peter Zenger was very important because it established the principle of freedom of the press.
10. The document that lists the reasons the American colonies broke away from England is called the Bill of Rights.

DEPT. OF
EDUCATION

Constitutional Law 3

Wisconsin *v.* Yoder

406 U.S. 205, 92 S.Ct. 1526, 32 L.Ed.2d 15 (1972)

TOPIC—Action brought concerning the right to free exercise of religion under the First Amendment

FACTS—Members of the Old Order Amish faith in Wisconsin refused to send their children to public schools past the eighth grade. The Amish believe if they send their children to high school, their own salvation and that of their children will be in danger. Amish beliefs require members of that faith to make their living by farming or in ways closely related to farming. The Amish feel that high schools and colleges might give their children "worldly" ideas. These ideas conflict with Amish beliefs. The Amish are not against education through the first eight grades. They agree that their children must have some learning in order to be good farmers and citizens.

The Amish people in this case were convicted for violation of a state law requiring school attendance to age sixteen. The case was appealed to the United States Supreme Court.

QUESTION—Should a group of persons be made to attend public schools when such attendance is against their religious beliefs?

THE CONSTITUTION IN AMERICAN SOCIETY

The United States Constitution binds fifty separate states together. It establishes the government of the United States of America. The Constitution gives us the basic principles by which our legal system works. The laws made by our elected representatives in Congress are based on the Constitution. This means that our Constitution and laws represent the voice of the people of the United States.

The document itself is found in the National Archives in Washington, D.C. It is protected by a glass case and guarded at all times. But because the Constitution is a living document, it affects the day-to-day lives of the American people in many ways. It affects us when we read the newspapers or watch the evening news on television. It affects us when we attend school or when we receive paychecks. There is hardly any part of our lives that the Constitution of the United States does not touch in some way.

■ ***Outline of the Constitution*** It is important for you to have an understanding of what the Constitution really is. The outline of the Constitution shown below will help you in

learning about the parts of the Constitution that have a direct bearing on laws and our legal system. The entire Constitution can be found on pages 279–301.

A. Preamble

We the people of the United States, in order to form a more perfect union, establish justice, insure domestic tranquility, provide for the common defense, promote the general welfare, and secure the blessings of liberty to ourselves and our posterity, do ordain and establish this Constitution for the United States of America.

B. Main Body of the Constitution

ARTICLE I	The legislative branch of the government
ARTICLE II	The executive branch of the government
ARTICLE III	The judicial branch of the government
ARTICLE IV	Full faith and credit clause, privileges and immunities clause
ARTICLE V	Process for adding amendments
ARTICLE VI	Supremacy clause

C. Bill of Rights—Amendments I to X

AMENDMENT I	Freedom of religion, speech, press, assembly, and petition
AMENDMENT II	Right to keep and bear arms
AMENDMENT III	Quartering of troops
AMENDMENT IV	Right against unreasonable searches and seizures, no warrants without probable cause
AMENDMENT V	Grand jury, double jeopardy, privilege against self-incrimination, due process of law, and eminent domain

AMENDMENT VI	Rights of the accused—speedy public trial, jury trial, informed of charge, confrontation of witnesses, and assistance of counsel for the defense
AMENDMENT VII	Jury trial in civil suits
AMENDMENT VIII	No excessive bail, nor fines, nor cruel and unusual punishments
AMENDMENT IX	Listing of rights in the Constitution does not limit all other rights retained by people.
AMENDMENT X	Powers not delegated to United States, nor prohibited to states, are reserved to states or people.

D. Amendments XI to XXV

AMENDMENT XI	A state may not be sued by citizen of another state or citizen of foreign country.
AMENDMENT XII	Provision for election of President and Vice President
AMENDMENT XIII	No slavery or involuntary servitude except as punishment for crime
AMENDMENT XIV	Persons born or naturalized in United States are citizens of state where they reside; no state to abridge privileges or immunities of United States citizens; or deprive any person of life, liberty, or property, without due process of law; nor deny equal protection of the laws
AMENDMENT XV	Right of United States citizens to vote not to be denied on account of race, color, or previous servitude
AMENDMENT XVI	Income tax without apportionment according to census
AMENDMENT XVII	Election of senators by direct vote of people of state

AMENDMENT XVIII	Prohibition amendment—repealed by Twenty-first Amendment
AMENDMENT XIX	Woman suffrage
AMENDMENT XX	Abolishes short sessions of Congress; Congress to meet each year
AMENDMENT XXI	Repeals Eighteenth Amendment
AMENDMENT XXII	Limits presidential term of office to two elective terms
AMENDMENT XXIII	Presidential electors for District of Columbia
AMENDMENT XXIV	Eliminates poll tax in federal elections
AMENDMENT XXV	Presidential succession

■ ***Government under the Constitution*** The United States Constitution should not be confused with the constitutions of the fifty states. Most state constitutions are much like the federal Constitution, but they serve to set up each state's own government. As a general rule, state constitutions include many more detailed legal matters than does the United States Constitution. Nothing in a state constitution is allowed to conflict with the principles set forth in the federal Constitution. For example, a state cannot take from its citizens any one of their federal rights.

However, the writers of the Constitution wanted to limit the powers of the federal government. Perhaps of first importance in their minds was provision for a system of restraints on government actions. The Tenth Amendment states clearly that those powers not given to the United States by the Constitution are given to the states or to the people. The United States government is allowed to use only those powers that are given to it by the Constitution.

THE DISTRIBUTION OF POWERS IN OUR FEDERAL SYSTEM OF GOVERNMENT

Federal Government

Delegated powers

To raise and support armed forces
To levy and collect taxes
To borrow money
To coin money
To admit new states
To regulate interstate and foreign commerce
To govern territories and the national capital
To carry on foreign relations
To set up post offices

Implied powers

"To make all laws... necessary and proper for carrying into execution the foregoing powers...."

Federal and State Governments

Concurrent powers

To levy and collect taxes
To borrow money
To make and enforce laws
To provide for the general welfare
To set up courts

State Government

Reserved powers

To regulate intrastate commerce
To determine voter qualifications
To provide for public safety and morals
To establish local government
To carry on elections
To incorporate businesses
To issue licenses

The Constitution is the highest law of the land. This is set forth in Article III. But who decides what is legal under the Constitution? It has been stated that the Constitution "says what the Supreme Court says that it says." And this is true. It is the duty of the United States Supreme Court to decide legal questions based on the Constitution. The Supreme Court does not give advice or opinions. It only makes decisions on actual cases brought before it. The Supreme Court has the power to declare acts of Congress as well as state laws unconstitutional. In the case of *Marbury* v. *Madison* (1803) the Supreme Court first decided that a certain act of Congress was contrary to the Constitution. Since that time the Supreme Court has ruled on many acts of Congress and many more state laws to decide if they were constitutional.

■ ***Growth of federal powers*** Our society has become more and more complex since the Constitution was first written. Our problems have become nationwide in scope. So the idea of what powers the national government may use has grown a great deal. The growth, however, has been based exactly on the language of the Constitution. Article I, Section 8, Paragraph 18 gives Congress power "to make all laws which shall be necessary and proper." The leading case on this point is *McCulloch* v. *Maryland* (1819). In that case the State of Maryland placed a tax on the Bank of the United States. The bank refused to pay and Maryland sued to collect. During the trial, the State of Maryland questioned whether Congress had the power to set up a bank in the first place. The Constitution does not specifically give it that power. But Chief Justice of the United States John Marshall said that "the necessary and proper" clause of the Constitution gave Congress the power it needed. Congress is charged with the responsibility for such things as collecting taxes and supporting the armed forces. In order to do these things, Congress may use convenient means. But it may do so only as long as the means used are necessary, useful for the purpose, and proper. The Supreme Court decided that a bank is a convenient way for the government to handle its business.

■ ***Commerce clause*** Another reason for the growth of federal power is the "commerce" clause found in Article I, Section 8, Paragraph 3. The Congress shall have the power "to regulate commerce with foreign nations, and among the several states." A long list of United States Supreme Court decisions has added to federal powers under the commerce clause. This clause was put into the Constitution to end the strong rivalry among the states. Some states have natural advantages over other states. Some have fine ports. Others have mineral wealth. There were always economic battles between the states. The United States Supreme Court case that first decided the scope of the commerce clause was *Gibbons* v. *Ogden* in 1824. The State of New York had given a group of its citizens the right to run steamboats on waters in the state. People from neighboring New Jersey wanted to run steamboats on these same waters. The Supreme Court decided that to allow only the group in the State of New

York to use these waters and not allow citizens of New Jersey the same right was unconstitutional under the commerce clause.

The states do not always agree about what the national commerce powers are. Often they do not agree either about what police powers the states have in interstate commerce. In most cases where the two powers conflict, the Supreme Court has decided in favor of the federal government. Areas covered by the commerce clause have grown through the years. Today our lives are affected in many ways wherever there is interstate commerce. The commerce clause may affect the business where people work and the goods that they buy as well as the running of such places of business as restaurants, motels, and other public places all over the country. Under the commerce clause, the government has the power to regulate transportation by road, rail, or air. It has the power to provide flood protection. It can build dams, and it can keep dams from being built. It can also control industrial and agricultural production and prices. Today there are few areas that do not fall under the federal government's power to regulate commerce.

Edwards *v.* California

314 U.S. 160, 62 S.Ct. 164, 86 L.Ed. 119 (1941)

TOPIC—Action involving interstate commerce and state police power

FACTS—Mr. Edwards was a citizen of the United States living in California. His wife's brother, Mr. Duncan, lived in Texas. Duncan worked there with the Works Progress Administration. This was a relief program set up by Congress at the request of President Franklin Roosevelt. Duncan went to California to live with his brother-in-law Edwards in December 1939. He had left his job in Texas and had no money. Ten days after he got to California, Duncan began receiving financial help from the California state government. A short while later some people

---

interstate commerce Business or trade between two or more states or their citizens.

became unhappy about this man's coming from another state into California and having to be taken care of by the state. They remembered that the state had a law which said that a person could not bring someone into California from out of state when the newcomer had neither money nor a job. They brought the facts of this case into a California court. The court decided that Edwards did break the California law by bringing Duncan into the state. The question was appealed to a higher court. Finally, the United States Supreme Court accepted the case.

QUESTION—Under the federal Constitution, does a state have the right to use police power to keep a United States citizen from coming into its territory with neither job nor money?

Heart of Atlanta Motel, Inc. *v.* United States
379 U.S. 241, 85 S.Ct. 348, 13 L.Ed.2d 258 (1964)

TOPIC—Action involving interstate commerce and civil rights

FACTS—The appellant owned and ran the Heart of Atlanta Motel. This 216-room motel was located in downtown Atlanta. People could easily reach it from busy highways. The appellant had advertised the motel outside the state of Georgia. He had put ads in magazines sold all over the country. He had used more than fifty billboards and highway signs inside the state asking for guests. About 75 percent of the guests were from out of state. This meant that the motel was engaged in interstate commerce. Before the Civil Rights Act of 1964 was passed, the owner had always refused to rent rooms to blacks. He said that he meant to go on refusing. The United States government, through the Department of Justice, brought suit against the motel. The court found that the motel's racially discriminatory policy was against the law as stated in the Civil Rights Act. The owner appealed the case to the United States Supreme Court.

QUESTION—Does Congress have the constitutional power to regulate a privately owned business under the public accommodations sections of the Civil Rights Act of 1964?

■ ***Full faith and credit clause*** Another way the Constitution serves to regulate relations among the separate state governments is through the "full faith and credit" clause. This is found in Article IV, Section 1. It says that each state must respect the laws and court decisions of all other states. For example, if a marriage is legal in one state, it must be accepted as legal by all the other states. Also, if a person is found not guilty of a particular crime by the courts of one state, that person cannot be tried for the same crime in any other state.

■ ***Privileges and immunities clause*** The "privileges and immunities" clause in Article IV, Section 2, protects the rights of citizens as they visit or move from state to state. A citizen of the United States from one state can move to another state and at all times be sure of protection under state law. A citizen can live, work, and own property in any state. However, such a person must live in the state for a given length of time before being able to vote or hold office in that state.

Toomer *v.* Witsell
334 U.S. 385, 68 S.Ct. 1156, 92 L.Ed. 1460 (1948)

TOPIC—Action involving the privileges and immunities clause

FACTS—South Carolina law said that people living in that state had to pay a license fee of $25 for each boat they used for shrimp fishing within 3 miles of the state's coastline. A person who did not live in the state had to pay $2500 for each boat so used. This fee was cut to $150 if the person from outside the state had held a license for each of the three years before.

The fishing that South Carolina tried to regulate by the law in question is part of a larger shrimp-fishing industry. The waters used stretch from North Carolina to Florida. Most of the shrimp in these waters are migratory. They swim south in the late summer and fall and return north in the spring. There was no federal law about fishing in these waters, so the four states most interested had gone their own ways in making laws. Many commercial shrimpers, including those from out of state, liked to start fishing off the Carolinas in the summer. They then followed the shrimp down the coast to Florida.

Some of the shrimpers from Georgia felt that the fees charged by South Carolina were much too high. They felt that this was not fair, and they brought their case to the federal district court. This court decided in favor of the State of South Carolina. The case was then appealed to the United States Supreme Court.

QUESTION—Under the privileges and immunities clause of the Constitution, does South Carolina have the right to penalize people from outside of the state for fishing within 3 miles of its coastline by charging them a higher fee than that charged to people who live in South Carolina?

■ ***Equal protection in the states*** The first ten amendments to the Constitution limit the powers of the federal government. The Fourteenth Amendment, on the other hand, has to do with the powers of the state governments,

not the federal government. The Fourteenth Amendment, along with the Thirteenth and Fifteenth Amendments, was passed following the War Between the States. Before the war, no state in the South or the North considered blacks to be citizens. The Fourteenth Amendment was passed in 1868 to make sure that black Americans received all their political rights as citizens of the United States. In the years since then, the Supreme Court has interpreted the Fourteenth Amendment to mean that the individual states must give to all their citizens the same rights already guaranteed by the federal government under the Bill of Rights.

The most important language in the Fourteenth Amendment is found in Section 1:

> All persons born or naturalized in the United States, and subject to the jurisdiction thereof, are citizens of the United States and of the State wherein they reside. No State shall make or enforce any law which shall abridge the privileges or immunities of citizens of the United States; nor shall any State deprive any person of life, liberty, or property, without due process of law; nor deny to any person within its jurisdiction the equal protection of the laws.

---

naturalize To admit to citizenship.

jurisdiction The legal authority of a court to try a case; power of those in authority.

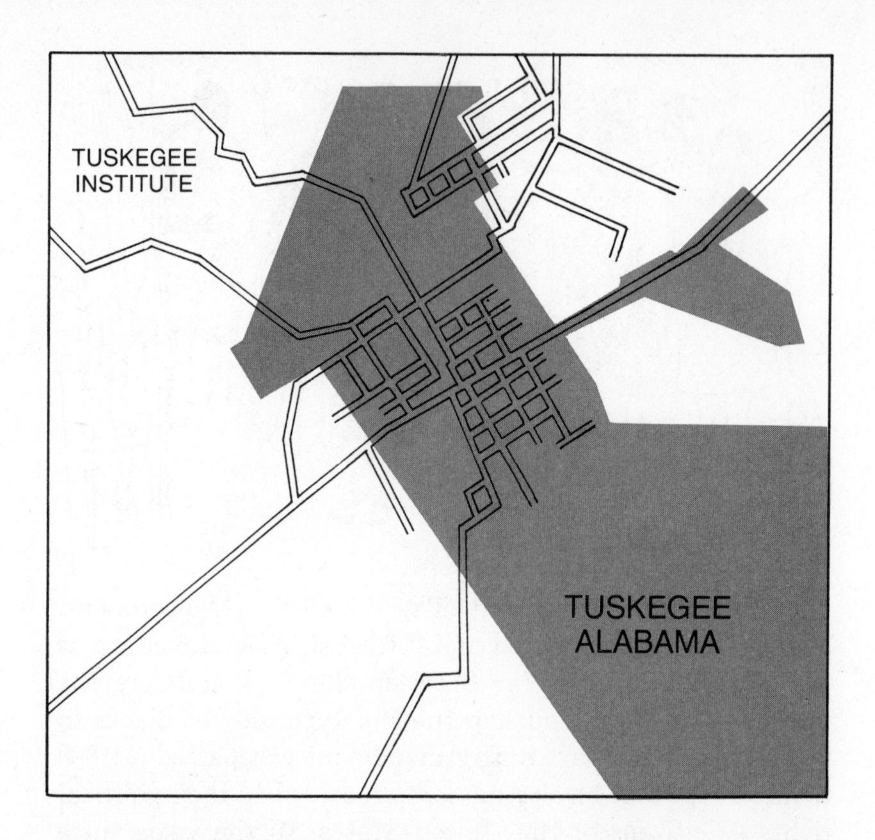

The phrase "due process of law" means all the proper steps and rights granted by the Constitution and the courts. It includes the right to a fair trial and the right to be represented by a lawyer. Due process assures people of fair and reasonable treatment in the judicial process. It protects them from arbitrary acts of judges or other officials. Due process has come to mean the idea of fair play for all under the law.

Gomillion *v.* Lightfoot
364 U.S. 339, 81 S.Ct. 125, 5 L.Ed.2d 110 (1960)

TOPIC—Action involving rights under the Fourteenth Amendment

FACTS—In 1957, the Alabama State Legislature passed a law that changed the boundaries of the city of Tuskegee. Before the law was passed, Tuskegee was square in shape. The law changed it into a strangely irregular, 28-sided figure. This was deliberately designed to exclude areas where large numbers of black people lived so that they could no longer vote in the city.

The new law had arranged the city's voting districts in a manner that kept all but 4 out of 500 blacks from voting in city elections. However, not one white voter was affected. A black citizen of Tuskegee sued on the grounds that the new law deprived him of his right to vote.

QUESTION—Does a state have the constitutional right to change a city's voting district lines in order to arrange the votes more heavily in one district than in another?

Green *v.* County School Board
391 U.S. 430, 88 S.Ct. 1689, 20 L.Ed.2d 716 (1968)

TOPIC—Action involving school desegregation and rights under the Fourteenth Amendment

FACTS—The school system in New Kent County, Virginia, had only two schools. One school was for white children and one was for black children. About one half of the 4,500 people in the county were blacks. Lately the school system had run under a "freedom of choice" plan. This allowed the pupils to choose the school they wished to attend. While the "freedom of choice" plan was working, not a single white child had chosen to attend the black school. A number of black children had entered the white school. But 85 percent of the black children still attended the black school. The record showed that 21 school buses ran overlapping routes to carry pupils to and from the two schools.

QUESTION—Can a school system go on using the "freedom of choice" plan when the plan is not doing what it is supposed to—in this case, desegregating the county schools?

---

voting districts Divisions of state, city, or county set up for purposes of voting.

THE BILL OF RIGHTS

The first ten amendments, known as the Bill of Rights, were added to the Constitution in 1791. They guarantee to every individual citizen certain fundamental rights and liberties. The writers of the Bill of Rights, as well as other American leaders of the time, did not want an all-powerful federal government. They feared that such a government might repeat the very evils that a revolution had been fought to escape. So the Bill of Rights was designed to protect the basic rights of a free people against federal actions. The first ten amendments, more than any other part of the Constitution, have kept alive the spirit of American independence. Today these rights remain important as safeguards against interference by government.

CIVIL LIBERTIES GUARANTEED TO ALL AMERICANS

■ ***First Amendment*** The First Amendment is concerned with four basic rights and liberties. These are freedom of religion, freedom of speech, freedom of the press, and freedom of assembly. The First Amendment protects citizens against federal laws that would interfere with the four freedoms. For a long time the Supreme Court held that the First Amendment applied only to the federal government and not to the separate states. However, as you read on page 71, since the Fourteenth Amendment was added to the Constitution, the Supreme Court has held that the Bill of Rights must apply to each state as well as to the federal government of the United States.

■ *Freedom of religion* was a right that the colonists were very concerned with protecting, because they remembered well the religious persecutions in Europe. They wanted to be sure that such persecutions could not happen in the United States. After the Revolutionary War, there were many religious groups in all the thirteen new states. Many of the citizens, especially in Virginia and the Carolinas, continued to belong to the Church of England. Some belonged to other Protestant churches such as Baptist, Methodist, Lutheran, Presbyterian, Congregationalist, and Quaker. Each religious group wanted to be sure that it had the right to follow its own beliefs without interference. Persons who were not members of any religious group wanted to have the right not to follow any religion if they so chose.

In 1802, President Thomas Jefferson stated that he thought the First Amendment was meant to build "a wall of separation between church and state." Others felt that the First Amendment was only meant to keep the government from favoring any one religion over another. In spite of this disagreement, it was clear that the Constitution intended to protect the right of every person to follow freely whatever religion he/she chose. Article VI, Paragraph 3 of the main body of the Constitution states that "no religious test shall ever be required as a qualification to any office or public trust under the United States."

Marsh *v.* Alabama

326 U.S. 501, 66 S.Ct. 276, 90 L.Ed. 265 (1946)

TOPIC—Action brought concerning right to free exercise of religious beliefs

FACTS—Mrs. Marsh was a member of Jehovah's Witnesses. She was handing out religious literature on the streets of a town in Alabama that was owned by a shipbuilding company. Marsh stood on the sidewalk near the post office as she was handing out the literature. In nearby stores the shipbuilding company had posted a notice that read as follows: "This Is Private Property, and Without Written Permission, No Street, or House Vendor, Agent or Solicitation of Any Kind Will Be Permitted." Marsh was warned that she could not hand out her literature without a permit. She was also told that no permit would be given to her. When she protested, she was arrested for violation of the Alabama Code. An Alabama law made it a crime to enter or remain on the premises of another after having been warned not to do so.

QUESTION—Does a person have the right to hand out religious literature on the streets of a company-owned town?

■ *The freedoms of speech and the press* were most important in the minds of the people after the Revolutionary War. Many of them had gone through a number of trying years during which they did not feel free to state their own feelings about English rule. They wanted to be sure that the Constitution protected their right of free expression. Democracy itself depends upon the people being able to talk freely about their own ideas on matters of public policy. The freedoms of speech and the press were necessary to guarantee the right of free expression needed for a democratic society. Freedom of speech includes the following.

1. Freedom of thought
2. Freedom of belief
3. Freedom to speak
4. Freedom to remain silent

Freedom of the press includes the freedom to write, draw, picture, or carve. The freedoms of speech and the press do not mean freedom to use the following kinds of speech or language.

1. Slanderous or libelous
2. Lewd or obscene
3. Profane
4. Meant to encourage criminal acts
5. Designed to plan and promote the overthrow of the government by force

---

United States *v.* O'Brien
391 U.S. 367, 88 S.Ct. 1673, 20 L.Ed.2d 672 (1968)

TOPIC—Action involving freedom of speech under the First Amendment

FACTS—On the morning of March 31, 1966, Mr. O'Brien and three friends burned their Selective Service cards on the steps of a Boston courthouse. Among the large crowd that gathered to watch were several agents of the Federal Bureau of Investigation. Right after the burning, members of the crowd began attacking O'Brien and his friends. An FBI agent led

O'Brien to safety inside the courthouse. O'Brien said that he had burned his card in order to try to win others to his antiwar beliefs. He was charged with willfully and knowingly mutilating, destroying, and burning his registration card in violation of the Universal Military Training and Service Act of 1948.

QUESTION—Does a person have the right to burn his Selective Service card as a means of expressing an idea?

Kovacs *v.* Cooper
336 U.S. 77, 69 S.Ct. 448, 93 L.Ed. 513 (1949)

TOPIC—Action involving free speech and a "captive audience"

FACTS—Mr. Kovacs was convicted of violation of a law of the city of Trenton, New Jersey. This law prohibited the use of sound amplifiers on city streets. The law stated

> . . . that it shall be unlawful for any person . . . held as a principal, agent or employee, to play, use or operate for advertising purposes, or for any other purpose whatsoever, on or upon the public streets, alleys or thoroughfares in the city of Trenton, any device known as

a sound truck, loud speaker or sound amplifier, or radio or phonograph with a loud speaker or sound amplifier, or any other instrument known as a calliope or any instrument of any kind or character which emits therefrom loud and raucous noises and is attached to and upon any vehicle operated or standing upon said streets or public places aforementioned.

Kovacs was using a sound truck for advertising purposes on a public street in Trenton. The case went to the United States Supreme Court.

QUESTION—Does such a law violate the rights of freedom of speech and freedom to give information to others?

Wood *v.* Georgia
370 U.S. 375, 82 S.Ct. 1364, 8 L.Ed.2d 569 (1969)

TOPIC—Action based on the right of free speech

FACTS—Groups of people with common interests—ethnic, racial, religious, economic, etc.—often vote for or against the same candidates or issues. This is sometimes called bloc voting. On June 6, 1960, a judge of the Bibb Superior Court in Bibb County, Georgia, ordered an investigation into the question of black bloc voting. The indications were that certain people running for office in the county had paid large amounts of money to get groups of black votes.

The following day Mr. Wood, elected sheriff of Bibb county, told the newspapers, "Whatever the judge's intention, the action . . . ordering an investigation of 'Negro bloc voting' will be considered one of the most deplorable examples of race agitation to come out of Middle Georgia in recent years." A month later Wood was charged with being in contempt of court based on the above statement. The case eventually went to the United States Supreme Court.

QUESTION—Does an elected officer have the right to freedom of expression about political acts?

---

contempt of court Lack of respect for the dignity or authority of the court or interference with its orderly administration of justice.

■ *Freedom to meet peaceably and associate together* is another right protected under the First Amendment. It is only when a group gathers for a purpose that is against the law or that endangers the running of state or national government that any limit is placed upon the freedom of assembly. The right of people to gather together and express themselves is fundamental to our idea of liberty. After the Revolutionary War, the people felt that the right of peaceable assembly, like the freedoms of speech and the press, lay at the foundation of the government they desired.

Adderly *v.* Florida
385 U.S. 39, 87 S.Ct. 242, 17 L.Ed.2d 149 (1966)

TOPIC—Action involving the freedoms of expression and assembly guaranteed under the First Amendment

FACTS—A group of students from a Florida university were arrested for protesting against racial discrimination at their school. The next day another group of students from the university went to the county jail to protest those arrests. The county sheriff, as legal custodian of the jail and jail grounds, tried to talk the group into leaving. He warned them that they must leave or he would arrest them for trespassing. Some left, but others stayed and were arrested. Thirty-two students were convicted of "trespass with a malicious and mischievous intent" upon the premises of a county jail. The case was appealed.

QUESTION—Did the students have the constitutional right under the "freedom of expression" clause to demonstrate on jail grounds after being asked by the sheriff to leave?

Edwards *v.* South Carolina
372 U.S. 229, 83 S.Ct. 680, 9 L.Ed.2d 697 (1963)

TOPIC—Action involving rights of freedoms of expression and assembly

---

trespass The unlawful act of entering another person's property without permission.

FACTS—Late in the morning on a March day, 187 black high school and college students met at a Zion Baptist church in South Carolina. From there they walked in groups of about 15 to the South Carolina State House grounds, which were open to the public. The students wanted to make known to the citizens of South Carolina that they were not happy with the way in which black people were being treated.

Thirty or more police officers were already on the State House grounds when the students arrived. At first the students were simply warned to remain peaceful. But later they were asked to leave within 15 minutes. They did not leave. Instead they began carrying signs bearing such messages as "I am Proud to be a Negro" and "Down with Segregation." They sang "The Star-Spangled Banner" and other patriotic and religious songs, while stamping their feet and clapping their hands. After the 15 minutes had passed, they were arrested and marched off to jail. The state trial court convicted them of breach of the peace. The case was appealed to the United States Supreme Court.

QUESTION—Did these students have the constitutional right to protest and demonstrate?

■ ***CBs and the First Amendment*** Is there any connection between the legal use of citizens band radios and the rights under the First Amendment of the Constitution of the United States? In the last few years huge numbers of homes and automobiles all over the country have grown "ears." Ears is the slang term for citizens band radio antennas. The CB antennas are the symbol of a new communication craze in America.

Like just about everything else that people do, there is a legal side to citizens band radio use. A CB user must become a licensed operator. She/he must use the equipment following rules and regulations set up by the Federal Communications Commission (FCC). Today there are well over thirteen

breach of the peace Unlawful disturbance of the public peace and quiet.

million citizens band radios in the United States. This means that roughly one out of every twenty citizens may talk over wireless radio to other CB users at any given time.

The citizens band radio as we know it today began in 1958. That year the FCC assigned certain available radio wavelengths for use as a new Citizens Band Radio Service, called Class D. The new radio service was for the most part meant for both personal and business use by private citizens, particularly in cases where there were no other ways of sending messages. This meant such uses as those needed in operating some large businesses, farms, and building projects. It was also useful for service or repair businesses, such as emergency road service. By 1959 the FCC had given out about 15,000 Class D station licenses to citizens band radio users.

In 1960 the FCC developed new rules designed to restrict citizens band radio communications to useful and "substantial" messages. Messages sent to random or unknown stations were not allowed. The sending of messages between two or more Class D stations was held to not more than five minutes at a time, which had to be followed by two minutes of silence. By 1963 the FCC noted that about 350,000 Class D radio users had received their licenses. The FCC also saw that there was a great deal of misuse of the Class D operating privileges. The FCC felt that the continued usefulness of the Citizens Band Radio Service was in danger. Their ideas for changes in the citizens band radio rules were made public, and interested persons were invited to give their own ideas to the FCC. In answer to this request, more than 2,500 persons gave their views to the commission. In 1965 the FCC again set up new rules meant to limit use of the Citizens Band Radio Service. One new ruling stated that the five-minute operating time had to be followed by five minutes of silence. The FCC reported that as of April 1965 there were more than 800,000 people who held licenses in the Citizens Band Radio Service. Applications were being filed at the rate of about 20,000 a month.

■ ***CB as a hobby*** By 1970, citizens band radio had been discovered by the hobbyists. These people saw CB as a form of entertainment. They wanted to take part in radio conversations just for the fun of it, and the twenty-three frequency channels set aside for citizens band radio became crowded with talk. Still more people began to use CB radios during the gasoline shortage. Truck drivers all over the country began using their CB radios to tell one another where they could get fuel and how traffic was running in certain places. The truck drivers gave themselves nicknames such as Sundance Kid and Boomerang. In March 1975, pressured by the hobbyists, the FCC lifted the restrictions against the use of CB as a hobby. In July 1976, the FCC increased to forty the number of frequency channels that could be used starting in 1977. Today, thousands of licensed CB users send their voices out legally in a continuing stream of small talk. Many CB users say that they enjoy using their CB radios while making long trips. Others say that CB radios can be put to helpful use. They can be used to report accidents or road problems and to help find lost persons. In a growing number of cases,

CB owners have helped police by reporting crimes. But for most CB users, their radios remain an enjoyable hobby.

Today's rules for the use of citizens band radios were developed by the Federal Communications Commission and are known as Part 95, Citizens Band Radio Service. Every citizens band radio owner must apply to the FCC for a license, which is good for five years. A person must be eighteen years of age or older in order to get a license. Copies of FCC Rules and Regulations (VI, Part 95) governing the Citizens Band Radio Service may be had from the Superintendent of Documents in Washington, D.C. Copies of these rules can also be obtained at many radio stores for a small charge.

Lafayette Radio Electronics *v.* United States
345 F.2d 278 (1965)

TOPIC—Petition for review of Federal Communications Commission regulation

FACTS—On April 26, 1965, a new rule of the FCC was to go into effect. The new rule stated that citizens band radio stations could not be used "for engaging in radio communications as a hobby or diversion, i.e., operating the radio station as an activity in and of itself." The Lafayette Radio Electronics Corporation, which made citizens band radios, challenged this rule. The company asked the United States Court of Appeals for the Second Circuit to issue a temporary restraining order to prevent the new rule from becoming effective. The company said that the rule violated the First Amendment right to freedom of speech and expression.

Representatives of the FCC told the court that the Citizens Band Radio Service was intended for messages between businesses and delivery trucks or cars. It was meant for use in vehicles in and around large factories, building projects, and farms or ranches. It was also meant for the use of such people as campers, hunters, and explorers. The FCC said that the

---

temporary restraining order A court order whereby an action or a law will not be enforced or permitted until a full court hearing on the subject is held.

service was meant for serious messages and was not meant to be used just for fun.

QUESTION—Does the federal government have the power to regulate and limit the use of citizens band radio messages?

Gagliardo *v.* United States
366 F.2d 720 (1966)

TOPIC—Action involving conviction of uttering obscene, indecent, or profane language by means of radio communication

FACTS—Mr. Gagliardo and Mr. Sartain were talking to each other over their citizens band radios in Las Vegas, Nevada. At one point they began to argue. Sartain said that Gagliardo started to swear and make certain insulting statements. Gagliardo was charged with being in violation of the Federal Communications Act of 1934. This act provides as follows:

> Whoever utters any obscene, indecent, or profane language by means of radio communication shall be fined not more than $10,000 or imprisoned not more than two years, or both.

The United States District Court for the District of Nevada tried the case. The jury found Gagliardo guilty of violating the above regulation because he used obscene language over the citizens band radio.

Gagliardo appealed his case on two counts. He said that his use of citizens band radio involved only messages within one state. The normal range of a CB radio is from 10 to 25 miles. This would mean that messages from Las Vegas, Nevada, would not cross Nevada state lines. There had been no evidence presented that Gagliardo's messages were, in fact, heard outside of Nevada. Gagliardo also said that his case should not have been tried in a federal court at all, but in a state court, since the messages were not sent across state lines.

QUESTION—Does the federal government have the constitutional right to regulate citizens band radio communications?

■ ***Second Amendment*** Those who wrote the Bill of Rights were used to having a militia, or citizen army, which could be called on in times of trouble. The Minutemen had served well during the Revolutionary War. The framers of the Bill of Rights did not want to maintain large standing armies. They did want to keep the federal government from interfering with the right of citizens to bear arms in local militias. Therefore they wrote the Second Amendment into the Bill of Rights. Because of this amendment, the states are free to make their own rules about citizens having and using guns. There have been only a few cases that have come before the courts about rights under the Second Amendment.

■ ***Third Amendment*** During early American history, the colonists were required to quarter English soldiers in their homes. The colonists resented this and remembered it well. The Third Amendment was put into the Bill of Rights to make sure that the new government could never force citizens to allow soldiers to live in their homes. Today the Third Amendment is only of interest as a part of our history. Our government, under the Constitution, has never tried to make citizens house soldiers in their own homes.

■ ***Fourth Amendment*** "The right of the people to be secure in their persons, houses, papers, and effects, against unreasonable searches and seizures, shall not be violated, and no warrants shall issue, but upon probable cause, supported by oath or affirmation, and particularly describing the place to be searched, and the persons or things to be seized." The Fourth Amendment protects every person against unreasonable searches of his/her person, home, and place of

---

search warrant A written order by a judge directing that certain places or persons be searched in order to seize particular items for use as evidence in a court trial.

probable cause Reasonable cause; the existence of sufficient facts and circumstances to cause a reasonable person to believe a crime has been committed.

business. It also protects against unreasonable arrest, or the seizure of papers and other personal property.

The Fourth Amendment was made a part of our Bill of Rights because, as colonists, the American people had suffered a great deal from what they thought to be unjust and unreasonable uses of the power to search and seize by the British government. Customs officers, for example, had the right to break into and search any buildings they pleased. All they needed was a paper called a *writ of assistance.* This paper was a kind of general search and seizure warrant, or written authorization, to deal with prohibited or smuggled goods. Abuse of these writs in the colonies reached a peak in the 1760s. A Massachusetts lawyer, James Otis, Jr., resisted these searches as a form of tyranny. "A person with this writ," said Otis, "may enter all houses, shops, etc. at will and command all to assist him." But, said Otis, "a man's house is his castle, and while he is quiet [law-abiding] he is as well guarded as a prince in his castle." When the Continental Congress of 1774 asked the king to do something about unjust and arbitrary rules and laws, it gave as one example the abuse of search and seizure powers by the king's officers.

The right to be secure in their persons, houses, papers, and other property from government search and seizure had long been a part of the rights and liberties of English people. It was part of the tradition of common law. In the sixteenth and seventeenth centuries, however, sweeping powers of search and seizure were developed under the strong Tudor and Stuart kings. These powers were used by the Crown, and later by Parliament, to control people and ideas. In 1476, William Caxton set up a printing press in England. Within fifty years the government began to censor many kinds of printed matter. Search and seizure powers were broadly used to keep material that the king did not like from being printed. The Stationers Company, the printers' guild of London, was given the right to search, seize, and burn any books that were printed in England or brought into the country without the permission of the government.

During the seventeenth century, wide use of oppressive search and seizure powers went on. James I, King of England from 1603 to 1625, began the use of writs of assistance as general search and seizure warrants to deal with smuggled goods. These writs were widely used by later Stuart kings and by Parliament to attack and control their enemies. During the reign of William and Mary (1689–1702) the writs were stopped for a time because the searches were a heavy burden on the people. In the eighteenth century, the general search warrant came to be thought of as illegal and unconstitutional in England. William Pitt, prime minister from 1756 to 1761 and from 1765 to 1768, spoke out strongly against such searches, calling them unreasonable and unjust. "The poorest man," Pitt said, "may in his cottage bid defiance to all the forces of the Crown. It may be frail—its roof may shake—the wind may blow through it—the storms may enter—the rain may enter—but the King of England cannot enter; all his forces dare not cross the threshold of the ruined tenement!"

Our Constitution was written in 1787. By that time all the written state constitutions already had clauses that

---

 guild An association of people with similar interests or jobs.

restricted the right of the government to search and seize. It had been easy for the thirteen colonies to speak out against the searches and seizures made by the British Crown during its long rule. The question now was how the new government was to deal with searches and seizures among a free people. When and how should the government go about searching a citizen or seizing personal belongings?

Our country's founders knew that to fight crime and enforce laws, some searches and seizures would be needed. But they felt that such searches and seizures should not be unreasonable. And the government's right to seize should be based on *probable cause.* The Fourth Amendment protects people from unreasonable seizure of their persons, papers, and personal property. A legal officer cannot issue a warrant to search and/or seize unless there are very good reasons to believe the person to be searched has property that is illegally held, or has done something against the law. The search warrant must state in detail the place to be searched. It must also tell in detail the person or thing to be seized.

To say that there must be probable cause for a warrant means that there must be much more than just strong suspicion. It means that the warrant must be based on facts that would cause a reasonable person to believe there has been an act against the law.

Denville Twp COURT

COUNTY OF MORRIS

SEARCH WARRANT

STATE OF NEW JERSEY)
)SS:
COUNTY OF MORRIS)

TO: Any Law Enforcement Officer

Det/Sgt William Brown having personally appeared on this date before me, Judge of the Denville Twp Court assigned in and to the County of Morris, State of New Jersey, upon an application for the issuance of a search warrant on the ground that he has probable cause to believe that in and upon certain premises within the Twp of Denville in this County and State, to wit, the premises known as 42 Elm Road and more particularly described as follows: residence of John Doe Single family wood frame dwelling, color Blue with white trim, front and side entrance, no garage and circular driveway.

and the person(s) of John Doe

there has been and now is located certain property

(a) obtained in violation of the penal laws of the State of New Jersey;

(b) possessed, controlled, designed, intended for use in connection with the violation of the penal laws of the State of New Jersey;

(c) which has been used in connection with the violation of the penal laws of the State of New Jersey;

(d) which constitutes evidence of or tends to show the violation of the penal laws of the State of New Jersey,

said property consisting of Narcotics, Controlled Dangerous Substances and/or related paraphernalia.

AND the Court having taken the affidavits of Det/Sgt William Brown

and having examined under oath the following witnesses:

And the court being satisfied from the foregoing that grounds for granting the application exist,

NOW, THEREFORE, YOU ARE HEREBY COMMANDED to enter and search, with the necessary and proper assistance, the premises hereinabove named, and to search with the necessary and proper assistance said person(s) as set forth above, for the property specified serving this warrant and making the search and to take into your possession all such specified property which may be found on the said premises or on such persons(s), to the end that the same may be dealt with according to law.

YOU ARE FURTHER COMMANDED in the event that you seize any of the above described articles, to give a copy of this warrant, together with a receipt for the property so seized, to the person from whom it is taken or in whose possession it is found, or in the absence of such person to leave a copy of this warrant, together with such receipt, in or upon the premises from which the said property was taken.

Form- P100

Who may issue a search warrant? It has come to be understood that search warrants can be legally issued only by a judge or other magistrate. This is done so that a disinterested person may decide if there is a legal need to invade a person's privacy. When a search warrant has not been duly signed by a judge or other magistrate, it carries no power and is without force of law.

A search warrant is not required if the time needed to get it would allow the suspected offender to get away. Neither is it needed if the extra time would allow evidence to be moved or destroyed. People and items in cars, boats, and planes, for example, may be searched and seized by officers of the law without a warrant if the officers have good reasons for believing a law has been broken and the persons involved plan to run away.

When making a lawful arrest, an officer of the law may search the person arrested. Items of evidence found near the place of the arrest may be seized. Also, law officers may stop a person for investigation if they have reasonable grounds to believe a crime has been or may be committed. When a law officer holds someone in order to investigate, he/she may pat down, or "frisk," the citizen in order to show up hidden weapons. This "stop and frisk" act is allowed in order to protect the safety of the officer as well as that of nearby citizens. Of course, whenever a person agrees to be searched or to have his/her property searched, that person gives up the Fourth Amendment rights—for that occasion only.

The courts of our land are still dealing with the question of what should be the correct meaning of the terms *unreasonable* and *probable cause.* When a crime is committed, the government must have some way to get evidence that can be used in court to convict the guilty person. But making searches of citizens and their belongings can only be done when the proper authority states this is reasonable and based upon probable cause. Court decisions continually reshape the requirements for legal searches and seizures to obtain

---

magistrate The judge of a court that has limited authority.

evidence that will be accepted in courts of law. The changes made in our search and seizure laws are good examples of how laws are changed to better serve the needs of the people and preserve their rights.

The first important case dealing with rights under the Fourth Amendment was *Boyd* v. *United States* (1886). George and Edward Boyd were New York City merchants who had agreed to sell the United States government plate glass of a certain quality. The glass was for use in a federal courthouse and post office under construction in Philadelphia. As part of the agreement, the government said that the Boyds could bring the glass into the country without paying importation taxes. The Boyds brought in far more plate glass than they needed to satisfy their agreement with the government. They then had on hand a great deal of plate glass on which they had not paid duty. The government brought action against the Boyds to force them to pay taxes on the glass that was not needed for the government building. In court the judge directed the Boyds to hand over their papers that would show the exact amount of glass they had brought into the country. The Boyds objected, but did so, and the jury decided in favor of the government.

The case was appealed to the Supreme Court of the United States. This Court reversed the decision of the lower court. It found that the proceedings against the Boyds were unconstitutional. Ordering them to show their personal papers amounted to an illegal search under the Fourth Amendment. It is not necessary for someone's premises to be entered in order for a search to exist. If someone is made to produce books or papers to be used as evidence against that person, that is also a violation of the Fourth Amendment.

A rule was established in *Boyd* v. *United States* that evidence gotten by means of an unconstitutional search cannot be used in federal courts. Later this came to be known as the *federal exclusionary rule* because it excluded evidence got-

---

importation tax A charge imposed by the government for bringing certain goods into this country from another country.

ten illegally. The term *exclusionary rule* was first used in the case of *Weeks* v. *United States* (1914). The Weeks case also first recognized the right to search without a warrant as a part of an arrest. As late as 1961, the Supreme Court in *Mapp* v. *Ohio* (1961) decided that the exclusionary rule applies to the states as well as the federal government under the Fourteenth Amendment. Therefore evidence gotten by illegal searches and seizures cannot be accepted in either federal or state courts.

The right to search an automobile without a warrant was first recognized in *Carroll* v. *United States* (1925). The Carroll case applies also to airplanes and boats. The Supreme Court decided that an officer of the law may search vehicles without a warrant if there is reason to believe they hold illegal items. Later, in *Harris* v. *United States* (1947), the Supreme Court established the "plain view" doctrine. In the words of the court,

> It has long been settled that objects falling in the plain view of an officer who has a right to be in the position to have that view are subject to seizure and may be introduced in evidence.

It was in 1968, in the case of *Terry* v. *Ohio* (see page 96), that the Supreme Court decided that law officers may stop and frisk citizens when the officers think some illegal act is going on.

We have followed some of the changes in search and seizure laws since the kings of England first used them. As in other areas of law, we can expect changes to follow as people refine present laws and pass new ones to serve society.

Mapp *v.* Ohio
367 U.S. 643, 81 S.Ct. 1684, 6 L.Ed.2d 1081 (1961)

TOPIC—Action involving illegal search and seizure

FACTS—On May 23, 1957, three police officers in Cleveland, Ohio, wanted to question a certain person about a bombing. This person was reported to be hiding in Miss Mapp's home. Without a search warrant, the police forced their way into her house. Once inside, they found obscene materials during the course of their widespread search of the house. These materials were used to convict Mapp of "having in her possession certain lewd and lascivious books, pictures and photographs." The case was appealed to the United States Supreme Court.

QUESTION—Can evidence taken in violation of the search and seizure rulings of the Fourth Amendment be used to convict a citizen of a criminal charge?

Stoner *v.* California
376 U.S. 483, 84 S.Ct. 889, 11 L.Ed.2d 856 (1964)

TOPIC—Action involving illegal search and seizure

FACTS—On the night of October 25, 1960, the Budget Town Food Market in Monrovia, California, was robbed by two men. One of the men was described by witnesses as armed and as wearing horn-rimmed glasses and a gray jacket. Soon after the robbery, a checkbook belonging to Mr. Stoner was found in the parking lot and turned over to the police. Two of the stubs in the checkbook showed that checks had been drawn to the order of the Mayfair Hotel in Pomona, California. Following this lead, the officers learned from the Pomona Police Department that Stoner had a criminal record. They got a picture of him from the Pomona police, which they showed to the two people who had seen the robbery. They both stated that the picture looked like the man who had carried the gun. On the basis of this information the officers went to the Mayfair Hotel in Pomona at 10 o'clock on the night of October 27. They had neither search nor arrest warrants. This is what happened according to one of the officers.

> We approached the desk, the night clerk, and asked him if there was a party by the name of . . . Stoner living at the hotel. He checked his records and stated "Yes, there is." And we asked him what room he was in. He stated that he was in Room 404 but he was out at this time. We asked how he knew that he was out. He stated that the hotel regulations required that the key to the room would be placed in the mail box each time a guest left the hotel. The key was in the mail box and the clerk therefore knew he was out of the room. We asked him if he would give us permission to

> enter the room, explaining our reasons for this. . . . We explained that we were there to make an arrest of a man who had possibly committed a robbery in the city of Monrovia, and that we were concerned about the fact that he had a weapon. He stated "In this case, I will be more than happy to give you permission and I will take you directly to the room."

The officers entered and made a careful search of the room and everything in it. They found a pair of horn-rimmed glasses, a gray jacket, and a .45 caliber automatic pistol. Its clip and several cartridges were in the bottom of a bureau drawer. Stoner was arrested two days later in Las Vegas, Nevada, and returned to California for trial on the charge of armed robbery. The gun, the cartridges and clip, the horn-rimmed glasses, and the gray jacket were all used as evidence against him at his trial and Stoner was convicted. The case was appealed to the United States Supreme Court.

QUESTION—Can a hotel clerk, under the Fourth Amendment's search and seizure rulings, allow the search of a guest's room?

Terry *v.* Ohio

392 U.S. 1, 88 S.Ct. 1868, 20 L.Ed.2d 889 (1968)

TOPIC—Action involving illegal search and seizure rights guaranteed under the Fourth Amendment

FACTS—Police officer McFadden testified that while on duty in plain clothes in downtown Cleveland at about 2:30 in the afternoon of October 31, 1963, he noticed two men standing on a corner. He had never seen the two men before and was not able to say exactly what first drew his eye to them. However, he stated that he had been a police officer for 39 years and a detective for 35 of those years. He said it had been his job for 30 years to move around downtown Cleveland watching for shoplifters and pickpockets. He said that he would "stand and watch people or walk and watch people at many intervals of the day." He explained that his powers of observation had grown over the years.

Officer McFadden became suspicious that the two men might be "casing a job, a stick-up." He added that he feared that they may have had a gun. At one point a third man came along and talked to the first two men. Officer McFadden came up to the three men, told them he was a police officer, and asked for their names. When the men "mumbled something," Officer McFadden grabbed the defendant, Mr. Terry, and spun him around so that they were facing the other two men. McFadden patted down the outside of Terry's clothing, and found a pistol in the left breast pocket of his coat. Terry was charged with carrying a concealed weapon and the lower court found him to be guilty as charged. The case was appealed to the United States Supreme Court.

QUESTION—Since the Fourth Amendment gives people the right to be safe in their persons, houses, papers, and belongings against unreasonable searches and seizures, can a person be searched by an officer of the law if the officer has reasonable cause to believe the person's appearance and acts are suspicious?

Chimel *v.* California
395 U.S. 752, 89 S.Ct. 2034, 23 L.Ed.2d 685 (1969)

TOPIC—Action involving illegal search and seizure

FACTS—Late in the afternoon of September 13, 1965, three police officers searched the home of Mr. Chimel in Santa Ana, California. The officers had a warrant for his arrest for the burglary of a coin shop, but they did not have a search warrant. Chimel's wife let the officers into the house. The police waited 10 or 15 minutes, until Chimel returned home from work. When he walked in, one of the officers handed him the arrest warrant and asked for permission to "look around." Chimel objected, but the officers told him that they were going to search the house anyway based upon the lawful arrest warrant. They searched the three-bedroom house, including the attic, the garage, and a small workshop. The search lasted for nearly one hour. Things taken from the house, such as coins, several medals, and tokens, were used as evidence in Chimel's trial and he was convicted. The case was appealed to the United States Supreme Court.

QUESTION—Can the search of a whole house without a search warrant result in gaining legal evidence for an arrest and conviction?

■ ***Fifth Amendment*** Like the First Amendment, the Fifth Amendment has a number of different guarantees. Most of these have to do with protecting the rights of citizens accused of crimes. These rights include the right to an indictment by a grand jury and protection against double jeopardy and self-incrimination.

■ *"No person shall be held to answer for a capital or otherwise infamous crime, unless on a presentment or indictment of a grand jury."* Indictment by grand jury had been part of the English common law tradition for hundreds of years before the signing of the Declaration of Independence. As early as 1215, England's Magna Carta (Great Charter) stated that a "free" person should not be tried for a serious crime unless a group of that person's peers in the form of a grand jury has heard the facts and decided whether trial should be brought. Paragraph 39 of the Magna Carta stated that "no free man shall be seized or imprisoned, or stripped of his rights or possessions, or outlawed or exiled, or deprived of his standing in any other way, nor will we proceed with force against him, or send others to do so, except by the lawful judgment of his equals or by the law of the land." It is not surprising, then, that the Fifth Amendment to the Constitution should state that it is the right of a person to be brought before a grand jury before being legally charged with a serious crime.

---

indictment by grand jury A formal or written charge, presented by a grand jury to the court, on the basis of which an accused person is brought to trial.

double jeopardy Trial of a person for a second time for the same crime in the same jurisdiction. The Fifth and Fourteenth Amendments make such a trial unlawful unless there is an appeal from a conviction.

self-incrimination Implying the guilt or wrongdoing of oneself.

capital crime A criminal offense punishable by death.

■ *". . . nor shall any person be subject for the same offence to be twice put in jeopardy of life or limb."* The Fifth Amendment states that a person cannot be tried twice by the federal government for the same crime. This means all crimes—felonies, or serious crimes; and misdemeanors, or lesser crimes. This rule protects a person from living through a long period of worry and expense brought on by having to appear in court over and over for the same offense. It does away with the chance of an innocent person being convicted if that person is forced to continually offer a defense against the same charge. Of course, when a person is tried and convicted but appeals the case to a higher court, the earlier conviction may be set aside. That person might then be tried a second time based upon what the appeal court decides. But, in general, once a court has tried a person and delivered its verdict, that person cannot be tried again for that particular crime.

A person may give up this right and ask to be tried a second time. Also, the government reserves the right to try a citizen a second time for a higher offense. For example, a person might be convicted of assault and battery. If later the victim dies, a trial for murder can then take place.

Green *v.* United States
355 U.S. 184, 78 S.Ct. 221, 2 L.Ed.2d 199 (1957)

TOPIC—Action involving double jeopardy provision of the Fifth Amendment

FACTS—Mr. Green was charged with having committed arson by intentionally setting fire to a house. He was also accused of causing the death of a woman in this fire. If this was true, it amounted to murder in the first degree. This could have been punished by death. Green entered a plea of not guilty to both charges and a trial was held in the District of Columbia. The jury was told that it could find him guilty of either first or second degree murder. It found him guilty of murder in the second degree. Later, in an appeals court, his conviction was dropped because the court decided there was not enough evidence. Still later, he was tried again for setting the fire. This time the charge was murder in the first degree, and he was convicted. The case was appealed to the United States Supreme Court.

QUESTION—Under the double jeopardy provision of the Fifth Amendment, can a person who has earlier been convicted of second degree murder be tried again and given a sentence for first degree murder?

---

assault An unlawful, deliberate threat to use force or attempt to physically harm someone.

battery The actual and unlawful use of force by one person on another.

murder in the first degree The deliberate, planned killing of someone; the killing of someone during the commission of a serious offense.

murder in the second degree The malicious killing of someone, without deliberate planning.

■ *"... nor shall be compelled in any criminal case to be a witness against himself."* The right against self-incrimination is one of the most important of the Fifth Amendment. A person charged with a crime has the right not to be called in court as a witness against himself/herself. All through history, confession has sometimes been obtained through unjust pressure and even torture. So this protection has been set up to make sure that guilt cannot be established through confession.

A person who is called as a witness against the accused can be made to take the witness stand. But once on the stand, such a person may use the right not to testify on the grounds that it may incriminate him/her. A person appearing before a congressional committee hearing also has this right against self-incrimination.

---

congressional committees Members of Congress formed into temporary groups to investigate matters of national concern; also, permanent committees to pass on legislation that will be presented to the House or Senate.

United States *v.* Wade
338 U.S. 218, 87 S.Ct. 1926, 18 L.Ed.2d 1149 (1967)

TOPIC—Action involving right against self-incrimination under the Fifth Amendment

FACTS—In 1964 a man with a small strip of tape on each side of his face entered a bank in Eustace, Texas. He pointed a pistol at the cashier and the vice president of the bank, who were the only persons there at the time. He made them fill a bag with the bank's money and give it to him. He then drove away with his helper who had been waiting in a car. Mr. Wade was arrested for the bank robbery. FBI agents, without notice to Wade's lawyer, arranged to have the two bank workers look at a lineup of Wade and five or six other people. The people in the lineup had to wear strips of tape on their faces. Each one had to say "Put the money in the bag." The bank workers identified Wade as the robber and he was convicted. The case was then appealed to the United States Supreme Court.

QUESTION—Is a person's rights against self-incrimination violated by having to be in a lineup?

■ *"... nor be deprived of life, liberty, or property, without due process of law."* Due process, as has already been discussed (page 71) in relation to the Fourteenth Amendment, means a number of things: (1) A person must be given notice that proceedings against him/her are to take place. (2) A person must be given a chance to prepare for the trial. (3) The trial must be held in a fair and impartial way. In short, due process means all the protections given in the Constitution and all the other guarantees that have come to be accepted through common law and through our courts. When it can be shown that due process of law was not followed, the accused may be given a new trial or set free.

All these protections guaranteed under the Fifth Amendment were intended to limit the powers of the federal government. However, as you know, the Fourteenth Amendment assured citizens that the states also must respect these rights.

Frontiero *v.* Richardson
411 U.S. 677 (1973)

TOPIC—Action involving the due process clause of the Fifth Amendment and civil rights.

FACTS—According to a federal law, a male member of the armed forces may claim his wife as a "dependent" whether or not she is in fact dependent upon him for any part of her support. A woman in the armed forces, however, may not claim her husband as a "dependent" unless he is in fact dependent upon her for over one half of his support.

Sharron Frontiero, a lieutenant in the United States Air Force, applied for housing and medical benefits for her husband, Joseph Frontiero, on the grounds that he was her dependent. Such benefits would automatically have been granted the wife of a male member of the armed forces. Lt. Frontiero's application was denied on the grounds that she failed to show that her husband was dependent upon her for more than one half of his support. The case finally went to the United States Supreme Court.

QUESTION—Does a female member of the United States military services have the right to claim her husband as a "dependent" in order to get increased housing allowances and medical and dental benefits on an equal basis with male members of the armed services?

■ *"... nor shall private property be taken for public use, without just compensation."* Also under the Fifth Amendment, the federal government is prevented from "taking" property from a private citizen without paying the owner a fair price. The government cannot take private property except for a public use. It must then pay the owner the fair market value of the property. This is known as the *right of eminent domain.*

■ ***Sixth Amendment*** Trial by jury was brought to England by the Normans. During the Middle Ages, jurors were neighbors of the accused person. They appeared at court to testify as to the good or bad character of that person. However, they did not really decide the outcome of the trial by giving a verdict. But by the time of the American Revolution, juries in this country did in fact decide the outcome. They could decide if a party was innocent or guilty. One of the charges made against King George III in the Declaration of Independence was that the colonists, in many cases, were not allowed a trial by jury. The Sixth Amendment states that "In all criminal prosecutions, the accused shall enjoy the right to a speedy and public trial, by an impartial jury of the State and district wherein the crime shall have been committed, ... to be informed of the nature and cause of the accusation; to be confronted with the witnesses against him; ... and to have the assistance of counsel for his defense."

---

confront witness To challenge the testimony of a witness.

counsel Lawyer employed or appointed to represent and advise someone in legal matters.

The Sixth Amendment gives a person the right to a speedy public trial. But the Supreme Court has interpreted this to mean that the legal processes leading to the trial will be orderly. In *United States* v. *Ewell* (1966) the Court held that the seventeen months that had passed between the arrest and the hearing did not violate the speedy trial right of the Sixth Amendment. The Court also stated that so long as the wait before the trial is not purposeful on the part of the legal system, or oppressive, the defendant cannot complain.

A person charged with a crime has the right to a fair trial with an impartial judge and jury. An "impartial jury" is made up of persons who would not discriminate against anyone because of race, creed, color, or position in life. They must also not have prejudged the defendant.

In criminal trials the accused has the right to face the witnesses against him/her and to be present in court when they testify. The accused also has the right to cross-examine them and question what they said during their testimony. These rights are based partly upon the idea that it is not as hard to lie about people behind their back as it is while looking directly at them.

Under the Sixth Amendment, the accused has a right to have the help of a lawyer. If the accused is an indigent, that person has the same right to be represented by a lawyer as a person who is able to pay for a lawyer's services. The court must see to it that the lawyer is paid by the state. In federal cases the federal government pays the lawyer. This right to have a lawyer begins when a person is taken into custody or otherwise has his/her freedom taken away. It continues until the court makes a final determination about the case. The right to have a lawyer holds also when cases are appealed to higher courts. The right to be represented by a lawyer, however, holds only for criminal cases.

---

cross-examination The questioning of a witness by the party against whom the witness was called, to test the truthfulness of that witness's testimony.

indigent A person without money or property.

determination A court decision settling or ending a legal dispute.

Gideon *v.* Wainwright

372 U.S. 335, 83 S.Ct. 792, 9 L.Ed.2d 799 (1963)

TOPIC—Action involving right to counsel

FACTS—Mr. Gideon was charged with having broken into a poolroom in Panama City, Florida. Under Florida law such an offense is a crime punishable by more than one year in jail. Gideon appeared in court without a lawyer. He explained that he was too poor to pay a lawyer, and he asked the court to appoint one for him. The judge answered Gideon as follows:

> Mr. Gideon, I am sorry, but I cannot appoint counsel to represent you in this case. Under the laws of the state of Florida, the only time the court can appoint counsel to represent a defendant is when that person is charged with a capital offense. I am sorry, but I will have to deny your request to appoint counsel to defend you in this case.

Gideon then acted as his own lawyer during the trial. He was convicted and sentenced to five years in the state prison. The case was appealed to the United States Supreme Court on the grounds that the defendant was not represented by a lawyer. It was claimed that this lack of representation violated due process and caused an unfair trial.

QUESTION—Must a defendant who is poor be given a lawyer in a case involving a minor crime?

Douglas *v.* California
372 U.S. 353, 83 S.Ct. 814, 9 L.Ed.2d 811 (1963)

TOPIC—Action concerning right to counsel

FACTS—Mr. Meyes and Mr. Douglas were both to be tried in a California court for committing thirteen felonies. The crimes included robbery, assault with a deadly weapon, and assault with intent to commit murder. These men were too poor to pay a lawyer, so the court selected one to defend them. At the beginning of the trial the defending lawyer stated that the case was complicated. He said he was not prepared to represent the men. Meyes and Douglas then dismissed him and asked the judge to provide other counsel. The judge refused, and both men were convicted and given prison terms.

The case was appealed to the California District Court of Appeals. Douglas and Meyes were still not able to hire their own lawyer and asked the court to provide them with counsel for their appeal. The court stated that it had gone over the record and decided that no good at all could be served by giving them a lawyer. The appeals court upheld the decision of the lower court and the case was then appealed to the United States Supreme Court.

QUESTION—In order to conform to the provisions of right to counsel under the Sixth Amendment, must the court appoint a lawyer so that a defendant may appeal a case if he/she so wishes?

Escobedo *v.* Illinois
378 U.S. 478, 84 S.Ct. 1758, 12 L.Ed.2d 977 (1964)

TOPIC—Action involving due process and right to counsel

FACTS—In January 1960, Mr. Escobedo was arrested and questioned by the Chicago police about the murder of his brother-in-law. His lawyer, who had come to the police station, was not allowed to talk to him.

The police later testified in court that Escobedo had no record of earlier dealings with the police. They said he "was handcuffed" in a standing position, that he "was nervous, he had circles under his eyes and he was upset." They said he was "agitated" because "he had not slept well in over a week."

Escobedo had not been told of his constitutional right to remain silent, and he made some damaging statements during the police questioning. Later in court, Escobedo said that during the course of the police questioning he had asked over and over to speak to his lawyer, but was told that his lawyer "didn't want to see" him. The testimony of the police officers confirmed these accounts.

The court convicted Escobedo of murder based upon what he had said to the police during his questioning. The case was appealed to the United States Supreme Court.

QUESTION—Does a person accused of a crime have the right to see a lawyer before being questioned by the police?

Estes *v.* Texas
381 U.S. 532, 85 S.Ct. 1628, 14 L.Ed.2d 543 (1965)

TOPIC—Action brought to guarantee due process of law

FACTS—Mr. Estes was a well-known business person. He was charged with obtaining money by fraud. Estes asked that telecasting, radio broadcasting, and the taking of moving or still pictures not be allowed at his trial. A hearing was held before

fraud Cheating.

the trial to decide what to do about this. At the hearing the court was jammed with reporters, photographers, and television camera operators. The hearings were broadcast and televised live, and parts of the television tapes were later shown on the evening news. The State of Texas decided to let the trial judge rule on Estes' request. The trial judge ruled that television and news pictures would be allowed during Estes' trial.

Later it was found that four persons picked as jurors had seen or heard at least part of the pretrial hearing on television and radio. Estes was found guilty by the jury, and appealed on the grounds that the news coverage prevented him from having due process of law.

QUESTION—Can there be due process of law where there is widespread news coverage of court proceedings?

Miranda *v.* Arizona
384 U.S. 436, 86 S.Ct. 1602, 16 L.Ed.2d 694 (1966)

TOPIC—Action concerning right to counsel under the Sixth Amendment and right against self-incrimination under the Fifth Amendment

FACTS—On March 13, 1963, in Phoenix, Arizona, Mr. Miranda was arrested for kidnapping and rape. He was taken to the police station for questioning. However, he was not told that he had the constitutional right to remain silent and to see a lawyer. Two hours later the officers came out of the room where they had been questioning him, with a written and signed confession. At the top of the paper was a typed statement that the confession was made of his own free will. It said it was made "with full knowledge of my legal rights, understanding any statement I make may be used against me."

At Miranda's trial, the written confession was accepted as evidence over the objection of his lawyer. The officers also testified to an earlier spoken confession made by Miranda during the police questioning. Miranda was sentenced to 20 to 30 years in prison.

On appeal, the Supreme Court of Arizona held that Miranda's constitutional rights were not violated when the police got his confession. The higher court agreed with the conviction of the lower court. The court made a strong point of the fact that Miranda did not specifically ask for a lawyer. The case was then appealed to the United States Supreme Court.

QUESTION—Can statements gotten from a person through police questioning without the presence of his/her lawyer be used as evidence?

Sheppard *v.* Maxwell

384 U.S. 333, 86 S.Ct. 1507, 16 L.Ed.2d 600 (1966)

TOPIC—Action involving right to a fair trial

FACTS—Mrs. Sheppard, the wife of a well-known doctor, had been murdered, and her husband seemed to be the chief suspect. The news media complained about Dr. Sheppard's lack of cooperation. They said he had refused to take a lie detector test. They also claimed that Sheppard's important family had thrown up a protective ring about him. There was a great deal of publicity about the case both before and during his trial. The public was very interested in Sheppard's trial and it became a big news story. However, much of the material printed or broadcast about Sheppard and his trial was one-sided and inaccurate.

The jurors were out for five days and four nights to decide on a verdict. The telephones had been removed from their rooms, but they were allowed to make calls on others that were nearby. They could place the calls themselves, and no record was kept of what was said. The jurors were able to talk to people who might influence them. Such people might offer opinions on the case. Or they might offer information that was not brought up at the trial.

The jury finally returned a verdict of murder against Sheppard. The case was appealed.

QUESTION—Has the Sixth Amendment's right to a fair trial been violated when there is too much news coverage of what goes on during a trial?

Williams *v.* Florida
399 U.S. 78, 90 S.Ct. 1893, 26 L.Ed.2d 446 (1970)

TOPIC—Action involving the right to a twelve-person jury trial

FACTS—Mr. Williams was brought before a Florida court on a charge of robbery. He was tried by a six-person jury and sentenced to prison for life. Williams appealed the case on the grounds that his rights under the Sixth Amendment had been violated because he had not been tried by a twelve-person jury. The Florida District Court of Appeals agreed with the lower court and rejected Williams' claim. Williams then appealed to the Supreme Court of the United States.

QUESTION—Does a person have a right to be tried by a twelve-member jury under the Sixth Amendment?

Baldwin *v.* New York
339 U.S. 66, 90 S.Ct. 1886, 26 L.Ed.2d 437 (1970)

TOPIC—Action involving trial of a person who committed a misdemeanor

FACTS—A police officer said that he saw Mr. Baldwin remove a loose package from a woman's purse on a crowded escalator. Baldwin was charged with jostling. According to New York state law, jostling occurs when a person intentionally places a hand in or near another person's pocket or purse. A year in prison is the maximum punishment for this act.

Baldwin was brought to trial in the New York City Criminal Court. He asked for a jury trial, but was refused. The reason was that the New York City Criminal Court Act stated that ". . . all trials in the court shall be without a jury." Baldwin was sentenced to prison for one year. He appealed the case, but the New York Court of Appeals agreed with the lower court. The case was then appealed to the United States Supreme Court.

QUESTION—Does a person charged with a misdemeanor punishable by a one-year prison term have a right to trial by jury?

Illinois *v.* Allen
397 U.S. 337, 90 S.Ct. 1057, 25 L.Ed.2d 253 (1970)

TOPIC—Action concerning the right of the accused to confront witnesses

FACTS—Mr. Allen was charged with armed robbery and tried by an Illinois jury. The evidence against him showed that after ordering a drink in a bar, he took $200 from the bartender at gunpoint.

During the trial Allen used vile and abusive language. The judge warned him about this many times. At one point Allen said to the judge, "When I go out for lunchtime, you're going to be a corpse here." The judge said, "One more outbreak of that sort and I'll remove you from the courtroom." This warning did not stop Allen and he went on talking back to the judge. He said, "There's not going to be no trial either. I'm going to sit here and you're going to talk and you can bring your shackles out and straight jacket and put them on me and tape my mouth, but it will do no good because there's not going to be no trial." After more such remarks, the judge ordered the trial to go on without Allen in the room. Allen was sentenced to 20 to 30 years in prison. He appealed his case to the United States Supreme Court. He said that since he had not been allowed to remain in court all through his trial, he was not able to confront the witnesses against him. This, he said, deprived him of his rights under the Sixth and Fourteenth Amendments.

QUESTION—Does a defendant have the right to be present in court during the trial no matter how he/she has been acting?

■ ***Seventh Amendment*** Article III, Section 2, of the Constitution calls for trial by jury in criminal cases. This right is guaranteed again in the Sixth Amendment. When the Bill of Rights was written, however, there was nothing in it about jury trials in noncriminal cases. The Seventh Amendment was written into the Bill of Rights to guarantee jury trial in noncriminal cases where the money damages asked for are more than $20. This amendment applies only to trials in federal courts. States do not need to have jury trials in noncriminal cases unless the state constitution requires it.

The right to jury trial as promised by the Seventh Amendment is guaranteed in cases that involve such matters as legal agreements, debts, and injuries to people or property. There is, however, no right to a jury trial in suits of this kind against the government. This right to a jury may be given up by the parties to a controversy if they choose to do so. Also, federal court judges may set aside the jury's verdict when not enough facts are presented to support the conclusion reached by the jury.

■ ***Eighth Amendment*** The Eighth Amendment guarantees to each citizen that "Excessive bail shall not be required, nor excessive fines imposed, nor cruel and unusual punishments inflicted."

■ *"Excessive bail shall not be required."* A person who has been accused of certain offenses may be released from jail while waiting for trial if that person posts bail. This means that the accused puts up a certain amount of money as security for appearing in court on the day of the trial. If that person fails to appear, he/she must give up the money. The person is also subject to arrest again.

Not every person accused of a crime is freed on bail. Generally speaking, a person accused of a crime such as murder is not allowed to post bail. But the Eighth Amendment says that those who are so freed must not be charged beyond their ability to pay. The amount of bail needed in any given case is set by the judge of the court. Some of the things a judge considers when setting the amount of bail are the kind of crime committed and the general character and record of the accused. The judge also considers the accused's ability to raise money.

Carlson *v.* Landon
342 U.S. 524, 72 S.Ct. 525, 96 L.Ed. 547 (1952)

TOPIC—Action involving bail for aliens

FACTS—Several members of the Communist party of the United States were being held in custody in California. They were not citizens and they were being held while waiting to see if they would be deported. Under the Internal Security Act of 1950 the United States Attorney General had the power to hold them without bail. However the aliens asked to be allowed to post bail. The case was sent to the United States Supreme Court.

QUESTION—Do aliens have the same right to the Eighth Amendment's guarantee of bail as do American citizens?

■ *"... nor excessive fines imposed."* If the court fines a citizen, the Eighth Amendment guarantees that the amount of the fine cannot be so high that he/she will find it impossible to pay. It is up to the judge of the court to decide how much the fine will be.

Tate *v.* Short
401 U.S. 395, 91 S.Ct. 668, 28 L.Ed.2d 130 (1971)

TOPIC—Action brought to question fines given

FACTS—On nine traffic charges, an indigent in the state of Texas had been given fines adding up to $425. Texas law said that those who could not pay should be jailed for the time needed to satisfy their fines at the rate of $5 a day. This meant that the indigent in this case would have had to serve an

---

alien A foreign-born person who is not a citizen of the country in which he/she lives.

deport To send an alien back to the country from which he/she came when the presence of that person is considered undesirable.

85-day term in jail. The case was appealed to the United States Supreme Court.

QUESTION—Are the Eighth Amendment rights of a person who has no money violated when he/she is forced to serve time in jail rather than pay a fine because that person has no money?

■ *"... nor cruel and unusual punishments inflicted."* You may think these words would not apply to our system of justice today. But the problem is still with us. It may come in the form of having the date of an execution put off time after time. There is also the question of whether or not the death penalty itself might be thought of as cruel and unusual. The Eighth Amendment protects people against being punished in ways that are too hard relative to the offense. One Justice of the Supreme Court said that it guarantees "the principle of civilized treatment."

Louisiana ex. rel. Francis *v.* Resweber
329 U.S. 459, 67 S.Ct. 374, 91 L.Ed. 422 (1947)

TOPIC—Action brought concerning cruel and unusual punishment

FACTS—Mr. Francis had been sentenced to be electrocuted by the State of Louisiana. However, when the attempt was made to carry out this sentence, the machinery would not work. Francis brought suit for release from his sentence. He sued on the grounds that at this point execution would deny him due process of law because of the right against double jeopardy in the Fifth Amendment and the right against cruel and unusual punishment in the Eighth Amendment.

QUESTION—Does a person have the right to be freed from sentence because of the failure of the execution machinery? Does setting a new date for electrocution violate a person's rights under the double jeopardy rule of the Fifth Amendment? his/her rights under the Eighth Amendment? the due process rule of the Fourteenth Amendment?

Powell *v.* State of Texas
392 U.S. 514, 88 S.Ct. 2145, 20 L.Ed.2d 1254 (1968)

TOPIC—Action involving cruel punishment

FACTS—Mr. Powell was tried in a Texas court and found guilty of breaking a state law against being drunk in public. The defendant, who drank large amounts of wine every day, got drunk once a week. He had already been convicted of public intoxication about a hundred times. Upon appeal to a higher court, he said that he suffered from chronic alcoholism. For that reason, he said, he could neither handle his drinking nor control his public behavior. The case was finally appealed to the United States Supreme Court.

QUESTION—Is a person who suffers from alcoholism liable for violating a law that makes it illegal to be drunk in a public place?

RIGHTS OF AN ACCUSED PERSON

No unreasonable arrest.

To remain silent under police questioning.

To see a lawyer.

To be told of exact charges.

No forced confession or use of evidence obtained illegally.

No excessive bail.

To a fair jury trial.

To confront and cross-examine witnesses against oneself.

Not to act as witness against oneself.

If acquitted, no second trial for same crime.

If convicted, no cruel or unusual punishment.

To appeal.

■ ***Ninth Amendment*** The Ninth Amendment is intended to make sure that the people are able to keep all their fundamental rights. This means rights other than those stated in the first eight amendments of the Bill of Rights. Exactly what these rights are has not been decided by the Supreme Court based upon case law. However, one of them is often called the right to privacy.

■ ***Tenth Amendment*** The Tenth Amendment states strongly that the powers not given by the Constitution to the national government must remain with the states or the people. However, in modern times, the federal government has become involved in activities affecting the states and the citizens more than the framers of the Constitution or the Bill of Rights could have imagined. The growing part the government plays in caring for the general welfare of the people has tended to weaken the original intent of the Tenth Amendment.

■ ***The living Constitution*** You have discovered as you studied this chapter that the Constitution is an instrument of great flexibility. It is full of life and possibilities. Its limits and powers are subject to continual reinterpretation by the United States Supreme Court, acting upon real cases involved with human rights and government actions and regulations. It provides for deciding matters of great national importance at the highest levels of government. And it protects the rights and liberties of all the people in their homes and everyday lives.

The United States Constitution was written in 1787 for what was mostly a farming nation of less than four million people. It is still a living force that allows an industrial nation of well over two hundred million people to live in freedom under the law.

Reviewing the Chapter

Law-Related Terms

Full faith and credit clause *P. 69*
Privileges and immunities clause *P. 69*
Due process *Pp. 72, 305*
Probable cause *P. 86*
Federal exclusionary rule *Pp. 92–93*
Self-incrimination *P. 98*

Review Questions

1. What role does the Supreme Court play in relation to the Constitution? *P. 65*
2. **(a)** Why was the commerce clause put into the Constitution? **(b)** List some powers of the federal government under this clause. *Pp. 66–67*
3. **(a)** How are people protected by the full faith and credit clause? **(b)** How are they protected by the privileges and immunities clause? *P. 69*
4. Name the four basic rights guaranteed under the First Amendment. *P. 75*
5. **(a)** What protections are guaranteed by the Fourth Amendment? **(b)** Explain what probable cause means in relation to a search warrant. *Pp. 86–89*
6. What rules or principles were established in these cases: **(a)** *Boyd* v. *United States*? **(b)** *Gideon* v. *Wainwright*? **(c)** *Escobedo* v. *Illinois*? *Pp. 92–93, 106–107, 108, 269–270*
7. **(a)** What rights of a person being arrested were set forth in the decision in *Miranda* v. *Arizona?* **(b)** Which Justices dissented and why? *Pp. 110–111, 270–271*
8. Why is the Constitution sometimes called the "living Constitution"? *P. 120*

Chapter Test

From the list below, select the answer that best completes each statement. Write your answers on a separate paper.

Gideon v. *Wainwright*
full faith and credit
federal exclusionary
Miranda v. *Arizona*
self-incrimination
Supreme Court
press
federal
probable cause
due process

1. The ______ decides legal questions based on the Constitution.
2. The ______ government has the power to regulate commerce between the states.
3. Under the ______ clause, each state must respect the laws and court decisions of all other states.
4. ______ of law assures fair and reasonable treatment in the judicial process.
5. The First Amendment guarantees freedom of speech, ______, religion, and assembly.
6. There must be ______ before a search warrant can be issued.
7. Under the ______ rule, evidence obtained by illegal searches and seizures cannot be accepted in federal or state courts.
8. Under the Fifth Amendment, a person is guaranteed protection against ______.
9. ______ established the right of a person accused of a minor crime to be provided an attorney if he or she cannot afford one.
10. According to ______, a person has the right to have an attorney present while being questioned by the police.

ON SCHOOL

Torts 4

Wire *v.* Williams
270 Minn. 390, 133 N.W.2d 840 (1965)

TOPIC—Personal injuries caused by negligence

FACTS—Diane Wire was a second-grade pupil at a public school in Minnesota. Ms. Williams was Diane's teacher. It was her duty to watch over a second-grade class in physical education. At 2:30 P.M. on May 8, 1961, Diane was jumping rope while the teacher was on duty as part of the regular class program. The rope being used was some six feet in length with a wooden handle on each end. Each pupil was allowed to go on jumping until the rope was stepped on by the person jumping or was stopped because it hit that person's foot. At the time Diane was jumping, one handle of the rope was being held by the teacher. Diane's feet came down upon the rope, pulling the wooden handle out of the teacher's hand. The handle flew toward Diane, hit one of her front teeth, and also caused other injuries. Diane sued. The trial jury decided that the teacher was not negligent. The case was appealed.

QUESTION—Is a teacher responsible for a child's injuries in the normal course of performing exercises not thought to be dangerous?

WHAT IS A TORT?

The word *tort* means "wrong" or "injury." A tort is not the same thing as a crime. A crime is an offense against the public at large. A tort, on the other hand, is a harmful act against an individual. Some acts against individuals, however, are crimes. Murder is such an act. Although murder is a harmful act against an individual, it is also considered a threat to society. It is therefore a crime. In cases involving a crime, the state takes action by bringing criminal charges. In tort cases, it is up to the person wronged or injured, not the state, to bring suit against the person who did the wrong. In criminal cases, a person found guilty of a crime may be punished by imprisonment and/or a fine, or both. In tort cases, the court must decide (1) if there really has been a wrong or an injury and (2) who is at fault or liable for the wrong. The court may then order the person who did the wrong to pay damages (money) to the injured party.

Tort law is based on one of three grounds: (1) intentional aggression, (2) negligence, and (3) strict liability. Intentional aggression may consist of interference with one's land or personal property. It may involve injury or harm, either physical or mental, to a person. Negligence consists of someone's doing an act without using due care or failing to do an act that the law says must be done. Strict liability is concerned with the duty a person has when doing something that is by its very nature dangerous to others.

INTENTIONAL AGGRESSION

There are many acts that are considered acts of intentional aggression. Such acts are known as intentional torts. Assault, battery, the causing of emotional distress, false imprisonment, and trespass are all intentional torts.

■ ***Assault*** For an intentional tort of assault to happen, a person must have intentionally and wrongfully started a force directed toward the injured party. This must have been done without the consent and against the will of the victim. Because of the action, the victim must be frightened about his/her safety. For example, David shakes his fist at Pete and

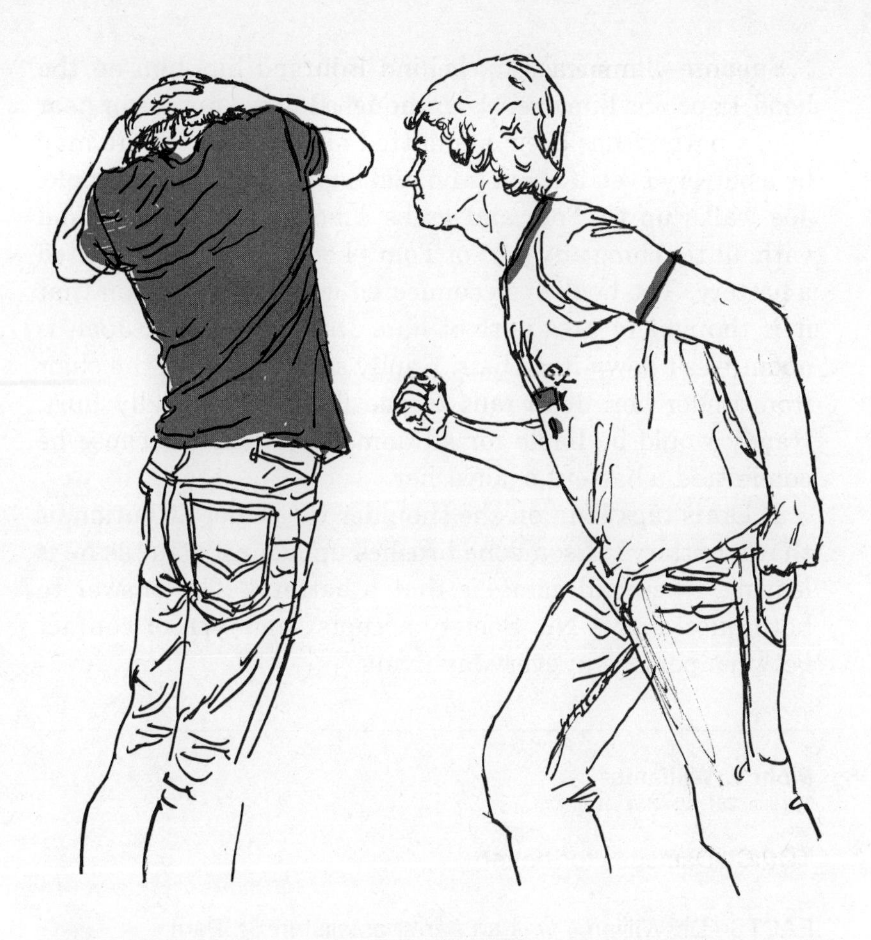

threatens to hit him. This is an assault. Pete is frightened, as any reasonable person would be. Pete has every right to believe he is in danger of being hurt.

Spoken words, looks, or gestures alone are not assaults. Suppose Betty says to Pat, "You are about to be killed." That is not an assault. An interesting exception to the rule occurs if Pat is blind. If a statement such as the one above is made to a blind person, it is an assault.

■ ***Battery*** A battery is different from an assault. Generally, it involves a harmful or an offensive touching of another person, but without the fear that is often caused by an assault. In assault cases, a person is put into a state of fright. In battery cases, there is an actual touching of another.

Suppose Jim sneaks up behind Bob and hits him on the head, knocking him out. Even though Bob did not see or hear Jim, a battery has been committed against Bob. There may be a battery even if there is no real bodily hurt. For example, Joe walks up to Tom and grabs a book from Tom's hand without touching any part of Tom's body. Joe has committed a battery. The book is so connected with Tom's person that it is thought of as a part of him. In another case, Joan is about to sit down in a chair. Randy suddenly pulls the chair from under her. Joan falls to the floor and is badly hurt. Randy would be liable for all damages to Joan because he committed a battery against her.

If Doris taps Pam on the shoulder to get her attention, is that a battery? If someone brushes up against Paul as he is leaving a baseball game, is that a battery? The answer to both questions is No. Society accepts that type of contact between persons in everyday living.

Mohr *v.* Williams
95 Minn. 261, 104 N.W. 12 (1905)

TOPIC—Damages for battery

FACTS—Dr. Williams was an ear specialist in St. Paul, Minnesota. He examined Mrs. Mohr and told her she needed an operation on her right ear. After she was placed under an anesthetic and while she was unconscious, Williams made a complete examination. He discovered that there was a far more serious condition in the left ear than in the right ear. After talking with Mohr's family doctor, Williams operated on her left ear. Mohr had not been told before the operation that there was anything wrong with her left ear. The operation was successful and good for the patient. However, after it was over, Mohr brought action for battery.

QUESTION—Shall a doctor be liable for battery when he/she performs an operation on a patient different from the one planned?

Lamb *v.* Woodry
154 Or. 30, 58 P.2d 1257 (1936)

TOPIC—Damages for assault and battery

FACTS—On October 30, 1934, Mrs. Lamb, who lived in Oregon, bought a heating stove for $8.50. She signed an agreement whereby she would have the stove paid for by December 3 of that year. By April 8, 1935, some money still had not been paid. The defendant, Mr. Woodry, went to Lamb's home. He pushed Lamb aside and forced her to give up the stove.

QUESTION—Does the seller of goods have a right to take back property if he/she cannot do so peacefully and without using force?

Clayton *v.* New Dreamland Roller Skating Rink, Inc.
14 N.J. Super. 390, 82 A.2d 458 (1951)

TOPIC—Battery arising out of a fall on defendant's premises

FACTS—In October 1948, Mrs. Clayton and her husband went to the New Dreamland Roller Skating Rink as paying customers. While skating, Mrs. Clayton fell and suffered a broken left arm. She claimed that the fall was caused by chewing gum on the skating rink floor. She was taken to the first aid room of the skating rink. Mr. Brown, who worked there, tried to set Clayton's arm. Later, Brown was asked whether he was a doctor. He said that he was not a doctor but, as a prize-fight manager, he knew about such matters.

Clayton was taken to a hospital, where X rays were taken and doctors reset her arm. Because of damage done as a result of Brown's actions, bone grafts had to be made. Clayton's arm also needed plates and screws. Clayton sued Brown.

QUESTION—Is there a battery when an unskilled person tries to treat a person who has been hurt?

Fisher *v.* Carrousel Motor Hotel, Inc.
Supreme Court of Texas, 424 SW.2d 627 (1967)

TOPIC—Damages for a battery

FACTS—Mr. Fisher was a mathematician with the Data Processing Division of the Manned Spacecraft Center near Houston, Texas. He was invited by the Ampex Corporation to attend a meeting at the Carrousel Motor Hotel in Houston. The invitation included a luncheon. The guests were asked to answer the invitation by telephone. Fisher called and accepted. After the morning meeting, the guests went to the dining room to eat. The luncheon was buffet-style. Fisher stood in line with others waiting to have their plates filled. As Fisher was about to be served, a worker in the hotel, a Mr. Flynn, grabbed the plate from Fisher's hand. He said that Fisher, a black, could not be served. Fisher sued the motor hotel.

He testified in court that he had not been touched and did not suffer fear of physical harm. However, he said that Flynn's act had highly embarrassed and hurt him in front of his associates. The trial jury found the Motor Hotel liable for the actions of its employee, Flynn. Fisher was awarded damages for his humiliation and indignity. The Motor Hotel appealed the case. The Court of Civil Appeals found that there was no battery because there was no physical contact. Fisher than appealed to the Supreme Court of the State of Texas.

QUESTION—Has a battery been committed when there is no actual contact with a person's body but only with something held in the hand?

Jones *v.* Fisher
42 Wis. 2d 209, 166 N.W.2d 175 (1969)

TOPIC—Assault and battery

FACTS—The Fishers owned and ran a nursing home in Wisconsin. Mrs. Jones worked at the nursing home. She cared for the residents during the night hours, gave medicines, and prepared and served breakfast. She also did some cleaning work in the kitchen. The Fishers felt Jones was a good worker, and they were fond of her.

In September 1967, Jones was told by her dentist that she needed false upper teeth. The Fishers lent Jones $200 to help pay her dentist bill. Shortly after she got the upper plate, Jones quit working for the Fishers. About a week after she quit, she returned to the nursing home to get a check for $48 for her last week's work. Mrs. Fisher tried to get Jones to return to work at the nursing home. Jones refused. Mr. Fisher asked when Jones was going to pay back the $200. She told him he could take $20 out of the $48 check. She said she would pay the rest at the rate of $20 per month. Mr. Fisher said she would have to pay the whole amount in three days or leave the upper plate at the nursing home. Jones would not agree to this, and the two parties began arguing. Jones tried to run from the room. Mr. Fisher grabbed her arms, forcing them in back of her. Mrs. Fisher grabbed at Jones's face and mouth and took out the upper plate. Then Mr. Fisher let Jones go, and she ran out of the nursing home.

After leaving the home, Jones walked to the police station and reported what had happened. A police officer went to the nursing home. He got the teeth and gave them back to Jones. Jones sued.

QUESTION—Is the taking of personal property from a person by force justified to get the payment of a loan?

■ ***Emotional distress*** Lately many courts have come to accept the intentional causing of emotional distress or mental anguish as a tort. In such a tort there is an intentional act of frightening or distressing another person in such a way as to cause mental anguish. Dan, just for a joke, tells Paula that her brother has been in an accident. Dan says her brother is dying in the hospital. As a result, Paula has a nervous breakdown. If she sued Dan for damages, she would probably win the case and collect a great deal of money from Dan.

mental anguish Injury that includes all forms of mental pain for which a person may be legally compensated. Examples are deep grief, distress, anxiety, and fright.

■ ***False imprisonment*** The confining of one person by another so as to prevent that person's freedom of movement is called false imprisonment. The confinement must be almost total. It must also be against the will of the victim. The person must know that he/she is so confined. Paul may be asleep in his room when Don locks the door. If Don unlocks the door before Paul tries to leave the room, Paul would not know about his short imprisonment. If Paul did not know that he was locked in, the law would not accept that he had been falsely imprisoned. There can be no false imprisonment if there is a reasonably safe means of escape. The law encourages the person who is falsely imprisoned to try to escape. If someone is hurt while escaping, damages may be paid for injuries.

Bird *v.* Jones
7 Q.B. 742, 115 Eng. Rep. 668 (1845)

TOPIC—Damages for false imprisonment

FACTS—Mr. Jones, the defendant, blocked off a part of Hammersmith Bridge. This bridge was generally used as a public footway but was now blocked off in order to seat people to view a boat race. Mr. Bird, the plaintiff, said that he had a right to walk along the road. Bird was stopped by Jones, but started to climb over the obstruction anyway. Two police officers, hired to keep order during the boat race, stopped him and told him that he could not pass that way. But, they said, he was free to go back to the regular road to get to the other side of the bridge. He refused to do so and remained where he was obstructed for about one-half hour.

QUESTION—Is there false imprisonment when a person's freedom of movement is blocked on a public road?

Drabek *v.* Sabley
31 Wis. 2d 184, 142 N.W.2d 798 (1966)

TOPIC—Damages for false imprisonment

FACTS—The plaintiff, Thomas Drabek, ten years old, lived with his parents on Highway 67 in Wisconsin. On February 23, 1964, shortly before 6:00 P.M., he and four other boys were throwing snowballs at passing cars. As Dr. Sabley drove by, his car was hit by a snowball apparently thrown by one of the boys. Sabley stopped his car. The boys ran, but Sabley caught Tom. Holding Tom by the arm, Sabley took him to the car and told him to get in. Sabley asked and was told Tom's name, but he did not ask where Tom lived. With Tom in his car, Sabley drove into the village. He found a police officer and turned Tom over to him. Later action was brought against Sabley for false imprisonment, based on Tom's being made to enter and remain in Sabley's automobile.

QUESTION—Is the false imprisonment of a minor by a citizen justified on the grounds of self-defense?

■ ***Trespass*** The tort of trespass may involve either personal possessions or land or both. A person may be liable for

minor A person who is under the age at which he/she may exercise certain civil and personal rights.

the tort of trespass to another's personal property. When a person, without an excuse, intentionally interferes with the possession, ownership, or use of another person's personal possessions, the law says she/he must return the property or pay for it. John has some cane poles lying in his yard. Bill, his neighbor, takes the poles. Bill does not mean to steal. He just believes John would not mind his taking the poles for his own use. If John sues Bill, he may recover the poles. If the poles have been damaged, John would receive payment. Bill has trespassed on John's possession of the poles.

Catherine and Jill are neighbors. The limbs of Jill's plum tree hang over Catherine's boundary line. Catherine picks plums from the part of the plum tree hanging over the boundary line. Jill asks Catherine to return the plums. Catherine says that she has a right to have them. The law would make Catherine return the plums, or their reasonable value to Jill, the owner of the plum tree.

Liability for the tort of trespass to land arises when a person enters land owned by another and remains on the land in spite of the owner's wishes. The owner of land has the right to the use of the ground, the air above the ground, and the soil underneath. Recently, however, the "air age" has forced a change in the law. An airplane may fly above a person's land and it is not thought to be trespassing. However, airplanes must fly high enough not to interfere with normal use of the land below. Josh owns a small farm on which he raises cattle. Every day Rufus, his neighbor, takes off over and over again in his airplane and flies low over Josh's land. The loud noise causes Josh's cattle to become so frightened that they stampede and several of the cattle are hurt. Rufus's act is a direct invasion of Josh's land. So Josh can sue Rufus to make him pay for the damages to the cattle.

Harrison *v.* Wisdom
54 Tenn. 99, 7 Heisk 99 (1872)

TOPIC—Damages for trespass to personal property

FACTS—The city of Clarksville, Tennessee, is about 30 miles from Fort Donelson. After the fall of Fort Donelson in February 1862, during the War Between the States, a public meeting of the citizens of Clarksville was held at the mayor's office. The citizens decided to destroy all the liquor in town before the federal army arrived. They did this to keep the federal soldiers from becoming drunk. If the soldiers got drunk, they might harm the property and citizens of the town. A. B. Harrison was one of the persons whose liquor was destroyed. Harrison brought suit against the citizens of Clarksville who had taken part in destroying the liquor.

QUESTION—When there is immediate danger to the public safety, can personal property belonging to a person be taken from that person?

Ploof *v.* Putnam
81 Vt. 471, 71 A 188 (1908)

TOPIC—Damages caused by attempted trespass

FACTS—The defendant, Mr. Putnam, owned a small island in Lake Champlain with a dock built on the water. On November 13, 1904, the plaintiff, Mr. Ploof, was sailing on the lake. With him were Mrs. Ploof and their two children. A sudden and violent storm placed the sailboat and its passengers in great danger. Ploof saw Putnam's dock, headed the sailboat toward it, and tied the boat to the dock. A servant of the defendant felt that the boat did not belong there. He untied the boat and it was driven onto the shore by the storm. The sailboat, and everything in it, was destroyed. The Ploofs were thrown into the lake, and all of them were hurt.

QUESTION—Does a person have the right to enter land and make use of personal property belonging to another for the purpose of survival?

Longenecker *v.* Zimmerman
175 Kan. 719, 267 P.2d 543 (1954)

TOPIC—Damages for trespass

FACTS—Mrs. Longenecker and Mrs. Zimmerman owned adjoining homes. They had been neighbors for about five years. In September of 1950, Zimmerman, without Longenecker's permission, hired a tree surgery company to trim three cedar trees. Longenecker felt the trees were destroyed by improper pruning. The trees had a sentimental value for her and were also valuable for both shade and beauty. Longenecker felt each tree was worth $150 to $200. She sued Zimmerman, claiming trespass.

At the trial Zimmerman said that she had been mistaken as to the boundary line. She believed the trees were on her land. In fact, the trees were some two or three feet over the boundary line, on Longenecker's land.

QUESTION—Is a person entitled to damages for trespass in a situation where the other party did not know that a trespass was involved?

■ ***Defense of land or personal property*** People have a right to defend their land and personal property by reasonable force that will not cause serious injury to the trespasser. Before any act of defense is made, the owner or renter should ask the invader to stop trespassing. If the demand is ignored, the property owner may threaten to use greater force than would really be necessary to discourage the intruder. However, the use of force likely to cause serious injury or death is not justified to defend land or personal property. The only exception is in the defense of a person's home when the owner or renter fears that the invader means to do her/him bodily harm.

Any act done in defense of land or personal property must be done at the time the land is trespassed upon or the property is taken. Or it must be done while the owner or renter is

trying to catch the thief or invader. Once there has been a crime, the owner or renter must depend upon officers of the law to catch the trespasser or to return the property.

■ ***Self-defense*** Under most state laws, one has the legal right to defend oneself under certain conditions: (1) The aggressor has acted in such a way as to cause a person to believe she/he is about to be hurt. (2) Defensive acts taken would, under the circumstances, appear reasonable to the average person.

There is no duty to retreat when the force is threatened, unless the threatened act is just careless. In cases where a reasonable person would expect that death or serious harm is being threatened, that person may use the same amount of force that the aggressor uses.

The right of self-defense does *not* apply in the following cases.

1. The threat of danger has passed.
2. The defensive force is more than the average, reasonable person would use to defend himself/herself.

---

aggressor One who starts an attack or a quarrel.

3. There is an injury to a third person during the act of self-defense. For example, Albert attacks Bill. Bill pushes Herman into the path of danger. Bill is legally responsible if Herman is hurt.
4. A person is properly held or arrested by an officer of the law.

A person may legally come to the defense of a third person. At one time the law gave this right only when the victim was a member of one's immediate family. Today the law encourages people to give aid even to strangers who are in danger.

State *v.* Preece
116 W. Va. 176, 179 S.E. 524 (1935)

TOPIC—Action based on manslaughter charges

FACTS—Mr. Fine, 49 years old, was of medium height and weighed 150 pounds. He worked in the yards of the Norfolk and Western Railway at Williamson, West Virginia. About 7 A.M. on February 10, 1934, he left the yards with Mr. Wolford, age 22. They went to buy a pint of whiskey, which they drank. Then they went to a place on Fourth Avenue, where they bought another pint of whiskey and drank that too. Fine then decided that he wanted to see Mr. Ferguson, who lived at the home of Mr. Preece on Fifth Avenue. They went to Preece's home and asked if they could come in. Preece did not know them or what they wanted and told them to leave. Fine started up the stairs toward Preece saying that he would kill him. Thinking that Fine had a gun, Preece went into his apartment and got his own gun. Preece then shot and killed Fine. Fine, however, actually had no weapon.

QUESTION—Is a person allowed by law to use extreme measures to protect his/her home and/or person when threatened?

---

manslaughter The unlawful taking of a life without malice, voluntarily or involuntarily. Examples are crimes of passion and accidents that result from criminal carelessness.

NEGLIGENCE

Intentional torts, such as assault and battery, are based upon the idea that an aggressor means to do harm to another person. Negligence, on the other hand, is not based on intended harm. It is based, rather, on the duty that each person has to act in a careful and responsible manner when others are involved. The law expects each of us to act with due care for the safety of others and their property. Due care is measured by what the average, reasonable person would do under the circumstances. In negligence cases the fact that the defendant did not mean to hurt the plaintiff most often makes no difference. The point is whether a reasonable person would have been able to prevent the harm done.

• Mr. Hawkins collapsed in a store from a heart attack. As he fell to the floor he pushed a woman down, causing her to break a leg. Was Hawkins negligent and liable for the harm done to the woman? The answer is No. Under the circumstances, Hawkins was not able to show due care.

• Dr. Brown operated on Mr. Green to remove his appendix. Green continued to have pains. He went to another doctor.

That doctor discovered a clamp had been left in Green's side. Can Green collect from Brown for negligence? Probably. Every doctor must use the care and skill that the average doctor ought to have.

Negligence is a relatively new principle of tort law. It has been accepted for little more than one hundred years. Earlier, people lived largely on farms in the country. They did not often come into contact with one another. Today the number of people has grown. People live closer together in cities. We are in contact with dozens of people each day. So the standard of due care has become very important in order to protect the welfare of everyone.

In court cases dealing with negligence, the main question is how much care should have been shown by one person to another in the particular situation and whether that amount of care was shown. It is the duty of the judge to explain to the jury what negligence and due care are under the law. The jury serves as a group of average, reasonable men and women. The members of the jury think over the facts of the case in order to decide whether the defendant used as much due care as the average, reasonable person would have used in the same situation.

In negligence cases in which a child has caused the harm, the test is whether the child used the care and caution that the average, reasonable person of her/his age, intelligence, and experience would have shown under the circumstances.

Davies *v.* Mann

Exchequer 10 M. & W. 546, 152 Eng. Rep. 588 (1842)

TOPIC—Damages for negligence

FACTS—Mr. Davies tied together the front feet of his donkey and turned the animal out to graze along a public highway. The donkey was eating at the side of the road when Mr. Mann came along in his wagon at a fast pace. He knocked the donkey down and killed it. Davies sued Mann for the value of his donkey.

QUESTION—If a person is negligent by having an animal near a road, does that negligence keep the person from recovering damages?

King *v.* Smythe
140 Tenn. 217, 204 S.W. 296 (1918)

TOPIC—Damages for negligence

FACTS—Dr. Smythe was a surgeon in Memphis, Tennessee. He owned a car that he used in his work and for the pleasure of his family. His son, Frank, was a 24-year-old medical student. He often drove the car without asking his father first. In this case, the son drove the car negligently. He damaged the automobile owned by Mr. King.

QUESTION—Is the owner of a car liable for the negligence caused by a member of his/her family?

Cohen *v.* Petty
62 App. D.C. 187, 65 F.2d 820 (1933)

TOPIC—Injury caused by negligence

FACTS—Mr. Petty was a real estate agent. He took care of Jeannette Cohen's property and collected rents for her. One day, Petty was driving an automobile in which Cohen was a passenger. Seated in the front seat of the car beside Petty was Mrs. Petty. Cohen, a retired schoolteacher, and her sisters were in the rear seat. The people in the car had known each other for a number of years. Petty was driving along at about 25 to 30 mph when he neared a curve in the road. He was heard to say to his wife, "I feel sick." She said in a frightened voice, "Oh, what is the matter?" Petty's head had fallen back and his hand had left the wheel. He had fainted. Right after that, the car left the road and crashed. Cohen was hurt in the accident and sued Petty for negligence. In court Petty said that he had never fainted before. He said that as far as he knew he was in good health.

QUESTION—Is a person liable for harm done to others when something unforeseen causes him/her to lose physical control?

Zelenko *v.* Gimbel Brothers, Inc.
Sup. Ct. of N.Y., 158 Misc. 904, 287 N.Y.S. 134 (1935)

TOPIC—Damages based on negligence

FACTS—Ms. Zelenko became ill while shopping in Gimbel Brothers store in New York City. Some employees of Gimbel Brothers took her to a sickroom, where she was left for six hours. The employees did nothing else to help her nor did they try to get her medical aid. Later the woman died. Action was brought by the administrator of Zelenko's estate.

---

real estate agent A person who buys, sells, or rents property in behalf of another person for a fee.

administrator A person who has the legal authority to manage, settle, or dispose of the estate of a dead person, a minor, an insane person, or any legally incompetent person.

QUESTION—Does one who has no duty to aid another have a duty to act with care when aid is offered?

Kuhns *v.* Brugger
390 Pa. 331, 135 A.2d 395 (1957)

TOPIC—Damages for personal injuries caused by negligence

FACTS—Early on July 23, 1953, Albert Kuhns and George Brugger, both twelve years old, went fishing with their grandfather. They returned to their grandfather's cottage about 3:30 P.M. without him and entered his bedroom. In a spirit of play, Brugger picked up a gun and pointed it at Kuhns. At that moment Miss Fries, a greataunt, entered the bedroom and ordered Brugger to put away the gun. He did so, but a few minutes later he went to his grandfather's dresser and found another gun, in the top left drawer. The gun was loaded. Later, Brugger said, "I took it [the pistol] out, took it out of the holster,

took it in my hand. I believe I had my finger on the trigger. And I pulled the slide back, and then the shot occurred." The bullet entered Kuhn's body. It hit his spinal cord, paralyzing the lower part of his body. He could no longer walk and needed constant care and medicine. He would never be able to hold a job. Kuhns sued Brugger. The trial court returned a verdict against Brugger.

Brugger appealed on the grounds of his age. It was stated that he was incapable of negligent conduct at age twelve. Therefore he was not liable for the injury done.

QUESTION—May a child be held liable for negligent acts?

■ ***Responsibility of property owners*** Many negligence claims are about questions of due care in the ownership and use of personal property and land. Property owners have a duty, set by law, to show a measure of due care for the safety of those who enter or use their property. People who enter the property of another are of three kinds. A *trespasser* comes on to the property of another without permission. A *licensee* comes on to the property of another with the owner's permission. A licensee may be a guest visiting a friend or relative. An *invitee* comes on to the property of another as an invited business guest. That person has been invited onto the premises for some kind of activity or business. An invitee may be there to do business directly with the owner of the property. Or she/he may be there as a member of the public at large. For example, an invitee may be a customer of a store or bank.

An invitee must get the highest standard of due care. In the case of an invitee, the property owner is responsible for any dangerous condition on the premises. The owner is responsible for warning a licensee of any hidden dangers on the property. But the law does not say the owner must point out dangers that anyone could see. Is the person who delivers the milk an invitee, or a licensee? As a landowner, would you owe more due care to that person, or to a neighbor making a friendly visit?

An owner owes very little due care to a trespasser. The owner or occupier of property may use reasonable and necessary force to remove a trespasser from the premises. But she/he must not intentionally hurt the trespasser.

Sheehan *v.* St. Paul & Duluth Railway Company
U.S. Cir. Ct. of App., Seventh Cir. 76 F. 201 (1896)

TOPIC—Damages for negligence

FACTS—On October 30, 1894, in Carlton, Minnesota, Mr. Sheehan, a stranger in town, was seeking work. Soon after noon he went down the railroad tracks with three other men. One of them gave Sheehan 50 cents to buy tobacco and whiskey in the village. He was on his way to do this when his foot became caught in an iron cattle guard. Sheehan stated that at the time he had had two drinks of whiskey. While Sheehan was trying to free his foot, a train pulling 16 empty flatcars was switching tracks. The train crew did not see Sheehan until the train was almost upon him. Later Sheehan stated,

> I was trying to free my foot without hurting myself, and could not do it. I had all the skin off my ankle here, and I could not get out. I put down my hand to untie the shoe, and I could not put my hand down further than the lacing of my shoe, and I got my finger down, and tried to loose it. I seen the train at the depot steaming, and I didn't know what way she was coming.

Two witnesses said the train was moving at about 3 mph. An expert testified that at that speed the train could be stopped in 100 feet. The engineer, fireman, and brakeman testified that on hearing Sheehan's cries, every means was used to stop the engine. But snow had made the rail slippery and prevented fast braking. It was too late to stop the train from running over Sheehan's foot. Sheehan sued the railway company.

QUESTION—Does a property owner have a duty to care for a trespasser when the owner does not know a trespasser is there?

Chicago B & Q Railroad Company *v.* Krayenbuhl
65 Neb. 889, 91 N.W. 880 (1902)

TOPIC—Damages caused by negligence

FACTS—Mr. Krayenbuhl worked for the Chicago B & Q Railroad Company. He and his family lived in a small house near the railroad station. His son, Leo, aged four, often went on property owned by the railroad in the village of Palmer, Nebraska. He went there to play on a railroad turntable.

The railroad company had a policy that the turntable should be locked at all times when not in use. But this was often ignored by railroad workers. On October 20, 1895, Leo and several other children found the turntable was not locked or guarded. As the children were playing on the turntable, Leo's foot was cut off above the ankle. His father sued the railroad company for him for personal injuries based on negligence of the railroad company. Krayenbuhl won the case but the railroad company appealed.

QUESTION—Does the owner of property have a duty to care for children trespassers?

Kavafian *v.* Seattle Baseball Club Association
105 Wash. 215, 177 P. 776 (1919)

TOPIC—Damages for negligence

FACTS—Mr. Kavafian had bought a grandstand ticket for a baseball game in Seattle, Washington. He had been to the ball park five or six times before. When he arrived, there were empty grandstand seats behind a screen provided to protect the spectators from stray balls. Kavafian chose to sit in a place that was not behind a screen. During the game a foul ball struck Kavafian on the knee and hurt him. Kavafian sued. The trial court decided that Kavafian was an invitee to the ball park and could expect that his seat was reasonably safe. The Association appealed.

QUESTION—Is a spectator at a baseball game who chooses to sit in an unscreened spot able to recover damages for injuries?

Palsgraf *v.* Long Island Railroad Company
248 N.Y. 339, 162 N.E. 99 (1928)

TOPIC—Damages for personal injury caused by negligence

FACTS—Mrs. Palsgraf was waiting on a train platform for a trip to Rockaway Beach. While she stood there, two men ran by to catch a train as it was pulling out. The first man jumped on board easily. But the second man had trouble boarding the train as it moved away. He was helped by a guard on the platform who reached forward to help him on while another guard pushed him from behind. As the man got on the train, a package he was carrying fell to the ground. The package held fireworks that blew up, creating a shock so great that it knocked over some scales. The scales fell on Palsgraf and hurt her. She sued the railroad.

QUESTION—Is the railroad liable to Palsgraf for injuries that she received?

Laube *v.* Stevenson
137 Conn. 469, 78 A.2d 693 (1951)

TOPIC—Damages for negligence

FACTS—Mr. and Mrs. Stevenson owned a one-family house in Naugatuck, Connecticut, where they lived with their small child. On January 27, 1949, Mrs. Laube, Mrs. Stevenson's mother, was a guest in the Stevenson home. Mrs. Stevenson asked her mother to go down to the cellar to get a blanket for the baby. Laube had used the cellar stairs once, about a year before, but she did not know that they were now in a dangerous state. The upper part of the stairway had a landing covered with smooth, slippery linoleum. There was no handrail on either side, nor was there a light at the top of the stairway. A vacuum cleaner stood on one side of the landing and an ironing board was hanging loose on the wall. The Stevensons knew the state the stairs were in, but they gave Laube no warning. Laube went carefully toward the staircase and felt for a handrail. She put a hand on the wall to steady herself, but she was not able to do

so. Her right hand touched the vacuum cleaner. Her left hand touched the ironing board. She then stepped from the landing onto the step below. The stairs themselves were in an unsafe condition. Laube stumbled on them, fell, and was badly hurt. She sued.

QUESTION—Is a landowner liable for injury to a licensee?

King *v.* Lennen
53 Ca. 2d 340, 348 P.2d 98 (1959)

TOPIC—Damages for negligence

FACTS—Mr. Lennen owned a private swimming pool about 30 feet from a public street in Los Angeles County. Along the street side Lennen had built a concrete block wall with an opening 4 feet wide directly across from the pool. On another side there was a wood rail fence with openings through which children could readily enter. Lennen allowed his cow, two dogs, and three horses to move about freely near the pool. The animals and the pool could be easily seen by children. Children were attracted by what they saw and often entered the grounds to play with the animals around the pool. The water in the pool was $3\frac{1}{2}$ feet deep in the shallow end and 9 feet at the deep end. At the time in question, the water in the pool was so dirty that one could not tell how deep it was by looking into it.

Boyd King, one and one-half years old, lived with his parents near the Lennen property. Several times Lennen's teen-age daughter had been hired by the Kings as a baby-sitter. In order to entertain Boyd, she would bring him to the Lennen home and let him play with the animals near the pool. One day Boyd had been invited to play on Lennen's grounds. Later in the day, Boyd's body was found in the bottom of the pool. Boyd's father sued Lennen for negligence.

QUESTION—Can a landowner be held liable for a child's drowning in a swimming pool on the owner's land?

Lemon *v.* Edwards
Ct. of App. of Ky., 344 S.W.2d 822 (1961)

TOPIC—Damages based on negligence

FACTS—A gravel road runs from the main highway through Mr. Edwards's land to an area on the shores of Kentucky Lake. On an evening in July, during a rainstorm, Mrs. Lemon was driving along this road from her family's cabin toward the main highway. A large tree on Edwards's land fell across the top of Lemon's automobile. It crushed the car and hurt her badly. She sued Edwards. In court she said that the tree had been dead for several years and that Edwards was negligent in not having had it removed. Edwards did not live on his piece of densely wooded land. But the evidence showed that he visited his land four or five times a year. Little use was made of the gravel road other than by persons owning camps along the shore of the lake. The trial court gave a verdict in favor of the defendant, Edwards. Lemon appealed the case.

QUESTION—Does the owner of country land have a duty to keep trees on the land from falling into a public road?

STRICT LIABILITY

Laws dealing with strict liability most often have to do with three kinds of torts: (1) damage done by domesticated animals or wild animals under a person's control; (2) damage resulting from highly dangerous acts such as blasting, drilling, or tearing down buildings; (3) injury caused by the use of products that are known to be dangerous to those who come in contact with them. People engaged in these activities are strictly liable for the results of their acts. This is true even if due care is shown.

Filburn *v.* People's Palace & Aquarium Company, Ltd.
25 Q.B. Div. 258 (1890)

TOPIC—Damages done by animal attack

FACTS—Mr. Filburn was at the People's Palace and Aquarium Company, Ltd., where elephants were being shown. An elephant attacked Filburn and hurt him. Filburn sued the company. The judge asked the jury to decide whether (1) the elephant was a dangerous animal, (2) the company knew the elephant to be dangerous, (3) Filburn brought the attack on himself. The jury answered all three questions in favor of Filburn. The decision was appealed.

QUESTION—Shall the owner of the elephant be held strictly liable for damages the animal causes?

Zarek *v.* Fredericks
U.S. Cir. Ct. of App., Third Circuit, 138 F.2d 689 (1943).

TOPIC—Injuries caused by dog bite

FACTS—A young boy, Vincent Zarek, was vacationing with his mother at a hotel in Pennsylvania. Vincent leaned over to pet a dog owned by Mr. Fredericks. The dog bit Vincent, its teeth striking close to the boy's eyelid. The bite left scars that might be permanent and caused a slight droop to the eyelid. A suit for damages was brought against Fredericks. It was claimed that the boy received injuries in the amount of $4,000 from the dog bite.

The dog was six years old at the time it bit Vincent. It had been trained as a watchdog but, as far as was known, had never bitten anyone before. The trial court decided against Zarek. The case was appealed.

QUESTION—Shall the dog's owner be held strictly liable for damages to the plaintiff?

Luthringer *v.* Moore
31 Cal. 2d 489, 190 P.2d 1 (1948)

TOPIC—Damages caused by gas fumes

FACTS—Mr. Moore had been exterminating cockroaches in the basement of a drugstore in Sacramento, California. About midnight on November 16, 1943, Moore released hydrocyanic acid gas to kill the insects. The next morning Mr. Luthringer, who worked in the store, arrived for the day's work, suffering from a cold. After entering the store, he went to another floor to put on his working clothes. Feeling ill, he returned to the main floor. He was soon overcome by the gas and lost consciousness. Luthringer was removed from the store and given aid by firefighters of the city. He was then taken to a hospital, where he was kept for 20 days. He remained in bed at home for another two weeks. He returned to work at the end of December 1943, but he was not able to do his work as he had before he was hurt. His heart missed beats, causing him to worry. He had a continuing cough and lost twenty pounds. He suffered from headaches and weakness up to the time of the trial in his suit against Moore. The jury gave a verdict in favor of Luthringer. The court granted him $10,000 in damages. The case was appealed.

QUESTION—Is an exterminator strictly liable for injuries resulting from his/her work?

Beck *v.* Bel Air Properties, Inc.
134 Cal. 2d 834, 286 P.2d 503 (1955)

TOPIC—Damages for injury to property

FACTS—Mr. Beck owned a lot at the bottom of a canyon on the outskirts of Los Angeles, California. He built a single family home on his lot. Bel Air Properties, Inc. was using bulldozers on land above and to the east of Beck's lot. There was a steep slope of hard-packed soil and rock between Beck's lot and where the bulldozers were working. The slope was thickly covered with trees and plants. The bulldozing was being done at the top of the canyon. After the bulldozing, heavy rain caused large amounts of loose soil and rocks to flow over Beck's land, damaging his house and lot. Beck sued Bel Air Properties, Inc. He said that they were strictly liable for the hazardous act of bulldozing.

QUESTION—Is bulldozing as part of developing building lots thought to be a hazardous act under the law?

Spano *v.* Perini Corporation
25 N.Y. 2d 11, 250 N.E.2d 31 (1969)

TOPIC—Damage to property resulting from blasting operations

FACTS—Ms. Spano owned a garage in Brooklyn, New York. The Perini Corporation was building a tunnel nearby for the city of New York. On November 27, 1962, the Perini Corporation set off 194 sticks of dynamite only 125 feet away from the Spano property. The Spano garage was wrecked as a result of the shock waves caused by the blasting. There was no physical trespass on to the property owned by Spano. Spano sued the Perini Corporation.

QUESTION—Is a person or company that engages in blasting activities strictly liable for damages done?

OTHER TORTS

Other torts are based upon combinations of intentional acts, negligent acts, and/or acts of strict liability. These include nuisance acts and libel and slander.

■ ***Nuisance*** A nuisance is an unreasonable interference by one person in the use and enjoyment of land belonging to another. While this appears to be much like trespass to land,

---

hazardous act A dangerous act that may result in harm or damage to person or property.

there is an important difference. Trespass threatens the proper possession of land. Nuisance has to do with the use and enjoyment of land. When a nuisance or disturbance threatens the owner's use and enjoyment of land, she/he may ask that the court order the person responsible to stop the acts involved. If the nuisance really damages the land, the owner may sue for damages. Acts amounting to a nuisance must cause a real and continuing interference with the use and enjoyment of land. A slight or temporary interference is not enough to justify seeking legal aid.

Rogers *v.* Elliott
146 Mass. 349, 15 N.E. 768 (1888)

TOPIC—Damages for nuisance

FACTS—Mr. Rogers sued Rev. T. P. Elliott, pastor of St. Peter's Roman Catholic Church in Provincetown, Massachusetts, for ringing the church bell. Rogers said the ringing caused him pain and suffering. At the time the bells were rung, Rogers was suffering from sunstroke and was in a highly nervous state. At the trial Dr. Birge testified as follows:

> I attended the plaintiff for sunstroke. I found him in convulsions, the sunstroke having resulted in congestion of the brain. He was living at his father's house almost directly opposite the church. I left him Saturday night, apparently comfortable; saw nothing to prevent his recovery. I went to see him the next morning, and found him worse than the night before.

Birge saw that when the church bell was rung, his patient was thrown into convulsions. After leaving his patient, Birge went across the street to tell Elliott what was happening. Elliott said he would not stop ringing the bell for anybody. Elliott told the church custodian to go on with the ringing.

QUESTION—Do acts that disturb only a highly nervous person cause a nuisance?

■ ***Libel and slander*** Everyone has the right to be safe in the enjoyment of a good reputation. Therefore, it is unlawful to tell a third person, untruthfully, that another person is, for example, a "criminal," "liar," "cheat," "drunk," or "coward." Such words may harm a person's reputation and may even damage that person's business or trade. For example, a banker who has been called a "cheat" may suffer a great deal and may even lose his/her job.

Libel is a false and/or malicious criticism or insult that is written or printed and distributed. Warren writes to Perry that "Mike is a murderer." If Mike is not a murderer, Warren may be guilty of libel. Slander is a false and/or malicious criticism or insult that is spoken and heard by a third person. Warren tells Perry that "Mike is a murderer." If Mike is not a murderer, Warren may be guilty of slander.

In cases involving libel or slander, the person writing or speaking must prove the truth of the statements made. If that person cannot prove that the statements are true, then he/she may be guilty of libel or slander. That person may then be liable for damages to the person whose reputation has been harmed.

Bennett *v.* Norban
396 Pa. 94, 151 A.2d 476 (1959)

TOPIC—Damages for slander

FACTS—On Saturday afternoon, December 28, 1957, Mrs. Bennett entered Lynn's Self-Service Store in Erie, Pennsylvania. She wanted to buy a purse. She selected one, but could not find anyone to wrap it for her. She moved on to look at some skirts an aisle or two away, carrying the purse with her. She was in a hurry to return to the hospital where her child was recovering from an operation. She soon put back the purse and left the store without buying anything.

Twenty feet beyond the store door, Bennett was overtaken by the assistant manager of the store. He was red-faced and angry. He put his hand on her shoulder and blocked her path. He ordered her to take off her coat, which she did. He then said "What about your pockets?" He reached into two pockets on

the side of her dress, but found nothing. He then took her purse from her hand. He pulled her things out of it and looked into it. He then put the things back into her purse and gave it to her. He mumbled something and ran back into the store. Passersby had stopped to watch the search take place. Bennett was distressed and humiliated. She sued.

QUESTION—Can the statements and acts of a store manager who frisks a customer before a group of bystanders cause an action for slander?

Fawcett Publications, Inc. *v.* Morris
Okl., 377 P.2d 42 (1962)

TOPIC—Damages for libel

FACTS—In a 1958 issue of *True* magazine there appeared an article called "The Pill That Can Kill Sports." It was about the use of amphetamines, "pep pills," and similar drugs by athletes all over the country. The article said that players on the 1956 Oklahoma football team used drugs.

All through their undefeated season, Dennis Morris was fullback on the alternate squad of the 1956 Oklahoma team. He sued Fawcett Publications, Inc. (publishers of *True*) for libel based on the article. He asked for damages in the amount of $150,000. Facts brought out in court showed that the substance given to the Oklahoma players was "spirits of peppermint." This was a harmless substance used for dryness of the mouth. There was no evidence that any member of the team had used amphetamines or narcotic drugs. The jury returned a verdict in favor of Morris. Fawcett Publications, Inc. was ordered to pay $75,000 in damages. Fawcett Publications appealed.

QUESTION—Can a member of a group sue for libel based on a magazine article talking about illegal drug use among members of that group?

Reviewing the Chapter

Law-Related Terms

Tort *Pp. 124, 309*
Assault *Pp. 124–125, 302*
Battery *Pp. 125–126, 302*
Libel *P. 156*
Slander *P. 156*

Review Questions

1. How is a tort different from a crime? *P. 124*
2. List five types of acts that are considered intentional torts. *P. 124*
3. **(a)** How much force may one use to defend land and personal property? **(b)** When does the right of self-defense *not* apply? *Pp. 136–138*
4. **(a)** What is due care? **(b)** How is due care measured? *Pp. 139, 304*
5. Cite cases to support your answers: **(a)** Is a car owner liable for the negligent acts of a family member while driving that car? **(b)** May a child be held liable for negligent acts? **(c)** Does a property owner owe due care to children trespassers? *Pp. 141–150, 273–274*
6. **(a)** Explain the three categories of people who come on to another's property. **(b)** To whom does the property owner owe the most due care? the least amount of due care? *Pp. 144–145*
7. What are three kinds of torts that involve strict liability? *P. 151*
8. **(a)** What is the main difference between nuisance and trespass? **(b)** In what way are libel and slander different? *Pp. 154–156*

Chapter Test

On a separate paper, write T *if the statement is true, and* F *if the statement is false.*

1. A tort is the same thing as a crime.
2. Assault and battery are both intentional torts.
3. People have a right to defend their land and personal property by reasonable force that will not cause serious injury to a trespasser.
4. The right of self-defense does not apply if the defensive force is more than the average, reasonable person would use to defend himself or herself.
5. In negligence cases, the main questions are how much care should have been shown in the particular situation and whether that amount of care was shown.
6. An automobile owner may not be held responsible for the negligent acts of a member of his or her family while driving that car.
7. A property owner owes the highest standard of due care to a trespasser.
8. An example of a tort involving strict liability is one in which damage is caused by an animal under a person's control.
9. People engaged in hazardous activities are liable for the results of their acts, even if due care is shown.
10. A false and/or malicious criticism or insult that is spoken and heard by a third person is called libel.

MOCH

Property 5

Bridges *v.* Hawkesworth
Court of Queen's Bench, 21 L.J., N.S., 75 (1851)

TOPIC—Action concerning ownership of lost property

FACTS—Mr. Bridges was a traveling salesperson. In October 1847 he visited a shop that was run by Mr. Hawkesworth. While in the shop, he noticed a small package on the floor. Bridges picked up the package and discovered that there was money in it. He left it with Hawkesworth to give back to the true owner. However, the true owner never came back to ask for the money. After three years Bridges sued to get the money back from Hawkesworth.

QUESTION—Was the money found by Bridges in Hawkesworth's shop lost property?

WHAT IS PROPERTY?

From the point of view of the law, property is anything that people can own. Owning property means the right to use, enjoy, and control something. All groups of people have some form of property ownership. But the objects of property—the things owned—and the property rights protected by law are different among societies and over time. In primitive societies, some things were accepted as belonging to an individual person. A hunter's spear, for example, was thought of as almost a part of the hunter. Control over other things, such as hunting grounds, was thought of as belonging to the whole tribe. In all societies, however, it came to be more and more accepted that each person's rights must be protected by law. There grew up the idea of a person's rights to his/her own property.

■ ***Land ownership in early England*** When William the Conqueror took over England, he announced that all the land belonged to him. Even those who had owned land before William became king now had to agree that they held all their lands only through him. King William and his successors granted large pieces of land to their nobles and knights. These people held their lands from the king in return for the services they gave him. The most important service they owed the king was military. If a noble was disloyal or refused service, the king could take the land away. Clearly, only the king *owned* the land.

Land held in return for service was called a fief, or a fee. To the nobles and knights who promised him loyalty and service, the king granted fiefs that were supposed to support them and their families. Usually the fief was a manor or group of manors. The manor was a large farm. Part of the farm or farms was kept for the person who held the fief. This person was called the lord of the manor. The rest of the manor was held by tenant farmers. These farmers held their land in return for services they gave to the lord of the manor.

This form of landholding—a part of what is called the feudal system—lasted many hundreds of years in English history. In the beginning, when military service was most important, only people who could serve as knights or soldiers were allowed to hold a fief. It became the custom for the whole fief to be passed from the holder to his firstborn son. This son would be the next holder. And since the fief was meant to support a knight, it could not be divided among many heirs but must be kept together. It was only when military service became less important that women were allowed to hold fiefs or to inherit them.

■ ***Owning land in America*** The breaking up of this system of holding land in return for services was taking place in England during the sixteenth and seventeenth centuries. This was just at the time the American colonies were being settled. More and more English landholders held their land either in fee simple or like those tenant farmers on the English manors who were called freeholders. When English landholders held land in fee simple, the only feudal duties or services that remained were the payment of a fixed yearly rent, called a quit rent, and an oath of loyalty to the person from whom the land was held. Lands held by freehold were also held free of all services except for a yearly quit rent.

It was the desire for land ownership that led the largest number of English people to settle in America. Good farming land in England was becoming scarce in the seventeenth century. America offered the possibility of acquiring large amounts of land. The colonists who came to North America from England looked upon themselves as English. They felt they were guaranteed all the rights and liberties of common law. They felt they had the same rights to own and inherit land as the people at home in England. Lands granted to the settlers in America, therefore, either were held of the king in fee simple or were held by freehold. The charters of all the English colonies set up forms of land ownership by freehold or fee simple. In colonial America, voting rights were based on ownership of property. The colonists did not bring over the rest of the old English feudal system. And after the Revolutionary War the new states slowly did away with quit rents. Also, as a general rule, the right of the firstborn son to get all the land owned by his father was also done away with. Citizens could own land simply by buying it.

Colonists from other countries such as Spain, France, and Holland made great contributions to what is now the United States of America. But American laws of land ownership developed for the most part from the old English common law. And old words like *fee simple* and *freehold* are still used. In fact, fee simple ownership in the United States today is the most common and most complete kind of land ownership that it is possible to have.

■ ***Basic property rights*** Jeremy Bentham, an English philosopher, once said, "Property and law are born together. Before laws were made there was no property. Take away laws and property ceases." In 1829, Joseph Story, a Justice of the United States Supreme Court, wrote, "The fundamental maxims of a free government seem to require that the rights of personal liberty and private property should be held sacred."

---

fundamental maxim A basic and accepted general truth or principle.

WARRANTY DEED
INDIVID. TO INDIVID

This Warranty Deed *Made the day of A. D. 19 by*

hereinafter called the grantor, to

whose postoffice address is
hereinafter called the grantee:

(Wherever used herein the terms "grantor" and "grantee" include all the parties to this instrument and the heirs, legal representatives and assigns of individuals, and the successors and assigns of corporations)

Witnesseth: *That the grantor, for and in consideration of the sum of $ and other valuable considerations, receipt whereof is hereby acknowledged, hereby grants, bargains, sells, aliens, remises, releases, conveys and confirms unto the grantee, all that certain land situate in County, Florida, viz:*

Together *with all the tenements, hereditaments and appurtenances thereto belonging or in anywise appertaining.*

To Have and to Hold, *the same in fee simple forever.*

And *the grantor hereby covenants with said grantee that the grantor is lawfully seized of said land in fee simple; that the grantor has good right and lawful authority to sell and convey said land; that the grantor hereby fully warrants the title to said land and will defend the same against the lawful claims of all persons whomsoever; and that said land is free of all encumbrances, except taxes accruing subsequent to December 31, 19*

In Witness Whereof, *the said grantor has signed and sealed these presents the day and year first above written.*

Signed, sealed and delivered in our presence:

.... L.S.

.... L.S.

STATE OF
COUNTY OF

I HEREBY CERTIFY that on this day, before me, an officer duly authorized in the State aforesaid and in the County aforesaid to take acknowledgments, personally appeared

to me known to be the person described in and who executed the foregoing instrument and acknowledged before me that executed the same.

WITNESS my hand and official seal in the County and State last aforesaid this day of , A. D. 19

....

SPACE BELOW FOR RECORDERS USE

This Instrument prepared by:

Address

In our nation one of our great freedoms is the right to own, to buy, and to sell property. We expect the law to protect our right to use and control our property and to keep others from taking away that which rightly belongs to us. The Fifth Amendment to our Constitution states that no person shall be "deprived of life, liberty, or property, without due process of law."

■ ***Classes of property*** Property has been divided into two main classes. These are *real property* and *personal property.* Real property is land and all those things that are permanently attached to it. This is the kind of property we generally call real estate. All other things that are owned are called personal property.

These definitions may seem confusing. A car is just as "real" as a farm. The family house is more "personal" to the owner than shares of stock. But this is the way in which the law divides the two classes of things that people own. Therefore these definitions are very useful during our study of property.

PERSONAL PROPERTY

Personal property might include such things as cars, books, furniture, clothing, and jewelry. These are all things we can see and touch. But personal property might also include trademarks, copyrights, patents, and the goodwill built up by a business. These are things that we cannot touch but that we can own. What about an idea? Does the law say that an idea is personal property?

shares of stock Shares in the ownership of a corporation.

trademark A design or symbol that identifies the exclusive owner or manufacturer of an article.

copyright The legal protection of the works of artists and authors giving them the exclusive right to publish their works or to decide who may publish them.

patent A grant of exclusive right to an inventor, for a certain period of time, to make, use, and sell his/her invention.

goodwill In business, the favor or good reputation a store has established that is beyond the mere value of what it sells.

Belt *v.* Hamilton National Bank

U.S. Dist. Ct., District of Columbia, 108 F. Supp. 689 (1952)

TOPIC—Action concerning use of an idea

FACTS—Mr. Belt was in the advertising business. He thought of a plan for a radio program in which schoolchildren who could sing or play an instrument would take part. The program would be paid for by a business company, but would be controlled by local school authorities. Belt presented his idea to an officer of the Hamilton National Bank. He told the bank that if his idea was accepted, he expected to be paid. The bank decided to place such a program on radio, and hired Belt to do the planning and the first part of the work at a salary of $25 a week. There was an understanding that this agreement could be called off on two weeks notice. After two weeks the bank told Belt that his services were no longer needed. The program was on the radio every week for over a year and cost the bank about $47,000. Belt sued the bank for payment for the use of his idea.

QUESTION—Does the law provide for property right in an idea?

■ ***Ownership*** Some of the most important problems having to do with personal property are about possession or the right to possession. Possession is not to be thought of as owning something. One may get possession of something in a number of ways without owning it. When a person is in possession of personal property, such as a dog, a ring, or an automobile, the law will protect that person's possession against everyone except the true owner.

Ownership is a legally accepted relationship between the owner and the rest of the world with respect to a certain piece of property. The relationship involves certain rights. One of these is the right to keep all others from using or enjoying the property.

The usual way to obtain ownership of personal property is to buy it. There are other ways, however, by which one may acquire ownership. Ownership of a wild animal may be had by taking possession of it with the intention of keeping it. Until taken into possession, wild animals belong to no one. Ownership of personal property that is abandoned may also be had by taking possession with the intention of keeping it. This rule holds only if it is abandoned and not just lost or mislaid.

The difference between "lost" and "abandoned" goods depends on what happened when the owner of the goods last had them. If the owner had accidentally lost possession, the goods are "lost." If the owner has deliberately given up both ownership and possession of the goods, they are "abandoned." Abandoned goods belong to no one. The person who finds them may acquire ownership simply by taking such goods into possession.

Erickson *v.* Sinykin

223 Minn. 232, 26 N.W.2d 1972, 170 A.L.R. 697 (1947)

TOPIC—Action concerning lost or abandoned property

FACTS—Mr. Erickson was a house painter who had been hired by a hotel to paint rooms. While working in one of the rooms,

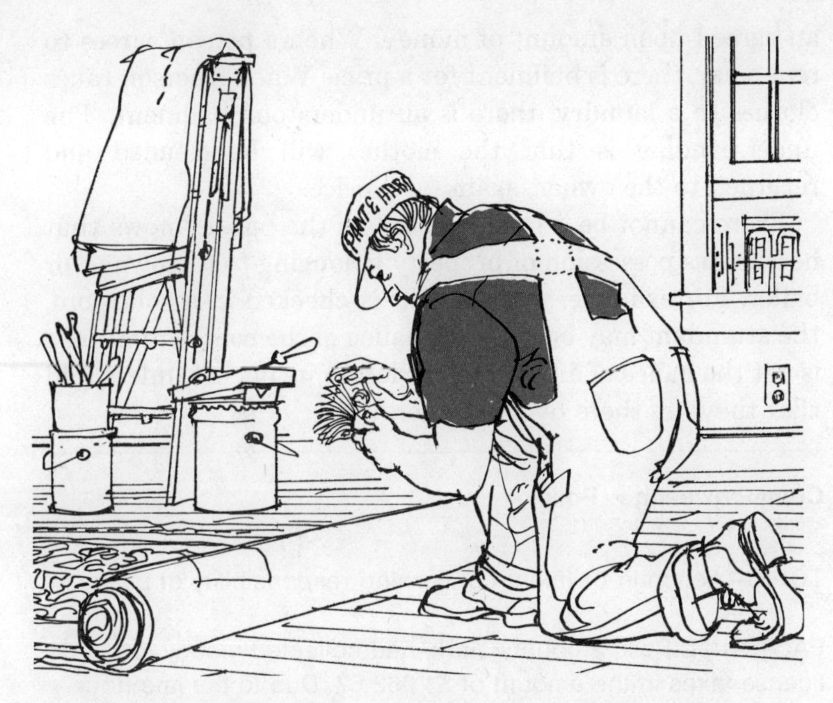

he discovered $760 under the carpet. He turned over the money to the hotel, which promised to try to find the true owner and return the money. The hotel kept the money, however, and Erickson sued to recover it.

During the trial it was found that the money had probably been under the carpet in the hotel room for more than fifteen years. No evidence was offered that the hotel had ever tried to give the money to the true owner after Erickson had turned it over to them.

QUESTION—Was the $760 abandoned property?

■ ***Bailment*** A bailment is also a legally accepted relationship. It takes place when one person leaves personal property with another for a certain purpose and under some sort of agreement. The property is left or delivered in trust with the understanding that it will be returned or accounted for when the purpose has been accomplished. The agreement may be either written or spoken. It may be either freely given or for an agreed-upon amount of money. When a person agrees to rent a car, there is bailment for a price. When a person takes clothes to a laundry, there is an understood bailment. The understanding is that the clothes will be cleaned and returned to the owner, again for a price.

There cannot be a bailment unless the bailee knows that he/she has possession of property belonging to the owner, or bailor. For example, when a coat is checked in a coatroom, the attendant may become the bailee of the coat. But he/she is not the bailee of any valuables left in its pocket unless told that they are there by the owner.

Commonwealth *v.* Polk
256 Ky. 100, 75 S.W.2d 761 (1934)

TOPIC—Action in bailment concerning responsibility of bailee

FACTS—Mr. Polk, a county clerk, had collected money for license taxes in the amount of $1,362.67. Due to the late hour of collection, the money could not be put in a bank. Instead, Polk placed it in a safe in his office. The safe, however, was not guarded and there was no insurance on the contents. During the night the safe was robbed and the money stolen. The Commonwealth of Kentucky sued Polk for the money.

QUESTION—Did Polk, as bailee, use necessary care to protect the property?

REAL PROPERTY

Earlier in this chapter you read that real property is land and all those things that are permanently attached to the land. Houses, barns, and office buildings are real property. So are trees, until they are cut down. Minerals, generally speaking, belong to the person who owns the land. Oil, gas,

---

county clerk An elected official of the county government who may be in charge of keeping property records, overseeing elections, and issuing certain licenses.

and water are also generally accepted as being parts of the land. So they, too, are real property.

■ ***Air rights*** Early common law held that the owner of the land owned all the space above the property as well as everything below it. It is now held, however, that because of air transportation, the owner should have the right only to that space above her/his land which would be necessary for the full use and enjoyment of the land. The airspace above that is held to be open and free for air travel.

Butler *v.* The Frontier Telephone Company
186 N.Y. 486, 79 N.E. 716 (1906)

TOPIC—Action concerning ownership of space above the land

FACTS—The telephone company had put a wire across Mr. Butler's land. The wire was in the air and did not touch the ground owned by Butler. Butler sued the telephone company to force it to remove the wire.

QUESTIONS—Did Butler own the airspace above his land?

Smith *v.* New England Aircraft Corporation
270 Mass. 511, 170 N.E. 385 (1930)

TOPIC—Action concerning ownership of space above the land

FACTS—Mr. Smith owned land near an airport. Planes had to fly low over his property in order to land. Smith sued the airport to keep the planes from flying over his land, claiming that he owned the airspace above the land.

QUESTION—Could Smith prevent airplanes from flying over his land?

Southwest Weather Research, Inc. *v.* Rounsaville
160 Tex. 104, 320 S.W.2d 211 (1958)

TOPIC—Action concerning right to natural rainfall

FACTS—Southwest Weather Research, Inc. owned airplanes, and its pilots flew over land owned by a number of ranchers. The weather company was seeding the clouds in the area in order to keep hail from forming. The ranch owners sued the company on the grounds that it was keeping natural rainfall from their land. They wanted the court to stop the company from seeding the clouds.

QUESTION—Did the ranch owners have a right to natural rainfall?

■ ***Adverse possession*** The most common way to acquire land in the United States is to buy it. But common law also allows ownership of land by adverse possession. When a person who is not the true owner of a piece of land uses it for a certain length of time as if she/he really does own it, that person becomes the adverse possessor of the land. In most states that length of time must be from fifteen to twenty-one years. During that time this person must live on the land perfectly openly. This is so that the true owner and everyone else would be given reasonable notice that she/he is claiming

to own the land. If during this time the true owner does not exercise rights of ownership in any way, the law allows the adverse possessor to become the true owner.

■ ***Zoning laws*** Many cities and towns have zoning laws. These are laws that regulate the uses that can be made of real property. Zoning laws are a way in which communities can plan how the land within their boundaries can be legally used to protect the best interests of the people who live there. These laws can also be used to protect the environment. Zoning laws often restrict the purposes for which certain property can be used. They may limit the kind and number of buildings that can be put up on it. They may also restrict the height of the buildings.

According to local zoning laws, certain parts of a city may be used for industrial or commercial pusposes. That is, factories, stores, or office buildings can be built on land in these parts of the city. Other parts of the city can be used only for residential purposes. That is, according to the zoning laws,

---

restrict To limit or place under special rules.

only homes can be built there. It is clearly very important for a person who plans to buy land to know whether there are any zoning laws that will affect the use it can be put to.

Bove *v.* Donner-Hanna Coke Corporation
236 App. Div. 37, 258 N.Y.S. 229, 179 N.E. 476 (1932)

TOPIC—Action concerning zoning restrictions

FACTS—Mrs. Bove bought land in a neighborhood that was zoned for industrial purposes. Mills, factories, and plants could be built in that neighborhood. Mrs. Bove built a store and a home on her land. Years later, the Donner-Hanna Coke Corporation built a coke oven across the street from Bove's land. She sued for damages because of the steam, dirt, and soot coming from the coke oven. She asked the court to stop the company from running its business in the neighborhood.

QUESTION—Did the zoning law protect the coke company?

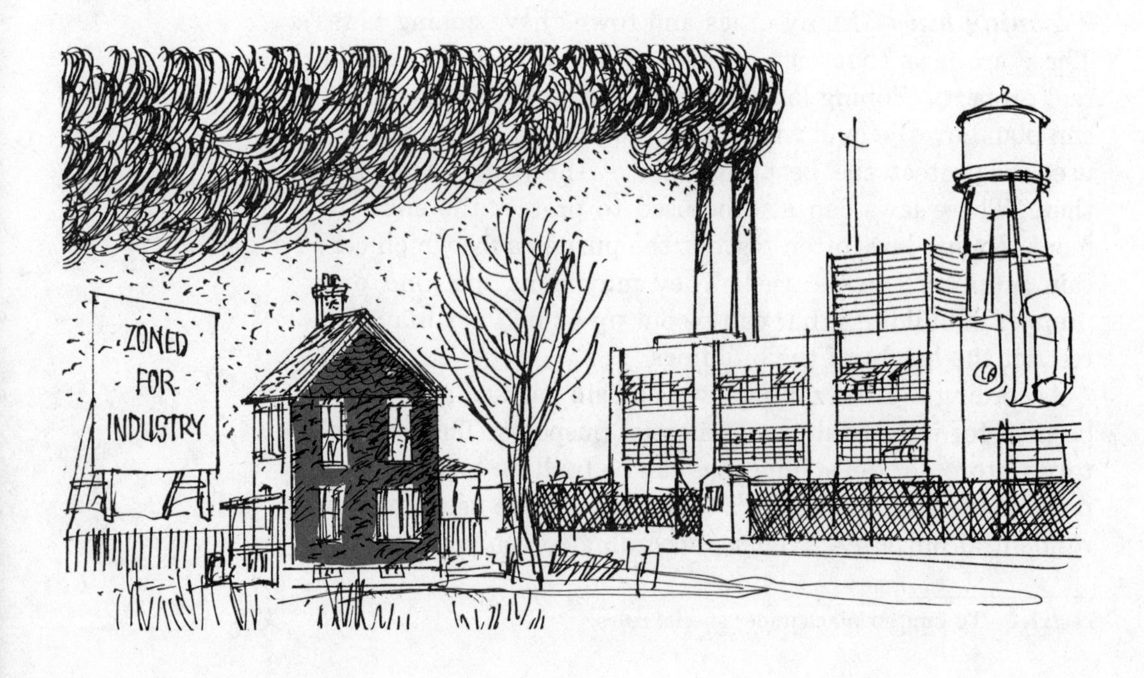

Cowling *v.* Colligan
158 Tex. 458, 312 S.W.2d 943 (1958)

TOPIC—Action concerning zoning restrictions

FACTS—Mrs. Colligan's neighborhood was zoned for homes only. However, she felt that her land would be worth four times as much if she could use it for commercial purposes. Mr. Cowling, a neighbor, sued to keep her from using her land for commercial purposes.

QUESTION—Could zoning laws prevent Colligan from using her land for commercial purposes?

EMINENT DOMAIN

The Fifth Amendment to the Constitution states that "No person shall be . . . deprived of life, liberty, or property, without due process of law; nor shall private property be taken for public use without just compensation."

Eminent domain is the power a government has to take private property for a public use. It may take land *only* for a use that is good for the public as a whole. And it must pay a fair and just price to the owner. Pipelines, railroads, highways, and public buildings have all been built on land that has been acquired in this way.

Cities and counties may decide that some buildings are so old and dangerous that they should be torn down. Under federal urban renewal laws, the city or county government can condemn such property. This means that the government can declare such property unfit for use as it is. It can then take over the property after a fair price is paid to the owners. The property may then be sold to private citizens who will rebuild and modernize the neighborhood. The rebuilding must be done according to a plan agreed to by the city or county. The federal government has given money to help pay for this kind of project.

Berman *v.* Parker
348 U.S. 26, 75 S.Ct. 98, 99 L.Ed. 27 (1954)

TOPIC—Action concerning right of city to condemn property

FACTS—The Bermans owned a department store in a neighborhood that the city had planned to rebuild. The city government had decided that many of the buildings in that part of the city should be torn down. The city government planned to use part of the neighborhood for low-rent housing. The Bermans sued to keep the city from taking their property. They said their property was commercial. It was not slum housing, and so the city had no right to have it condemned.

QUESTION—Could the city be prevented from taking the Bermans' property?

RENTING REAL PROPERTY

When you rent real property from someone, you become the tenant. The owner from whom you rent is called the lessor, or landlord. A tenant may rent an apartment or a house to live in. Or she/he may rent a building in which to run a business.

■ ***Lease*** The agreement that the tenant and the lessor come to about the property to be rented is called a lease. If the tenant plans to rent the premises for less than a year, the lease need not be written. However, most leases are in written form. A lease includes all the rights and responsibilities agreed upon by both parties. While there may be many more things agreed upon in a lease, most of them include at least the following.

1. The length of time the tenancy is to last
2. The amount of rent that must be paid and when it is to be paid
3. The services and repairs the owner must provide
4. The repairs and maintenance the tenant must take care of
5. Any other rules that both parties agree to (For example, a lease may say that no pets are allowed in a building.)
6. What the law allows the owner to do if the tenant does not live up to the terms of the lease

■ ***"Quiet enjoyment"*** Once a person has become a tenant, that person has the right to the "quiet enjoyment" of the premises. Quiet enjoyment means that a tenant has *almost* the same rights in the property as if she/he owned it. The owner must allow the tenant to live there without disturbance as long as she/he lives up to the terms of the lease. The owner cannot prevent the tenant from entering or leaving the premises. The owner cannot cut off the gas or water. And the owner must not allow other tenants to disturb her/him. A tenant may invite anyone onto the premises and do any-

---

tenancy The temporary occupying or possessing of land or buildings owned by another person.

thing there that is not against the law or forbidden in the lease. The owner does have the right to enter a tenant's premises for certain reasons such as to make emergency repairs. But, generally speaking, the law protects the tenant's rights to the "exclusive possession" of the rented premises.

The tenant, on the other hand, must not use the property for his/her own gain or advantage in any way that would lower or destroy its value. The tenant does not have the same right to make big changes in the property that the owner has. Nor does the tenant have the right to destroy the property.

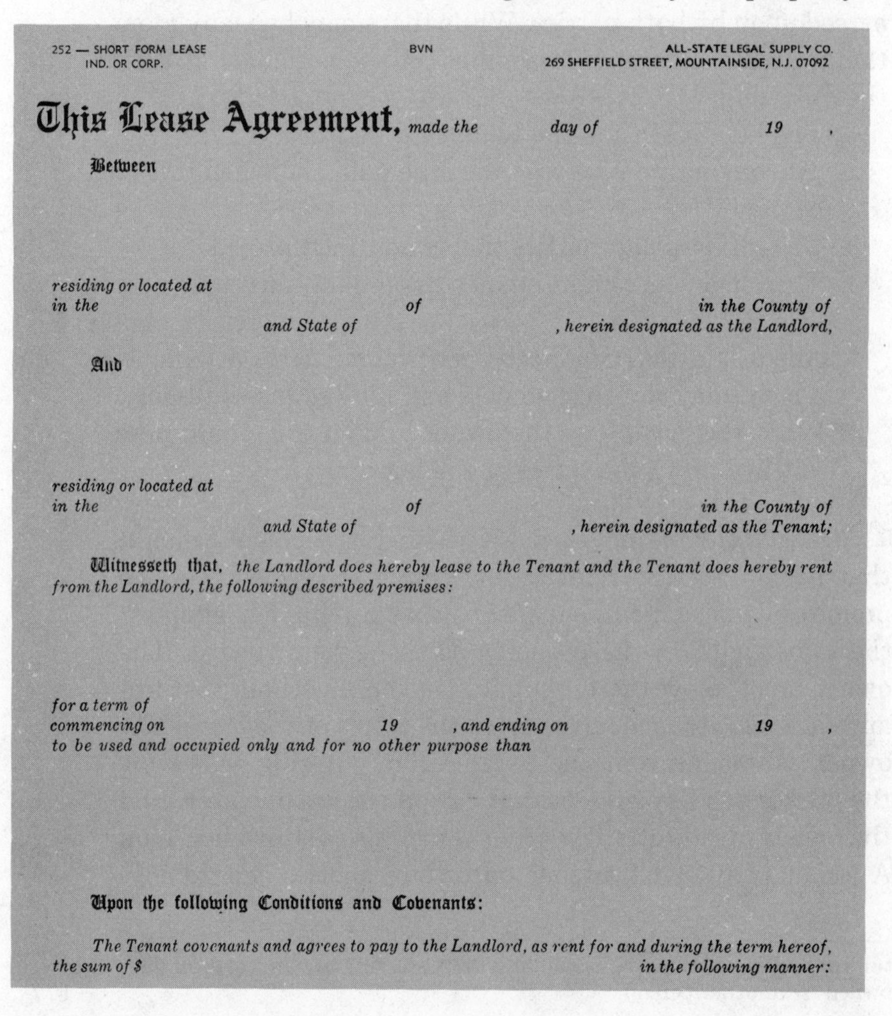
252 — SHORT FORM LEASE
IND. OR CORP.

BVN

ALL-STATE LEGAL SUPPLY CO.
269 SHEFFIELD STREET, MOUNTAINSIDE, N.J. 07092

This Lease Agreement, *made the day of 19 ,*

Between

residing or located at
in the of in the County of
and State of , herein designated as the Landlord,

And

residing or located at
in the of in the County of
and State of , herein designated as the Tenant;

Witnesseth that, *the Landlord does hereby lease to the Tenant and the Tenant does hereby rent from the Landlord, the following described premises:*

for a term of
commencing on 19 , and ending on 19 ,
to be used and occupied only and for no other purpose than

Upon the following Conditions and Covenants:

The Tenant covenants and agrees to pay to the Landlord, as rent for and during the term hereof, the sum of $ in the following manner:

And it is further agreed between the parties hereto, that if the building or buildings erected on the premises hereby leased shall be partially damaged by fire, the same shall be repaired as speedily as possible at the expense of the Landlord; that in case the damage shall be so extensive as to render the building untenantable, the rent shall cease until such time as the building shall be put in complete repair; but in case of the total destruction of the premises by fire or otherwise, the rent shall be paid up to the time of such destruction and then and from thenceforth this lease shall come to an end; provided however, that such damage or destruction be not caused by the carelessness, negligence or improper conduct of the Tenant or the Tenant's agents, representatives or employees.

This Lease shall be subject and subordinate at all times to the lien of any mortgages not exceeding the aggregate sum of

Dollars

now or hereafter placed on the land and buildings of which the leased premises form a part without the necessity of any further instrument or act on the part of the Tenant to effectuate such subordination; and the Tenant covenants and agrees to execute and deliver upon demand such further instruments evidencing the subordination of this lease to the lien of any such mortgage or mortgages as shall be desired by any mortgagee or prospective mortgagee. The Tenant hereby appoints the Landlord the attorney-in-fact of the Tenant, irrevocable, to execute and deliver any such instrument or instruments for and in the name of the Tenant.

And the Tenant further covenants that the Tenant will not assign this Lease, nor let or under-let the whole or any part of the premises, nor make any alterations therein, without the written consent of the Landlord, under penalty of forfeiture and damages; and that the Tenant will not occupy or use nor permit the said premises to be occupied or used for any business deemed extra hazardous on account of fire or otherwise, without the like consent, under the like penalty. The Tenant further covenants that the Tenant will permit the Landlord or the Landlord's agents or representatives to show the premises to persons wishing to rent or purchase the same; and on and after next preceding the expiration of the term, will permit "to let" or "for sale" notices to be placed upon the walls or doors of said premises, and remain thereon without hindrance or molestation; and also, that if the said premises or any part thereof shall become vacant during the said term, the Landlord or the Landlord's agents or representatives may re-enter the same either by force or otherwise without being liable to any prosecution therefor, and re-let the premises as the agent of the Tenant, and receive the rent thereof, applying the same first to the payment of such expenses as the Landlord may be put to in re-entering and re-letting, and then to the payment of the rent due by these presents; and the balance if any, to be paid over to the Tenant, who shall remain liable for any deficiency.

And the Tenant covenants and agrees to quit and surrender the premises at the expiration of the term hereof, in as good state and condition as they were at the commencement of the said term, wear from reasonable use thereof and damages by the elements excepted.

And the Tenant hereby further covenants that if any default be made in the payment of the said rent or any part thereof at the times above specified, or if default be made in the performance of any of the covenants or agreements herein contained, the said letting and the relation of Landlord and Tenant, at the option of the said Landlord, shall cease and terminate and the Landlord shall and may re-enter the premises and remove all persons therefrom; and the Tenant hereby expressly waives the service of any notice in writing of intention to re-enter, as may be provided for by any law or statute.

In all references herein to any parties, persons, entities or corporations the use of any particular gender or the plural or singular number is intended to include the appropriate gender or number as the text of the within instrument may require. All the terms, covenants and conditions herein contained shall be for and shall inure to the benefit of and shall bind the respective parties hereto, and their heirs, executors, administrators, personal or legal representatives, successors and assigns, respectively.

In Witness Whereof, the parties hereto have hereunto set their hands and seals, or caused these presents to be signed by their proper corporate officers and their proper corporate seal to be hereto affixed, the day and year first above written.

Signed, Sealed and Delivered in the presence of or Attested by

_______________ *Landlord*

____

_______________ *Tenant*

____

■ ***Ending a lease*** As you have read, American laws of land ownership grew out of the old English common law. This is also true of our laws about renting property. However, many changes have been made in these laws since they were first brought to America. In early common law, if the tenant failed to pay the rent, the owner generally did not have the right to throw him/her out. Neither did the owner have the right to end the lease before the agreed-upon date. The only thing the owner could do in most cases was to seize any personal property of the tenant found on the premises. This would be held until the rent was paid.

Today it is different. The lessor is allowed to end the lease if the tenant fails to pay the rent. While the laws vary in different states or communities, an owner can, as a rule, force a tenant who does not pay the rent to move out. A tenant can also bring the lease to an end under certain conditions. For example, an owner may not live up to the terms of the lease. She/he may allow the premises to become so run-down as not to be fit to live in. In that case, the law would probably allow the tenant to end the lease. However, because the laws are different in different places, it is best for both lessor and tenant to speak to a lawyer before trying to end a lease. Of course, an owner and tenant may always end a lease if they both agree to do so.

Reviewing the Chapter

Law-Related Terms

Personal property *Pp. 166, 307*
Real property *Pp. 166, 308*
Adverse possession *Pp. 172–173, 302*
Eminent domain *P. 175*
Tenant *Pp. 177, 309*
Lease *Pp. 177, 306*

Review Questions

1. In colonial America, who had the right to vote? *P. 164*
2. **(a)** Name the two classes of property. **(b)** Give examples of each. *Pp. 166, 307, 308*
3. What is the difference between lost goods and abandoned goods? *P. 168*
4. **(a)** What is a bailment? **(b)** Give two examples of bailment. **(c)** What condition must be fulfilled if there is to be a bailment? *Pp. 169–170, 302*
5. **(a)** Under early common law, who owned the airspace above land? **(b)** Why and how has that idea changed? Cite a case to support your answer. *Pp. 171–172, 276*
6. Explain how a person may obtain property by adverse possession. *Pp. 172–173*
7. **(a)** What are zoning laws? **(b)** What is their purpose? *Pp. 173–174, 309*
8. **(a)** Define eminent domain. **(b)** What two conditions are necessary for a government to use that power? *P. 175*
9. **(a)** What is a lease? **(b)** Explain a tenant's right to "quiet enjoyment." **(c)** What restrictions are there on a tenant's use of the property that he or she rents? *Pp. 177–178, 180*

Chapter Test

From the list below, select the answer that best completes each statement. Write your answers on a separate paper.

adverse possessor
bailment
personal property
zoning laws
voting
eminent domain
real property
lease
abandoned goods
tenant

1. In colonial America, ______ rights were based on the ownership of property.
2. Land and all those things permanently attached to it are ______.
3. Cars, books, jewelry, and furniture are examples of ______.
4. The finder of ______ may acquire ownership by taking them into possession.
5. There cannot be a ______ unless the bailee knows he or she has possession of property belonging to the owner.
6. A person who uses a piece of land for a certain period of time as if he or she really owned it may become the ______ of the land.
7. ______ may restrict the size and type of buildings a property owner can put on his or her land.
8. ______ is the power of a government to take private property for public use.
9. A ______ is a person who rents real property from its owner.
10. The agreement between a tenant and lessor about the property to be rented is called a ______.

Contracts 6

Supt. and Trustees of Public Schools of City of Trenton *v.* Bennett
27 N.J. Law 513, 72 Am. Dec. 373 (1859)

TOPIC—Action concerning breach of contract

FACTS—A builder, Mr. Bennett, contracted with the school board of Trenton, New Jersey, to put up a building on a certain lot for an agreed-upon price. Before the building was finished, the soil underneath it shifted and the building fell down. Bennett said he should not have to rebuild. The school board sued.

QUESTION—Can Bennett break the contract?

WHAT IS A CONTRACT?

A contract is an agreement between two or more people that the law will enforce. Behind every contract is the belief that most people want to do the right thing when they have dealings with other people. People who make a contract are expected to act in good faith.

Sometimes contracts have been enforced by religious authority as well as by the state. In the Middle Ages, for example, the Church looked upon promises people made as moral obligations. It was a serious matter to be brought before the Church courts to answer to charges of breaking a promise.

---

breach of contract The failure by a party to an agreement to perform any or all of the terms of the agreement for which he/she is legally responsible.

moral obligation A debt or responsibility that one feels bound to honor because of conscience or duty.

In many early legal systems, only contracts that followed certain forms and procedures were valid. In English common law, for example, a written contract had to have a common-law seal. This seal was a wax impression made by a metal device—sometimes a "signet ring"—and affixed to the paper on which the contract was written. This act of "sealing" was said to be the most solemn act of English common law. Although most states in our country have done away with the seal, we still speak of contracts as being "signed and sealed."

Today a contract is accepted as a legally binding agreement between two or more parties. The parties to a contract may agree to do something. Or they may agree not to do something. However, people who agree to something that is against the law cannot expect the courts to enforce such an agreement. For example, the law will not protect someone who agrees to buy illegal drugs or stolen goods or to murder someone. Such agreements are not true contracts.

■ ***Unilateral and bilateral contracts*** A contract involves at least two parties. A party may be one person. It may be a group of people. It may even be a corporation. If only one party makes a promise, then the contract is called a unilateral contract. Mary may tell Jane, "If you climb that mountain, I promise to give you $50." That is a unilateral contract. Only Mary made a promise. It is, however, a perfectly good contract. If Jane climbs the mountain, the courts will allow her to collect the $50 from Mary.

If both parties make promises, a bilateral contract has been made. Mary may say to Jane, "If you promise to climb that mountain, then I will promise to pay you $50." If Jane agrees to climb the mountain, both parties have made promises. A bilateral contract has been made.

■ ***Express and implied contracts*** The parties may make promises with words. This is called an express contract. Mary may say, "If you promise to climb that mountain, then I promise to pay you $50." That is an express contract.

The parties may by their acts or conduct indicate an agreement. This is an implied contract. Fred may ask a TV service person to come to his home and repair his TV. This is an implied contract. It is implied, or understood, that even though no one spoke about money, Fred has agreed to pay a reasonable fee for the TV service person's work. The law of contracts says that Fred has an obligation to pay the service person.

MAKING A CONTRACT

Generally a contract is legal if there has been an offer, an acceptance of the offer, a meeting of the minds, and the giving and receiving of a consideration.

■ ***Offer and acceptance*** Bill might tell a friend that he will sell her his history book. That is not an offer, but simply an invitation to bargain. If, however, Bill tells his friend that he will sell her his history book for $2, that is an offer. His friend may agree to buy it for that amount. That is an acceptance.

Suppose Margaret loses a valuable ring. She lets it be known that she will give a $5 reward for its return. She has made an offer. Someone hears about her offer. That person finds the ring and returns it to get the reward. That person's act is an acceptance of Margaret's offer.

Broadnax *v.* Ledbetter
100 Tex. 375, 99 S.W. 1111 (1907)

TOPIC—Action in contracts concerning offer and acceptance

FACTS—Mr. Ledbetter offered a $500 reward for the capture and return of an escaped prisoner. Mr. Broadnax did not know about the reward. But he captured the prisoner and returned him to the authorities. Later Broadnax found out about the

---

consideration Something of value given in return for a performance or promise of performance by another for the purpose of forming a contract.

reward. He said that even though he did not know about the reward at the time, he did return the prisoner and should get the money. He sued to get the $500.

QUESTION—Must Broadnax have known about the reward in order to collect?

■ ***Opinion, invitation, or offer*** The law states that, in order for a contract to exist, a reasonable person must believe an offer has been made. Sometimes there is much confusion over whether a real offer was meant or if an opinion was being expressed. Jim may say to Bob, "Your car is a beauty! It would be worth $5,000 to me!" Bob cannot decide that this is an offer. It is only a spoken opinion.

An invitation to make an offer must be distinguished from an offer. Jim may ask Bob, "Would you be willing to sell your car for $5,000?" Bob may answer, "No, I wouldn't sell it unless I could get $7,500 for it." Jim cannot then say, "Sold! I'll give you $7,500." The courts would hold that no offer was made by Bob. He was just voicing an opinion. Or, at the most, he was saying to Jim, "Make me an offer."

If the offer is clearly a mistake and the person who receives the offer knows or should know that it is a mistake, she/he cannot take advantage of it. Betty writes to Barbara offering to sell her business for $2,000. Barbara knows that there is a mistake. The amount should read $2,000,000. She cannot accept this offer and expect the contract to be valid.

Owen *v.* Tunison
131 Me. 42, 158 A. 926 (1932)

TOPIC—Action in contracts concerning offer and acceptance

FACTS—Mr. Owen wrote a letter to Mr. Tunison in which he offered to buy certain land and buildings that Tunison owned. He offered Tunison $6,000. Tunison answered by letter saying that he would not sell unless he could get $16,000. Owen wrote back saying that he would buy the land and buildings for $16,000. Tunison refused to sell, and Owen sued.

QUESTION—Was there an offer to sell?

You have seen advertisements many times. Is an advertisement an offer? Generally speaking, the answer is No. An advertisement is not a guarantee that you can buy an item for the advertised price. You may have seen advertisements with the words "Limited quantities available." A store, for example, may decide to sell ten tennis racquets for $20 each. It sells the ten racquets. You're the eleventh person to try to buy a racquet for $20. Does the store have to sell you a racquet for that price? No, it doesn't. What happens if a store puts an advertisement in a newspaper and the paper

---

valid contract A legally binding agreement that will be upheld by the courts.

makes a mistake in printing the price? It reads $3 instead of $30. Does the store have to sell the item for $3? Again, the answer is No.

Craft *v.* Elder and Johnston Company
Ct. of App. of Ohio, 38 N.E.2d 416 (1941)

TOPIC—Action in contracts concerning offer and acceptance

FACTS—The Elder and Johnston Company advertised a $175 sewing machine for sale at $26. Mr. Craft saw the advertisement in a newspaper and went to the store. He tried to buy the sewing machine for $26. The store would not sell it to him for that amount. Craft sued.

QUESTION—Is an advertisement such as this an offer to sell to the general public?

Lefkowitz *v.* Great Minn. Surplus Store
251 Minn. 188, 86 N.W.2d 689 (1957)

TOPIC—Action in contracts concerning offer and acceptance

FACTS—A store advertised the sale of fur stoles, each said to be worth $139.50. They were on sale for $1 each. The advertisement read "First Come, First Served." Mr. Lefkowitz was the first person to arrive at the store. He offered $1 for one of the furs, but the store refused to sell it to him. The people in charge said that they meant to sell to women only. Lefkowitz sued the store.

QUESTION—Was there an offer to sell that Lefkowitz could accept?

The decision in the Lefkowitz case shows how the interpretation of the law may vary from court to court. In this case, the court ruled that the advertisement was an offer. It said that the words "First Come, First Served" in the advertisement made a promise different from most advertisements. However, the Lefkowitz case is an exception. The general rule, as decided in the Craft case, is that an advertisement is *not* an offer.

■ ***Meeting of the minds*** For a contract to be valid, there must be a meeting of the minds. Each person must have a clear understanding of what exchange is meant in the agreement. Rita has a blue sweater she wishes to exchange for Maggie's yellow blouse. Maggie has two yellow blouses. One has long sleeves, the other short sleeves. Maggie, thinking Rita means the short-sleeved blouse, agrees to the exchange. But this is not the blouse Rita wanted. In this case there is no binding agreement, since there was not a meeting of the minds.

Raffles *v.* Wichelhaus
Court of Exchequer, 2 Hurl & Colt. 906 (1864)

TOPIC—Action in contracts concerning meeting of the minds

FACTS—Mr. Raffles agreed to sell some cotton to Mr. Wichelhaus. The cotton was to arrive in England on board a ship named *Peerless* sailing from Bombay, India. There were, however, two ships by that name. One was to leave Bombay for England in October. The other was to leave Bombay for England in December. Wichelhaus meant the ship leaving in October. Raffles meant the one leaving in December.

QUESTION—Was there a meeting of the minds? Did both parties contract for the cotton arriving on the same ship?

■ ***Consideration*** Most courts hold that for a contract to be valid there must be not only an offer, an acceptance, and a meeting of the minds, but also a consideration. By this is generally meant that which the promisor asks for in return for his/her promise. Ruth offered to buy William's stamp collection for $15,000. The stamp collection is the consideration William must give if he is to receive the $15,000.

binding agreement The strict legal responsibility of the parties to a contract to keep the terms of that contract or agreement.

Seller, ____

______________________, of ____, in consideration of ____ dollars, receipt whereof is hereby acknowledged, does hereby sell, assign, transfer and set over to Buyer, ______________________

______________________________________, of ______________________________________

______________________________________, the following described personal property, to-wit:

Seller hereby represents and warrants to Buyer that Seller is the absolute owner of said property, that said property is free and clear of all liens, charges and encumbrances, and that Seller has full right, power and authority to sell said personal property and to make this bill of sale. *All warranties of quality, fitness, and merchantability are hereby excluded.*

If this bill of sale is signed by more than one person, all persons so signing shall be jointly and severally bound hereby.

IN WITNESS WHEREOF, Seller has signed and sealed this bill of sale at ______________________

______________________ this ______________________ day of ______________________, 19____.

______________________________________ [SEAL]

______________________________________ [SEAL]

■ ***Contracts that must be in writing*** There are many contracts that are simply spoken agreements. A contract, however, does not have to be made in words. A promise can be made by certain acts. At an auction, a flick of a finger or a nod of the head may seal a contract. There are times, however, when it is better to have a contract in writing. Sometimes a contract *must* be in writing in order to be valid. If a contract by law must be in writing, a person acting as an agent for another cannot enter into such a contract for that person without written permission to do so.

Generally, the following kinds of contracts should be put in writing: (1) Those about the sale or purchase of real property. (2) Those about the sale or purchase of goods valued at $50 or more. (3) Those about the promise to be responsible for the debts or defaults of another. (4) Those in consideration of marriage. For example, person A is ill and needs special care. Person A promises person B, "If you will marry me and take care of me until I die, I will leave all my money and possessions to you." Person B then agrees to marry person A. (5) Those in which the terms of the agreement cannot be performed within one year from the date the contract was made.

Any question about whether a contract, written or spoken, can be enforced should be presented to a lawyer.

■ ***Credit cards*** We have said that contracts are made when two or more parties agree upon what they wish to exchange and the terms of the exchange. The use of credit cards is a modern way of arriving at a signed contract agreement. Under Section 1643 of the Truth-in-Lending Act 15 U.S.C. 1601-70 (1970), a credit card holder may be held liable for purchases bought with her/his card even if the card has

---

agent Someone authorized by another person to act for him/her.

default The failure to perform a duty that one is legally bound to perform.

credit card A card, issued by a bank, special company, or store, that entitles the holder to buy goods on credit rather than by paying cash.

been lost or stolen. Before there can be any liability, the company or bank that issues the card must give the card holder notice of the fact that he/she might be liable. A person whose credit card has been lost or stolen should give either written or spoken notice of the loss or theft to the issuer of the card. In any case, the holder of the card will not be held liable for more than $50 if the card is used without that person's knowledge. Sometimes as a courtesy to its customers, a card issuer may choose not to hold the card holder liable. The card holder then would not be liable for purchases made with the card after the issuer has been told about its loss, theft, or unauthorized use.

BREAKING A CONTRACT

Once a contract has been made, the law expects both parties to live up to the terms of their agreement. There must be a very good and sound reason for breaking a contract.

■ ***Breach of contract*** If a breach (breaking) of contract cannot be justified, the courts will not protect the party that breaks the contract. For example, on July 1 the Rich Building Company signs a contract to build a store for Mr. Smythe for $100,000 by January 1. Three months later the company refuses to finish the building. The company states that labor

unauthorized Not having legal or official approval.

and material costs are too high. It will not pay them to build the store for $100,000. That may be a breach of contract. The courts may decide that the building company did not have a good enough reason for failing to live up to its promise.

Whitman *v.* Anglum
92 Conn. 392, 103 A. 114 (1918)

TOPIC—Action concerning breach of contract

FACTS—Mr. Whitman contracted with Mr. Anglum to buy 175 quarts of milk each day from April 1, 1914, to April 1, 1915. On November 23, 1914, the city quarantined Anglum's cattle and the products of his farm. It was found that the cattle had hoof-and-mouth disease. Shortly after this, according to law, all the cattle had to be killed. Whitman demanded that Anglum deliver the milk he had promised. Anglum refused and Whitman sued.

QUESTION—Could Anglum be released from his contract to furnish 175 quarts of milk each day?

Surety Development Corp. *v.* Grevas
42 Ill. App.2d 268, 192 N.E.2d 145 (1963)

TOPIC—Action concerning breach of contract

FACTS—Mr. Grevas signed a contract with the Surety Development Corporation for the building of a prefabricated house. According to the contract, the house was to be finished on September 27, 1961. At 4:00 P.M. on September 27, Grevas arrived at the house. He found workers trying to finish the house. They were "slapping on siding, laying the floors, bulldozing the yard, hooking up the utilities." Grevas was told that the house would be ready by 5:30 P.M. However, Grevas refused to accept the house and he left right away. By 5:30 P.M. the house was just about finished. The building company sued Grevas.

---

quarantine To prevent the movement of people, animals, plants, or goods in order to keep them from spreading disease or pests.

QUESTION—Was there a breach of contract by the building company because the house was not finished by 4:00 P.M. on September 27?

■ ***Small claims courts*** Suppose you make a contract and then the other party to the contract does not live up to the terms of the agreement. The money involved is not enough to make it worth the expense of hiring a lawyer and going to court to sue the other party. Does that mean there is nothing you can do to get the damages you feel are coming to you? No. To deal with such situations, many states, counties, and municipalities have set up small claims courts.

The use of small claims courts is very simple. These courts charge fees of from $1 to $5 to help cover costs. The damage limits for small claims courts range from as low as $100 in New Orleans to as high as $2,000 in New Mexico. It is not necessary for either the plaintiff or the defendant to have a lawyer in these courts. Sometimes a party may choose to have a lawyer. However, if a party does not have a lawyer, the judge must ask searching questions to make sure that both claims and defenses are properly presented.

In most states, small claims courts do not allow jury trials. A few states, such as Illinois and Oklahoma, do allow jury trials. Sometimes the defendant in a small claims case chooses not to come to court. If she/he does not appear in court, then the plaintiff wins the case by default. In some states, the judgment of the small claims court is final and no appeal can be made. Most states, however, do provide for appeal into the regular court system.

As early as 1916, the city of Cleveland, Ohio, had set up a court to deal with claims of less than $35. In 1920, Oregon became the first state to have small claims courts in every county in the state. By 1955, over half the states in the country had established small claims courts.

Today, the most common type of claims brought before small claims courts has to do with consumer goods. Many

---

consumer goods Commercial products or things that satisfy people's wants.

Using the Small Claims Court

1. Go to the clerk of the court in the defendant's county and tell her/him your problem as quickly as possible. The clerk gives you a complaint form to fill out and charges you a small fee. The clerk may also help you fill out the form.
2. The clerk will set a date for your hearing and will see that the complaint is sent to the defendant.
3. On the date of the hearing, both parties are to appear in small claims court with any evidence or witnesses they may have and tell their stories to the judge.
4. The judge listens to both sides, considers any evidence presented, questions both parties, and makes a decision. If the judge decides that you are right, she/he orders the defendant to pay the amount you have asked for or an amount the court feels is fair.

claims are made against sellers or manufacturers for faulty goods or for misleading sales practices. Sellers of goods or services also bring claims to make buyers pay for the goods or services they bought. Claims may also be brought in connection with minor automobile accidents.

LACK OF CONTRACTUAL CAPACITY

Sometimes people enter into contracts and may not, for a number of reasons, be capable of understanding all that a contract involves. To protect such people and to prevent others from taking advantage of them, the law will often hold that they did not, at the time, have the capacity to make a contract. Any agreements they made, therefore, would not be valid.

■ ***Insane, drunken, or drugged persons*** A person who is insane or who is under the influence of alcohol or drugs may not be able to understand what she/he is doing. Any contract such a person signs will not be enforced.

---

clerk of the court A person employed by a court to keep records, schedule hearings and notify the parties, and perform many other duties depending on the activities of the court.

■ ***Minors*** A minor is a person under the age that the state has by law declared to be adulthood. The recognized age, usually between eighteen and twenty-one, varies from state to state. If minors marry, many states accept this as automatic adulthood.

A minor is seen by law as being too immature to enter into a business deal on equal terms with an adult. Most contracts made by a minor cannot be enforced. The aim of the law is to protect young people from being cheated by more knowing adults. However, this guardianship of minors by the courts is not a license for a young person to break any contract that she/he may no longer want to keep.

The law does hold minors fully responsible for some contracts if the young person lives alone without support from parents or guardians. Contracts entered into for necessary goods or services can be enforced. Necessary goods or services are such things as food, housing, and clothing. They also include basic education, medical services, or tools needed for making a living. Some states also have laws that bind a minor to a contract to give services as an actor or a professional athlete if the contract has been approved by a court.

Keser *v.* Chagnon
159 Colo. 209, 410 P.2d. 637 (1966)

TOPIC—Action for a breach of contract

FACTS—Mr. Chagnon signed a contract to buy a used Edsel automobile for $995 from Mr. Keser. Chagnon was a minor at the time. He was twenty years, eleven months old, but he told Keser that he was twenty-one. Two months after Chagnon reached twenty-one, he returned the Edsel. He tried to break the contract. Keser sued to make Chagnon pay what he still owed on the car.

QUESTION—Can a minor who misrepresents his/her age break a contract after reaching twenty-one?

Reviewing the Chapter

Law-Related Terms

Contract *Pp. 184, 303*
Unilateral contract *Pp. 185, 309*
Bilateral contract *Pp. 185, 302*
Express contract *Pp. 185, 305*
Implied contract *Pp. 186, 305*
Offer *Pp. 186, 307*
Acceptance *Pp. 186, 302*
Meeting of the minds *Pp. 191, 307*
Consideration *Pp. 191, 303*
Substantial compliance *P. 277*

Review Questions

1. Give an example of each of the following: **(a)** unilateral contract; **(b)** bilateral contract; **(c)** express contract; **(d)** implied contract. *Pp. 185–186*
2. What are the four conditions necessary for a valid contract? *P. 186*
3. Which condition necessary for a valid contract was missing in these cases: **(a)** *Broadnax* v. *Ledbetter?* **(b)** *Owen* v. *Tunison?* **(c)** *Craft* v. *Elder and Johnston Company?* **(d)** *Raffles* v. *Wichelhaus? Pp. 186–191, 276*
4. In *Craft* v. *Elder and Johnston Company* and *Lefkowitz* v. *Great Minn. Surplus Store,* the courts decided whether an advertisement was an offer. **(a)** What was the decision in each case? **(b)** Which decision is the general rule? *Pp. 188–190, 276*
5. What are the steps to follow to bring a case to small claims court? *P. 197*
6. List three situations in which a minor might be held fully responsible for a contract. *P. 198*

Chapter Test

On a separate piece of paper, write T *if the statement is true and* F *if the statement is false.*

1. An agreement in which both parties make promises is called a unilateral contract.
2. The four conditions necessary for a legal contract are (a) an offer, (b) an acceptance of the offer, (c) a meeting of the minds, and (d) the giving and receiving of a consideration.
3. If an obvious mistake has been made in a contract, the contract is not considered to be valid.
4. An advertisement is the same thing as an offer.
5. To be valid, a contract must be put into writing.
6. When a person uses a credit card to pay for something, no legal contract has been made.
7. One disadvantage of small claims court is that only the wealthy can afford to use it.
8. A contract made by a person who is insane or under the influence of drugs or alcohol cannot be enforced.
9. The purpose of the laws regarding minors and contracts is to protect minors from being cheated by adults.
10. Most contracts involving minors cannot be enforced.

Family and Juvenile Law

Tyrrell's Estate
17 Aug. 418, 153 P. 767 (1915)

TOPIC—Action involving legality of will

FACTS—Miss Tyrrell had lived and owned property in Arizona. When she died in Phoenix, Arizona, she left an unsealed envelope. On the outside of this she had written, "This is my last and only will to be acted upon by the Officers of the Humane Society in Phoenix. . . ." Tyrrell signed her name on the outside of the envelope.

Inside the envelope was a paper on which Tyrrell had written what was supposed to be her will. The paper was not signed. The envelope and the paper inside were offered in court as Tyrrell's last will.

QUESTION—Must a written will be signed by the person making the will?

MARRIAGE

What are the chances that one day you will marry? Do you know the legal side of marriage? What legal responsibilities do people accept when they marry? What rights do married persons have under the law? How does the law deal with problems affecting married persons?

Marriage is the legally accepted relationship of a man and a woman who have been joined as husband and wife. Marriage is a legal contract. As in all contracts, both parties must agree to the terms. These terms include many legal rights and duties. There can be no legally accepted change in this relationship without the approval of the courts. And this approval can only be obtained by following certain legal steps set forth in state law.

State laws decide the conditions that must be met in order to make marriages legal. These conditions vary from state to state. They include rules as to age, kinship between the parties, no already existing marriage, and a number of others.

In most states eighteen is the age at which people may marry without the consent of their parents. In some states the consent of parents is needed until the man is twenty-one and the woman eighteen.

Every state has laws that prohibit people from legally marrying certain close relatives. In some states marriage between more distant relatives, and even step-relatives or in-laws, is also not allowed.

A marriage license, issued by local authorities, is needed in all states. And in all but four states, before the license can be issued both parties must be given a blood test. This test is given to make sure they have no venereal disease.

Laws in all states say that after the license has been obtained, an authorized religious official, such as a minister, rabbi, or priest, may perform the marriage ceremony. In all states a legal official such as a judge or justice of the peace may also perform the ceremony. In a few states the governor or a city mayor may do this.

---

kinship A relationship based on blood ties rather than on marriage.

justice of the peace A judge who has limited powers and duties and presides over a court with limited jurisdiction.

MARRIAGE LICENSE — STATE OF NEW JERSEY

Good only for marriage in New Jersey—Invalid 30 days after date of Issuance
THE LEGAL FEE FOR THIS LICENSE IS $3.00

No. of License ....

Date of application .... at ............A.M. ............P.M.

County of .... {City, Borough or Township of ....

This is to Certify, That any person, religious society, institution or organization authorized by law to perform marriage ceremonies within the State of New Jersey, he or they, not knowing any lawful impediment thereto, is authorized to solemnize the rites of matrimony between

.... of ....
(Name of Male)

in the County of .... and State of New Jersey, and

.... of ....
(Present Name of Female)

in the County of .... and State of New Jersey.

In Testimony Whereof, I have hereunto set my hand and seal at

....

this .... day of ....

nineteen hundred and .... at ............A.M. ............P.M.

NOTE—This license, with stub attached, must be carefully preserved by the person receiving same and delivered in good condition to the person, religious society or organization authorized to officiate.

....
Registrar of Vital Statistics

....
(P. O. Address, including Zip Code)

■ ***Legal rights of wife and husband*** A legally married woman has the right to make contracts in her own name. She can also sue or be sued as an individual. She has the right to sell or give away property that she owns. A legally married man has all these rights, also. However, as a rule, property is acquired during marriage in the names of both husband and wife. It is then owned equally by both. Such property cannot be sold or given away unless both husband and wife agree. If either the wife or the husband dies, the one who is left receives full rights to the property that they owned together as a married couple.

Some states accept a widow's right of dower. This means that when the husband dies, the wife has the legal right to "the use and financial benefit" of her dead husband's real property. She has that right for as long as she lives and whether or not her husband made a will. Some states have laws giving a similar right to the husband. The husband then has the right to a share of his dead wife's real property during his lifetime. This is called the right of curtesy.

■ ***Parenthood*** The legal relationship of parent and child is formed by birth or adoption. Parents have a legal duty to support their children. They must also see to their general welfare. Parents, on the other hand, also have the legal right to the services of their minor children. When children work outside the home, parents have the legal right to their earnings. If someone hurts another person's child, the parent may bring suit for loss of services of that child.

Today many states and municipalities hold parents responsible for tort actions brought against their children. This is especially true in automobile damage cases where the driver is a minor child. It is also becoming more and more common in cases of vandalism and deliberate damage to

property. In most courts a parent and a minor child may not sue each other.

■ *Adoption* is a way provided by law by which the legal relationship of parent and child may be formed between adults and children who were not born to them. It is a formal process by which the adopting parents accept the duties and rights of natural parents. An adopted child has all the legal protection, rights, duties, and privileges of children born to their parents. The permission of a court, according to state law, is necessary for a legal adoption.

Adoption of a child breaks many legal ties with the natural parents. It places the legal responsibility for the child upon the adopting parents. In many states, however, a legally adopted child may inherit property from natural parents or other relatives.

■ ***Divorce*** The contract of marriage may be legally ended by the process called divorce. Courts may grant divorces for several reasons. The legal acceptance of these reasons differs from state to state. One widely accepted reason, or grounds, for divorce is infidelity on the part of either husband or wife. Other grounds are abandonment, desertion, and neglect. Still others are addiction to drugs, habitual drunkenness, and extreme cruelty. Some states also accept as grounds imprisonment of either husband or wife for more than three years.

Recently more and more states are allowing *no-fault* divorces. This means that it is not necessary for one partner to prove that the other was at fault. These states accept as grounds for divorce simply the agreement of both parties that the marriage relationship has completely broken down.

---

infidelity In divorce law, unfaithfulness of a man to his wife or of a woman to her husband.

abandonment In divorce law, the purposeful leaving of one's husband or wife without intending to return.

desertion In divorce law, leaving one's husband or wife without that person's consent and giving up all responsibilities and duties toward that person.

neglect In divorce law, the ignoring of responsibilities and duties.

■ *Support* Even a legal divorce often does not excuse the husband from having to support his former wife and his children. The general rule of the courts is that the support given must be at the level they enjoyed before the divorce. However, the courts may decide differently in the case of a woman who has a great deal of money of her own or a good job. They may decide that her former husband need not support her. In some recent cases the courts have decided that a wealthy wife who was the guilty partner in the divorce must support a poor husband. The main interest of the courts is to see that those people who depended on the marriage for a living are taken care of.

WILLS

A will is a legal document. In it a person can state the ways in which her/his property is to be disposed of upon death. The right to make a will leaving one's property as one chooses is a right belonging to the citizens of every state. And it is accepted as such by every state government.

■ ***Testate*** When a person dies leaving a will, that person is said to have died testate. He/she is known as the testator.

A will, once made, can be changed over and over again up until the death of the testator. When a person changes his/her mind about gifts made in the will, a new will should be written. The old one should be destroyed at that time. During a person's life, that person might make any number of wills.

When the person who made the will dies, the will must be reviewed by a probate court. This court makes sure that the will is legally acceptable. In order for the court to uphold a will, it must be made by a person who is legally "adult." Also, the will must be made by a person of "sound mind." The court wants to be sure that the person who made the will knew what he/she was doing and really planned to do it. Also, the court wants to be sure that such a person was not

---

probate court A special court that reviews the will of a dead person to make sure it is legally acceptable.

IN THE NAME OF GOD, AMEN

I, Jane Smith, residing at 42 West Adams Street in the City of Los Angeles, County of Los Angeles and State of California, being of sound and disposing mind, memory and understanding, and considering the uncertainty of this life, do MAKE, PUBLISH and DECLARE this to be my Last Will and Testament, as follows, hereby revoking all other and former Wills and Codicils by me at any time made:

FIRST: It is my Will and I do order that all my just debts and funeral expenses be paid as soon as conveniently may be after my death.

SECOND: I do give and bequeath the following:

(a) Unto my friend, William Jones, my 1974 Pinto.
(b) Unto my friend, Elizabeth Williams, my 10 carat Amythest ring.
(c) Unto my mother, Mary Smith, my dog, "Midget," a miniature collie-German shepherd.
(d) Unto my friend, Frank Kelly, my cats, "Trooper" and "Sweetheart."
(e) Unto my sister, Barbara Smith, my sapphire and pearl ring from my grandmother's estate.

THIRD: I do give, devise and bequeath all the rest, residue and remainder of my estate, both real and personal, in whatever the same may consist and wheresoever situate, to my beloved father and mother, John Smith and Mary Smith, in equal shares, share and share alike, or to the survivor of them.

FOURTH: In the event that my beloved father and mother, John Smith and Mary Smith, shall both predecease me, or in the event of a common disaster wherein they and I might perish together, I do give, devise and bequeath the rest, residue and remainder of my estate unto my beloved sister, Barbara Smith.

FIFTH: I do nominate, constitute and appoint my beloved sister, Barbara Smith, to be Executrix of this, my Last Will and Testament, to serve without bond or other security for the faithful performance of her duties. In the event that my beloved sister, Barbara Smith, shall predecease me or shall be unable to serve as Executrix hereunder, I do nominate, constitute and appoint in the alternative my father, John Smith, to serve as Executor of this, my Last Will and Testament, to serve without bond in this or any other State.

IN WITNESS WHEREOF, I, Jane Smith, Testatrix, have hereto subscribed my name and affixed my seal this 21st day of June, 1977.

Jane Smith (L.S.)

The foregoing Last Will and Testament was signed, sealed, published and declared by the above-named Testatrix as and for her Last Will and Testament, in our presence, who at the same time, have hereunto subscribed our names and residences as attesting witnesses the day and year aforesaid.

Joseph Brown — 193 Main St. Springfield, California

Ruth Wilson — 16 Winding Way Los Angeles, California

forced into doing something he/she did not want to do. A will must be properly signed by the person who made it. It must also be signed by two people who saw the will being signed by the testator. In some states three people must sign as witnesses. If all legal requirements are met, the court will uphold the will.

When a person dies testate, the court tries in every possible way to follow the intent of the will exactly. A well-written will makes everything clear. But often wills are written in a way that does not make wholly clear who is to get what. It is the duty of the court to decide as best it can the intent of the person who died. It is important that a will describe the wishes of the testator at the time of death as clearly as possible. It is really best to draw up a will with the help of a lawyer. The lawyer will make quite sure that everything is clear and in good order.

Balytat *v.* Morris
28 Ohio App. 2d 191, 276 N.E.2d 258 (1971)

TOPIC—Action involving right to inherit

FACTS—Mrs. Koehler, in her will dated July 14, 1970, directed that all of her property be sold and the money from the sale be given to charity. Her will also stated, "I have knowingly and intentionally failed to make any provision herein for my granddaughter, Susan Morris, who has shown me no affection over the years, and it is my express desire that she in no way share in my estate." The only other provision of Koehler's will was for the payment of her debts and expenses.

Koehler died on August 26, 1970, less than two months after she signed her will. An Ohio state law says that when a person wills an entire estate to charity, the will must be signed more than six months before the death of the testator. Koehler left no husband or children, so her granddaughter, Morris, was next of kin. Morris claimed the will was not valid. She took the case to court. The court found that based on the wording of the will, Morris could not inherit from her grandmother. The court ruled that the estate go to charity. The case was appealed.

QUESTION—Can the natural heir to an estate inherit what the testator planned to give to charity in a will signed less than two months before death?

■ ***Intestate*** If a person dies without leaving a will, that person is said to have died intestate. When this happens, each state has laws that outline to whom her/his property must go. Most states give the widow or widower the whole estate if the person who died left no living children, parents, brothers, or sisters. In some states, if a couple has living children, the surviving wife or husband receives one half of the estate. In other states he/she gets only one third. In either case, the rest is divided equally among the children. If no children are living, the grandchildren receive the share that their parents would have gotten.

State laws generally provide for and make clear the distribution of intestate estates among all possible heirs. The state also names an administrator to handle the distribution of every such estate according to those laws. But where there are no heirs, the whole estate goes directly to the state government.

STATE CODE*

TITLE 13. Descent and Distribution
ARTICLE 1. Descents

§ 1. Descent of real estate.—The real estate of persons dying intestate, as to such estate descends, subject to the payment of debts, charges against the estate, and the widow's dower, as follows:

(1) To the children of the intestate, or their descendants, in equal parts.

(2) If there are no children or their descendants, then to the father and mother, in equal parts.

(3) If there are no children or their descendants, and if there be but one surviving parent, then one half to such surviving parent, and the other half to the brothers and sisters of the intestate, or their descendants, in equal parts.

(4) If there are no children or their descendants, no brothers or sisters or their descendants, and if there be but one surviving parent, then the whole to such surviving parent.

(5) If there are no children or their descendants, and no father or mother, then to the brothers and sisters of the intestate, or their descendants, in equal parts.

(6) If there are no children or their descendants, no father or mother, and no brothers or sisters or their descendants, then the whole to the husband or wife of the intestate.

(7) If there are no children or their descendants, no father or mother, no brothers or sisters of their descendants, and no husband or wife, then to the next of kin to the intestate, in equal degree, in equal parts.

(8) If there are no children or their descendants, no father or mother, no brothers or sisters or their descendants, no husband or wife, and no next of kin to the intestate, then to the next of kin of the intestate's predeceased spouse in the same order of priority as provided for descent to the kin of the intestate.

(9) If there are no children or their descendants, no father or mother, no brothers or sisters or their descendants, no husband or wife, and no kin capable of inheriting, then it escheats to the state.

---

escheat The reverting of property to the state when there is no one else to legally inherit it.

* The laws for disposing of the property of people who die without leaving a will vary from state to state. The above "Descent and Distribution" rules represent the laws of only one state.

Reed *v.* Reed
404 U.S. 71 (1971)

TOPIC—Action involving the authority to act as administrator of an estate

FACTS—Section 15-312 of the Idaho Code (of laws) lists the classes of persons entitled to be administrators of a dead person's estate. One of the classes listed is "the father and mother" of the dead person. Section 15-314 of the Idaho Code, however, provides that "of several persons . . . equally entitled to administer, males must be preferred to females." Richard Reed, a minor, died in Idaho in March of 1967. He did not leave a will. Seven months after Richard died, his mother asked the probate court to appoint her as administrator of her dead son's estate. The estate had a value of less than $1,000. Before the date for a court hearing on the mother's petition, Richard's father asked the court to name him as administrator of his son's estate.

The probate court held a hearing on the two petitions. The court decided that Mr. Reed would be the administrator of Richard's estate. The court based its decision on the Idaho state law, which gives preference to male administrators.

Mrs. Reed appealed this decision. She and her lawyers claimed that the state law violated the equal protection clause of the Fourteenth Amendment. The appeals court cancelled the probate court decision and ordered the probate court to decide whether Richard's mother or father could do a better job of handling his estate. This order was never carried out because Mr. Reed appealed to the Idaho Supreme Court. This court reinstated the probate court order. Mrs. Reed then appealed to the United States Supreme Court.

QUESTION—Does the Idaho state law's preference in the sex of persons applying to be administrator of a dead person's estate deny equal protection of law and arbitrarily discriminate?

JUVENILE PROTECTION

Under early common law there was little difference between law for young people and law for adults. Early common law held that children under the age of seven were not legally responsible for a criminal act. It was felt that they were not capable of really meaning to commit a crime. However, from the age of seven up, children could be held liable, or legally responsible, for crimes. There were several cases of children under ten being hanged for serious crimes. Long ago young offenders were generally placed in the same jails and prisons that held hardened adult criminals. In the early 1800s the first reformatory school for young offenders was founded in Boston, Massachusetts. The first court for juveniles was set up in Chicago, Illinois, in 1889.

■ ***Who is a juvenile?*** The young offender of today is defined by law in each state. Most of these state laws say

---

reformatory school A penal institution to which young offenders may be sent for correction, training, and rehabilitation.

that a juvenile delinquent is a person up to sixteen or eighteen years old who does something that would be called a crime if it had been done by an adult. Also, juveniles may be held liable for behavior that is incorrigible or uncontrollable. They may also be legally responsible for truancy or for running away from home.

In re Gault
387 U.S. 1, 87 S.Ct. 1428, 18 L.Ed.2d 527 (1967)

TOPIC—Action involving juvenile proceedings

FACTS—At about 10:00 A.M. on June 8, 1964, Gerald Francis Gault, 15, was arrested in Arizona. He was arrested on a complaint by a neighbor, Mrs. Cooke. She said that Gault had made indecent telephone calls to her. At the time of his arrest Gault was on probation for another offense.

When Gault was arrested on June 8, he was placed in the Children's Detention Home. This was a kind of reformatory. Both of Gault's parents were working at the time he was arrested. They were not told of his arrest and did not find out until that evening. When she did find out, Gault's mother went to the detention home. There she was told why Gault had been arrested. At that time she was also told that there would be a hearing in juvenile court the next day.

At the hearing Gault was questioned by a judge. He had not been told that he had the right to remain silent. Neither had he been told that he had the right to have his lawyer present. No one was placed under oath to tell the truth, and no record was kept of what went on at the hearing. Cooke, who had made the complaint, was not present.

After the hearing, Gault went back to the detention home. He was kept there a couple of days and then taken home. On that

---

truancy Unreasonable absence from school.

juvenile court Court that handles charges against children under a certain age only, usually in an informal and nonpublic manner.

day, June 11, his mother was told in a note from the probation officer that another hearing would be held on June 15.

The Gaults asked that Cooke be present at this second hearing. This request was refused by the judge. No record was kept of this hearing, and no one was placed under oath. Gault was not represented by a lawyer. There was a great deal of disagreement about what had happened during the first hearing. The judge said that Gault had admitted part of the charges against him. But there was no real proof of what Gault had said under earlier questioning.

The judge sentenced Gault to the State Industrial School for six years, until he became 21. According to the laws of the State of Arizona, if Gerald Gault had been 18 years old, the heaviest sentence he could have gotten was a fine of $50 or less, or no more than two months in jail. The case was appealed to the Supreme Court of Arizona. This court agreed with the juvenile court's decision. The case then went to the United States Supreme Court.

QUESTION—Do juvenile courts have a responsibility to use due process of law rights guaranteed under the Constitution?

■ ***Juvenile courts*** After the first court for juveniles had been set up in 1889, judges across the land made tens of thousands of decisions about children who were brought before them for breaking the law. Before the Gault case in 1967, these decisions were made without using the same constitutional due process standards used with adults. In fact, in a few cases, young persons were given longer sentences than the law would have allowed for adults who had done the same thing.

---

probation The suspension of the sentence of a convicted offender, giving him/her freedom on the promise of good behavior and under the supervision of a probation officer.

probation officer An officer appointed to aid, supervise, and report on a convicted offender who is on probation.

In the Gault case the United States Supreme Court set the standard for using due process rights in juvenile cases. The Court stated that the Fourteenth Amendment due process rights should apply in juvenile proceedings that might result in the young person's being sentenced to an institution.

Today the justice system is trying very hard to improve juvenile courts. It is trying to make sure that young people accused of a crime are given all their constitutional due process rights before decisions are made. Only after proper hearings and procedures to ensure fairness to the accused do the courts decide the particular corrective measures necessary for each case.

In re Winship

397 U.S. 358, 90 S.Ct. 1068, 25 L.Ed.2d. 368, (1970)

TOPIC—Action involving a person's rights in juvenile court proceedings

FACTS—A 12-year-old boy named Samuel Winship was accused of stealing $112 from a woman's purse in New York. He appeared before a juvenile court charged with theft.

Some members of Winship's family said in court that he was at home at the time the money was taken. However, the judge decided that he was a "delinquent." He placed Winship in a training school for delinquents for at least 18 months and possibly for as long as six years. The judge stated that his finding of delinquency was based on the weight of the evidence presented. There was a New York state law that said a juvenile could be declared a delinquent if most of the evidence seemed to point to that conclusion. It was not necessary, as it is in adult criminal cases, that guilt be proved "beyond a reasonable doubt." The case was appealed to the United States Supreme Court.

QUESTION—Must juvenile courts prove guilt beyond a reasonable doubt in cases involving criminal acts?

Reviewing the Chapter

Law-Related Terms

Right of dower *Pp. 203–204, 308*
Right of curtesy *Pp. 204, 308*
Testator *Pp. 206, 309*
Intestate *Pp. 209, 306*
Probate court *P. 206*
Juvenile court *P. 213*
Probation *P. 214*

Review Questions

1. List four conditions that may have to be met for a marriage to be legal. *P. 202*
2. If property is acquired during marriage in the names of both husband and wife, what condition must be met if the property is to be sold or given away? *P. 203*
3. **(a)** What are the legal duties of parents? **(b)** What are the legal rights of parents? *Pp. 204–205*
4. Who has the legal responsibility for an adopted child? *P. 205*
5. **(a)** List seven grounds for divorce. **(b)** How is a no-fault divorce different from other divorces? *P. 205*
6. **(a)** What is the purpose of a probate court? **(b)** List the legal requirements that are necessary for the court to uphold a will. *Pp. 206–207*
7. **(a)** Before the decision in *In re Gault,* how were due process standards different for juveniles than for adults? **(b)** What principle was established in the Gault case? **(c)** According to the Gault decision, what rights are guaranteed to juveniles? *Pp. 213–215, 277–278*

Chapter Test

On a separate paper, write the letter of the answer that best completes each statement.

1. Property owned equally by husband and wife can be sold **(a)** only by the wife, **(b)** by either the husband or the wife, **(c)** only if both agree to sell.
2. A wife's right to benefit from her dead husband's real property during her lifetime is called the right of **(a)** curtesy, **(b)** dower, **(c)** eminent domain.
3. Earnings from the services of a minor child belong to the **(a)** parents, **(b)** child, **(c)** child and parents.
4. The legal responsibility for an adopted child belongs to the **(a)** natural parents, **(b)** adopting parents, **(c)** natural and adopting parents jointly.
5. Infidelity and abandonment are grounds for **(a)** adoption, **(b)** probation, **(c)** divorce.
6. The will of a dead person is reviewed by **(a)** an appeals court, **(b)** a probate court, **(c)** a probation officer.
7. To be legal, a will must be **(a)** clearly written, **(b)** recent, **(c)** signed.
8. A person who dies without leaving a will is said to have died **(a)** testate, **(b)** intestate, **(c)** in probate.
9. Due process standards for juveniles were established in **(a)** *Balytat* v. *Morris,* **(b)** *Reed* v. *Reed,* **(c)** *In re Gault.*
10. Juveniles are now guaranteed the due process right against **(a)** probation, **(b)** self-incrimination, **(c)** imprisonment.

SUPREME COURT
PROBATION

Judicial Procedures 8

JUSTICE SYSTEM

Legal process in the United States can be separated into three parts: (1) civil law, (2) criminal law, and (3) corrections. Most civil and criminal cases are decided in state rather than federal courts. How the "law" is applied in these cases is mostly governed by state constitutions, state laws, and state court decisions. Laws vary from one state to another. Clearly, then, the way the "law" works in your state may not be the same as in a neighboring state. It is important to remember this as you learn about the usual rules of procedure.

A civil case has to do with a dispute between private citizens. Or it may be between the government and private citizens. In a civil case, the dispute involves a legal right that one of the parties, the plaintiff, claims has been violated by the defendant. The plaintiff claims to have suffered some loss or injury caused by the defendant. As you learned in Chapter 4, "Torts," in a civil case there is usually no crime or criminal penalty. In a criminal case, the defendant is accused of breaking a law the violation of which has been defined as a crime by the state or federal government.

There are some cases that might call for both civil and criminal legal procedures. For example, suppose two people get into a fight. One or both may be prosecuted by the state in a *criminal action* for assault and battery. On the other hand, one of those people may sue the other in a *civil suit* for causing injuries. In the criminal case, the government is acting for the people. It is acting to protect the safety of the community. In the civil case, there is a question of private justice. The role of the court is that of a referee. It tries to see that the dispute is settled fairly. In both cases the decisions may call for the payment of money. In the civil case, the money would be paid by the defendant to the plaintiff as *damages*. In the criminal case, the money would be in the form of a *fine* paid by the defendant to the government.

The third part of legal process is corrections. Corrections deals with people who have been convicted of a crime. It has to do with the penalties for particular crimes. Corrections consists of whatever punishment or treatment the court imposes on the convicted person.

Civil Procedure

STARTING THE CASE

When a dispute between people arises, the parties may try to settle their own differences. They may try to settle without dealing with the courts. If they fail to agree, one party, generally the complaining party, or plaintiff, will see a lawyer.

Suppose Julia is in an automobile accident. She is hurt and her car is damaged. She believes the accident was John's fault. Julia wants John to pay her medical and car repair

---

judicial procedures The methods or rules by which justice is carried out within the legal system.

bills, and any other costs due to the accident. John says he did not cause the accident. He and his insurance company refuse to pay. Julia then asks George Adams, a lawyer, to represent her in the dispute. He listens to her story of the accident and tries to determine the extent of her losses and injuries. Then he decides what legal responsibilities John may have evaded that would make him owe Julia just compensation. A driver, for example, has a legal responsibility to drive within posted speed limits and to obey traffic lights. He/she has a legal responsibility not to drive with bad brakes or with broken headlights.

■ ***Complaint and answer*** Julia's lawyer writes out a complaint. This gives the facts that he believes make John responsible for Julia's injuries and the damage to her car. It also names the amount of money that Julia is asking John to pay. The complaint is filed with the clerk of the proper court. This means that the typed complaint is given to the person

---

compensation Amends made through payment of money to someone for loss or injury suffered by him/her.

COMPLAINT

Count I

1. Defendant, on or about January 1, 1974, executed and delivered to Plaintiff a promissory note whereby Defendant promised to pay to Plaintiff or order on May 1, 1975, the sum of Ten Thousand Dollars ($10,000), with interest thereon at the rate of eight percent per annum, and agreed to pay a reasonable attorney's fee for collection.

2. Defendant owes to Plaintiff Ten Thousand Dollars ($10,000) that is due on said note, and interest.

WHEREFORE, Plaintiff demands judgment against Defendant for the sum of Ten Thousand Dollars ($10,000), interest, attorney's fees, and costs.

Herman H. Hamilton, Jr.,
Attorney for Plaintiff

Of Counsel:

Capell, Howard, Knabe & Cobbs, P. A.
57 Adams Avenue
Montgomery, Alabama

Plaintiff demands trial by jury of this cause.

Attorney for Plaintiff

who is responsible for taking care of the court's official records. The clerk stamps the complaint with a certain number. She/he begins a file, or collection of papers, related to the case. All later papers connected with the case are filed with the clerk. They are stamped with the same number and placed in the file. This file becomes a public record and anyone is free to look at it upon request.

When the complaint is filed, Julia's lawyer can ask that a summons, or notice, be issued. This paper tells John that he is being sued. It directs him to appear and answer the complaint within a stated length of time. John is served with the summons along with a copy of the complaint. The sheriff or a deputy serves these papers on John. She/he might hand them over to John directly. Or they might be left at John's home with a member of the household. In this way, John is told of the nature of the case and he is brought under the control of the court.

Often a lawyer files a complaint with a court although she/he has every hope that the case will be settled out of court. There are several reasons for this. First, it shows serious intent on the part of the plaintiff. It sets the whole legal process in motion. Second, every civil and criminal action is subject to a statute of limitations. This means that there is a period of time following the event in question during which the plaintiff must file the complaint. The reason for this is that after a period of time witnesses may move away or die. Or they may forget what they saw. This makes it harder to prove what really happened. Also, the plaintiff may have the right to be paid for losses suffered. But he/she does not have the right to hold the threat of prosecution over the defendant's head forever. So Julia's lawyer must be very careful to learn the exact date of the accident. He must file the complaint within the time limit set by the statute of limitations.

Once John knows that he is being sued, he will want to have a lawyer, too. John's insurance company may hire a lawyer for him. John's lawyer, Elizabeth King, must now file an answer to the complaint. It must be filed within the period of time stated in the summons. If his lawyer fails to do this, the court can award Julia everything for which she is

---

deputy a person appointed as a substitute with power to act; an assistant who takes charge when his/her superior is absent.

prosecution The act or process of bringing a suit against, seeking to enforce by legal process; the act of beginning and carrying on a legal proceeding.

No. ________________

United States District Court

FOR THE

____

v.

SUMMONS IN CIVIL ACTION

Returnable not later than days after service.

____

Attorney for Plaintiff.

FPI—LK—6-23-53—80M—30

United States District Court

FOR THE

____

__________ DIVISION

CIVIL ACTION FILE NO.________

Plaintiff

v.

Defendant

SUMMONS

To the above named Defendant :

You are hereby summoned and required to serve upon

plaintiff's attorney , whose address

an answer to the complaint which is herewith served upon you, within days after service of this summons upon you, exclusive of the day of service. If you fail to do so, judgment by default will be taken against you for the relief demanded in the complaint.

____
Clerk of Court.

____
Deputy Clerk.

Date: [Seal of Court]

Note.—This summons is issued pursuant to Rule 4 of the Federal Rules of Civil Procedure.

suing. Not wanting this to happen, John and his lawyer answer the complaint. In this answer each statement made in the complaint must be admitted or denied. The complaint and answer are called *pleadings*.

Much of the legal process takes place *before* the case is set for trial. Most cases are settled by compromise, or agreement, between the parties. Those cases never come to trial. Usually the lawyers, after talking with their clients, meet or write each other. They discuss what compromise might be accepted by both parties. If they are able to agree, the dispute is settled out of court. The case is then dismissed by agreement of both parties.

Discovery Another important part of the legal process takes place before the trial. This is called discovery. During this stage, the parties may ask for information from each other. This may be given in either written or spoken statements, called depositions. From this information each party discovers what evidence and facts the other side plans to take to court. The statements of both parties and all witnesses are taken under oath. This is done before a public official called a notary public. The court reporter is also present. One of the main goals of the discovery is to settle what facts are agreed upon and what facts are still in dispute. It also allows statements to be taken from witnesses who cannot be present at the trial.

■ ***Pretrial conference*** It may become clear that John and Julia cannot compromise. They are not able to come to a settlement that is agreeable to both of them. The judge may then hold a pretrial meeting with the lawyers. The judge may do several things at this time. The first would be to further encourage a settlement out of court. If this does not work, the judge tries to narrow the issues that are in question. That is, she/he tries to get the parties to decide what things they can agree on and exactly what things are still in dispute and must be brought to court. The parties are not allowed to hide "surprise" issues or witnesses until the time of the trial. However, if new evidence is found by one party during the trial, it may be brought in. If this happens, the judge may call a recess. This gives the other party a chance to prepare a response to the new evidence.

GETTING READY FOR THE TRIAL

If the dispute is one of those few that cannot be settled at a pretrial stage, the judge will set a date for a trial.

■ ***Witnesses*** Both Julia and John want to prove their claims by strengthening their own testimony. They do this by getting witnesses who know the facts. These people are served with a subpoena. This is a written order directing

---

court reporter A person who is authorized to record court proceedings as they occur.

issue In a trial, a matter that is in dispute between two parties.

Witness Subpoena — Circuit Court of Leon County Case No.

STATE OF FLORIDA
COUNTY OF LEON

To All and Singular the Sheriffs of the State of Florida:

We command you to summon:

if .... be found within your county, to appear before the Hon. ....

.................., Judge of our Circuit Court for the County of Leon, Second Judicial Circuit of the State aforesaid at the Court House .... in Tallahassee at .... o'clock ....m. on .... the .... day of ...., 19..........., to testify and the truth to say on behalf of the ....

in a certain matter of controversy between ...., Plaintiff, and ...., defendant, and this you shall in no way omit.

Witness: PAUL F. HARTSFIELD, Clerk of said Circuit Court,

this .... day of ...., A. D. 19..........

(SEAL)

PAUL F. HARTSFIELD, Clerk

....
Attorney

By: ....
Deputy Clerk

them to appear in court at a given time and place. Refusing to do so may cause a person to be found in contempt of court. This could mean a fine or a jail sentence.

■ ***Plaintiff and defendant*** It is important to understand the part each of the people in a trial must play. The person who files the complaint is the plaintiff. In our case, this is Julia. Through her lawyer, Julia claims that John caused her injuries for which he is legally responsible. Julia must be able to prove that John evaded some responsibility toward her. She may have to prove that at the time of the accident he was driving his car in a negligent way. This would make him liable. She must also offer evidence showing how much injury and loss she suffered. She might show medical bills. She might bring photographs showing the damage to her car. She might also show loss of income while hurt and not able to work.

The defendant is the person the plaintiff is suing. In our case, this is John. At the trial John will try to show evidence that he was not negligent. He may try to show that Julia was also negligent. He may try to prove that Julia was not hurt as much as she claims. John may also wish to claim that the accident was, in fact, Julia's fault. He might even claim that she should be made to pay for *his* injuries and losses. If so, he will file a counterclaim.

■ ***Judge*** The judge has two main duties in the trial itself. One is to conduct the trial and keep order. The other is to make decisions about the law. If there is no jury, the judge listens to the facts and then gives the decision.

The judge rules on whether or not certain evidence can be accepted. There are strict rules governing what testimony and documents may be presented to the judge and jury. These rules are meant to make certain that the evidence presented is reasonably reliable. It must also be relevant, that is, directly related to the matters in dispute. Evidence

---

counter claim A claim by a defendant in response to a complaint; the purpose is to defeat that complaint.

that is unreliable or irrelevant might confuse or prejudice the jury. It could also waste valuable time. At the proper time, the judge instructs the jury in the rules of law that apply to the case before it.

■ ***Jury*** The persons who may serve on a jury are selected from the *jury roll*. This is a list of citizens who are eligible for jury duty. The selecting is done by a group called a jury commission. Each state has its own laws about the qualifications of jurors. These qualifications are usually very general. Among them are such things as citizenship, minimum age, good character, and sound health and judgment. No one can be disqualified solely because of race or sex. Serving on a jury is one of the most important duties and privileges of American citizens.

Before a court session that calls for jurors, the necessary number of names are drawn from the jury roll. More names are drawn than the exact number needed for the jury. These people will be part of a jury panel. It is from this group that the jury members for a particular trial will be chosen. The sheriff may send each person a summons instructing her/him to report for jury duty on a given date.

THE TRIAL

One of the most valuable liberties guaranteed to us by the Constitution is the right to a public trial. This is true whether a case is a civil suit or a criminal action. It is important, therefore, to understand something about trial procedure.

■ ***Selecting a jury*** The heart of our court system is a fair and impartial jury. To make sure of this impartiality, a pro-

---

irrelevant Not directly connected or related to the matter, topic, or issue being discussed.

prejudice To injure or damage by some opinion or action; to make someone turn against another.

disqualify To make unfit; to take away a power, right, or privilege.

cess has been set up allowing the parties in a case to remove suggested jurors from the panel. There are two ways of selecting the twelve (more or less) people who will serve on a petit jury. One way is always used in criminal cases, and sometimes in civil cases. This method is known as a struck jury. The lawyer for each party is given a list with an even number of names. The lawyers take turns striking names from the list. They do this until only the proper number of names remain.

In the other method, the names of the possible jurors are mixed together and placed in a container. Names are selected at random. When called, each juror takes a place in the jury box until there are the number used in that state. The judge or the lawyers may *challenge* jurors in order to remove them from the jury. Each lawyer is allowed to challenge a certain number of jurors without giving a reason. Any number, however, may be challenged for cause, or a particular reason.

---

petit jury A group of persons, usually twelve in number, sworn to decide on the facts of a case being tried.

challenge To dispute, to question the legality, to defy.

Among such reasons might be a close relationship between a juror and one of the parties in the case. Another reason might be that a juror has a special interest, perhaps financial, in the case. Or he/she might have already formed an opinion about the case or the parties. As one juror is rejected, another name is drawn. This goes on until both sides have agreed upon a jury.

A few alternate jurors may be chosen. This is in case one or two of the regular jurors cannot take part in the whole trial because of some personal or family emergency. The alternate jurors can then take their places to fill out the proper number. Sometimes, however, both parties may agree ahead of time that if one or two jurors have to drop out, the trial will go on with less than the original number.

When the jury selection has been completed, its members are sworn in. The case begins.

■ ***Presenting the case*** The lawyers make opening statements. Each one explains to the judge and jury what her/his side expects to prove through the evidence. Next, the evidence is presented. In our case, a civil damages suit, the plaintiff's (Julia's) lawyer makes the first opening statement. And he presents all of his party's evidence first. Julia must prove that she has a complaint against John that the law will accept. In other words, Julia must show that the injury about which she complains arose from the violation of a legal obligation owed her by the defendant. If she does not do so, John may move for a directed verdict in his favor. If this happens, the judge takes the case away from the jury and directs what its verdict shall be. This occurs when the evidence is so clearly in favor of one party that it forces only one logical decision.

When the plaintiff finishes, the defense presents its evidence. In our case, John's lawyer may present evidence showing that John did not do what Julia claims he did. Or she may try to show that Julia was also at fault. The first party, the plaintiff, is then allowed to try to disprove the defendant's evidence.

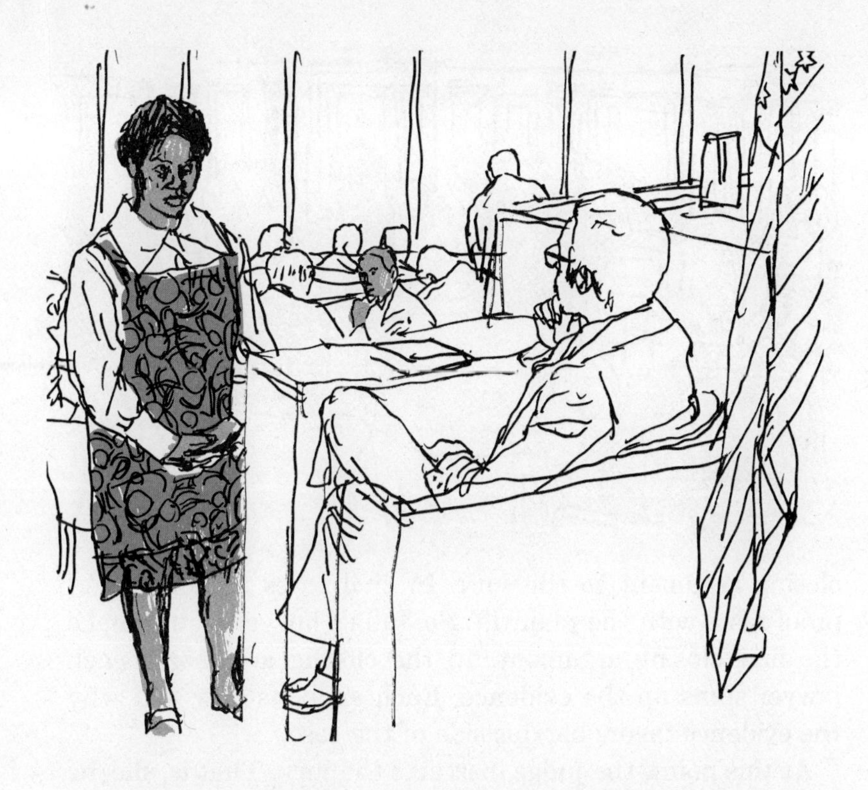

As each party presents a witness, that party's lawyer asks the witness questions to bring out information about the disputed facts. This questioning is known as direct examination. When the lawyer finishes questioning her/his own witness, the lawyer for the other side has the right to cross-examine that witness. Under the rules of court procedure, lawyers are allowed much more freedom on cross-examination than on direct examination. The idea is that if the lawyer for one party calls a witness, he/she expects the witness to present favorable evidence for that party. On the other hand, when cross-examining the other party's witness, the lawyer hopes to show errors in that witness's testimony. The lawyer may hope to show that the witness made a mistake. The lawyer may also try to prove that for some good reason the jury should not trust the witness's testimony.

■ ***Closing arguments and verdict*** When all the evidence by both parties has been presented, each lawyer may make a

closing argument to the jury. In civil cases the burden of proof rests with the plaintiff. So Julia's lawyer would make the first closing argument. In the closing arguments each lawyer sums up the evidence. Each explains how and why the evidence favors her/his side of the case.

At this point, the judge instructs the jury. That is, she/he explains to the jurors what rules of law they should follow as they decide which of the facts presented to them during the trial are true. For example, they might decide that it is a true fact that John went through a stop sign and caused the accident. Then they must apply the legal principle in which the judge instructed them. In this case, they would have to decide that John is guilty of negligence according to law. When the judge instructs the jury, each important issue is given careful attention.

After the judge instructs them, the jury members go into a private room to consider the evidence. They study and talk over all the facts until they reach a verdict. In criminal cases, state laws generally say that all jurors must agree on the

---

burden of proof The obligation to prove the truth of disputed fact(s) related to a case being tried before a court.

appellate court A court that does not hear the original trying of a case; cases are appealed to it from a lower court.

verdict. Most states do not demand such an agreement in civil cases. However, if the decision must be unanimous and the members cannot agree, then they are called a hung jury. The judge dismisses them and a new jury is called to try the case. However, in most cases the jury does reach a decision. The members then return to the courtroom to deliver their verdict to the court.

■ ***Appeal*** The losing party may feel that the verdict is wrong. If so, that party may choose to appeal. The case then goes to an appellate court. The time allowed for the appeal and the court to which it should be taken are governed by law. The appealing party is called the appellant. That party must present very clearly to the appellate court the reasons she/he feels the lower court verdict should be overturned. It is up to the appellant to show where the error was made at the jury trial.

The appellate court is made up of several judges. There is no jury and there are no witnesses. If this court takes the case, it does not try it again. Instead, it reviews the records of the original trial. It goes over the pleadings. It reads the testimony of the witnesses, which had been recorded during the original trial. The judges also read arguments written by the lawyers of both parties setting forth the reasons they believe the jury trial verdict should be confirmed or overturned. They may also listen to arguments from the lawyers. However, no new evidence can be brought in at the appellate level.

The appellate court does not look for errors of fact. It does not decide that the trial jury was wrong in its decision about which facts were true. The appellate court considers only strictly legal matters. It is interested in whether or not the trial jury applied the law correctly in reaching its verdict. It is interested in whether the trial judge might have made a legal error in accepting certain evidence. Or it considers whether that judge erred in his/her instructions to the jury.

If the appellate court decides to overturn the verdict, it may do one of several things. It may simply overturn the verdict, returning both parties to their positions before the jury trial. It may remand the case. This means sending it back to the trial court with orders to enter a certain new verdict. Or it may send the case back to the lower court for further proceedings, such as hearing more evidence. The appellate court may even send the case back for a new trial.

LEGAL AID

In many states, legal services are available free of charge to poor people who have legal problems of a civil nature. Such matters may include consumer complaints, family problems, debtor/creditor problems, landlord/tenant disputes, and the like. These free services are given by Legal Aid Societies or Legal Aid Clinics. Although the programs may take on different forms in different states, generally there are two kinds. There are legal aid programs paid for by the federal or state government. And there are such programs paid for by private funds. In many places county bar associations run the programs. The main idea behind all such programs is to help those citizens who need legal services in civil matters but who do not have the money to pay for their own lawyers. Help with legal problems is given to indigents by able lawyers who work full or part time for the legal services program.

Criminal Procedure

FELONIES AND MISDEMEANORS

There are two major kinds of criminal offenses. These are called felonies and misdemeanors. Felonies are the more serious. A felony is a crime punishable by a fine and a prison sentence of over one year, or by such a prison sentence alone. In a few cases, it may be punishable by death.

People who have once been convicted of a felony, even if the sentence is suspended, lose certain rights. They lose the right to vote and the right to serve on a jury. They cannot join any military service or work for the government. In many states they lose the right to hold public office. With few exceptions, the loss of these rights is permanent. People who have been convicted of a felony may also lose certain other privileges, depending upon the state. They may not be allowed to become barbers, engineers, or private detectives. They may not be permitted to be doctors, lawyers, or teachers. There are many other kinds of work they may never be able to get because of their conviction.

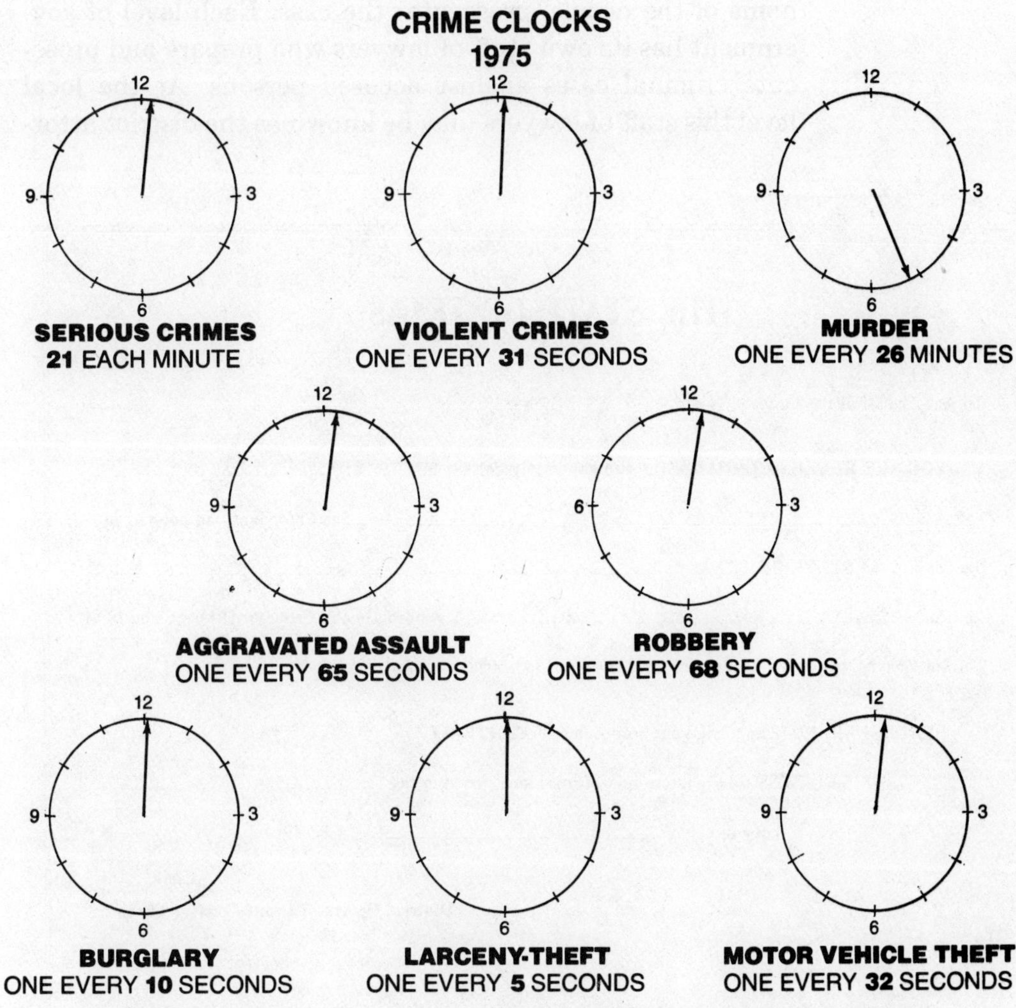

Adapted from Federal Bureau of Investigation annual report, Uniform Crime Reports for the United States.

Misdemeanors are less serious offenses. A traffic violation is a well-known example of a misdemeanor. Conviction for a misdemeanor does not as a rule mean the loss of rights and privileges as in the case of felonies.

ARREST An arrest is the act of taking into custody a suspected offender for possible criminal prosecution. A person who has been arrested and charged with a crime must face the whole law enforcement system. The government, acting in the name of the people, prosecutes the case. Each level of government has its own staff of lawyers who prepare and prosecute criminal cases against accused persons. At the local level this staff of lawyers may be known as the district attor-

D.C. 141 WRIT TO SERVE INDICTMENT

THE STATE OF TEXAS

To Any Sheriff of the State of Texas – GREETING:

YOU ARE HEREBY COMMANDED, to immediately deliver to ____________________

____________________ the defendant, in person, in

the case of the STATE OF TEXAS vs.____________________

____________ No.____________ pending in the Criminal District Courts of

Tarrant County, the accompanying certified copy of Indictment in said cause.

HEREIN FAIL NOT, and make due return hereof FORTHWITH.

WITNESS my signature and official seal, on this the ____________

day of ____________________ A.D. 19____ J. W. [illegible]

Clerk,

District Courts, Tarrant County, Texas

By____________________, Deputy

ney's office or the state's attorney. At the state level there is an attorney general's office. The federal government has the justice department.

An arrest may be made with a warrant or, under certain special circumstances, without a warrant. An arrest warrant is a written order directing the arrest of a certain person or of certain people. It can be issued by a court or by an official with the proper authority. An arrest is usually made by an officer of the law. But any other person can make a citizen's arrest. In some states, however, a citizen's arrest can be made for felonies only. Arrests for misdemeanors must be made by police officers. In the case of a minor misdemeanor such as a parking violation, the offender is not arrested. Instead, a summons is issued by a law officer.

To resist arrest is a criminal offense. This is true even though the person being arrested thinks the arrest is unlawful. However, if an innocent person is arrested unlawfully, that person may have grounds for a false arrest or false imprisonment civil suit.

Action to obtain a warrant to arrest a person and legally charge that person with a crime may be put into motion in several different ways. These are (1) a complaint, (2) an indictment, and (3) an information.

■ ***Complaint*** A private citizen or a law officer may wish to have someone arrested. That citizen or officer must "swear out a warrant" for the person believed guilty of some illegal act. The person beginning the action must sign a complaint under oath. That person must describe the alleged violation. And he/she must be willing to offer testimony to support the accusation. This is in line with the protection guaranteed by the Fourth Amendment (p. 86). If the judge or commissioner believes there is enough probable cause, or good reason,

---

citizen's arrest In certain circumstance, the legally acceptable arrest of another person by someone other than a duly sworn peace officer.

commissioner A representative of some level or unit of government. This person has both judicial and administrative powers.

WA 26751

The State of New Jersey
vs.

COURT	
COUNTY OF	N. J.
COURT DOCKET NUMBER(S) C–	COURT CODE NUMBER
COMPLAINT RESULT OF CASE RETURNED BY PROSECUTOR	PRIOR CASE DOCKET NUMBER C–

Defendant: ______

Address: ______

City, State: ______

COMPLAINT

Complainant: ______ (NAME OF COMPLAINANT) of ______ (IDENTIFY DEPARTMENT OR AGENCY REPRESENTED)

Residing at ______ (ADDRESS OF PRIVATE CITIZEN COMPLAINANT)

Upon oath says that, to the best of (his) (her) knowledge, information and belief, the named defendant on or about the

______ day of ______, 19___, in the ______ of ______ [MUNICIPAL CODE NO] ______ County of ______ N. J.
did;

Charge Number 1	Charge Number 2	Charge Number 3
N. J. S.	N. J. S.	N. J. S.

Subscribed and sworn to before me this ______ day of ______, 19______.

Signed ______ (NAME AND TITLE OF PERSON ADMINISTERING OATH) Signed ______ (COMPLAINANT)

To any peace officer or other authorized person: Pursuant to this warrant, you are hereby commanded to arrest the named defendant and bring (him) (her) forthwith before this court to answer the foregoing complaint.

Bail has been fixed by ______ in the amount of $ ______ or ______ (Specify condition of release, e.g. R.O.R.)

Date Warrant Issued ______

Court Appearance Date ______ Time ______ (AM) (PM) ______ SIGNATURE OF JUDGE OR CLERK

DATE OF INITIAL APPEARANCE

COURT ACTION (Cases wherein judgment or Conditional Discharge is entered in this court)

CHARGES	WAIVER INDT./JURY	PLEA	DATE OF PLEA	ADJUDICATION OR COND. DISCH.	DATE	JAIL TERM	SUSP.	FINE	SUSP.	COSTS	SUSP.	PROBATION TERM	COND. DISCHARGE TERM
Number 1													
Number 2													
Number 3													

OTHER ACTION BY THIS COURT

PROBATION TERM SUPERVISED ☐ YES ☐ NO

DATE		DEFENDANT DISCHARGED AS TO PROBABLE CAUSE. PROSECUTOR GIVEN PRIOR NOTICE.	2	DEFENDANT HELD FOR GRAND JURY. ORIGINAL COMPLAINT, RECORD, BAIL TRANSMITTED.	3	NO ACTION BY THIS COURT. COMPLAINT REFERRED TO PROSECUTOR.	INSTITUTION TO WHICH SENTENCED
4	Other (Specify)						

BAIL INFORMATION

DATE	AMOUNT BAIL SET	REL. ON BAIL 1	R-O-R 2	COMMITTED DEFAULT 3	COMMITTED WITHOUT BAIL 4	PLACE COMMITTED
SURETY COMPANY – PERSON POSTING BAIL – RELEASED IN CUSTODY OF – ADDRESS						

PROSECUTING ATTORNEY AND DEFENSE COUNSEL INFORMATION

PROSECUTING ATTORNEY	NONE 1	STATE 2	COUNTY 3	MUNICIPAL 4	OTHER 5	DEFENSE COUNSEL	NONE 1	RETAINED 2	PUBLIC DEFENDER 3	ASSIGNED 4	OTHER 5

MISCELLANEOUS INFORMATION

______ JUDGE ______ DATE

NJ/CDR-2 (REV 1/75)

ORIGINAL

she/he issues the warrant. This is then served on the accused person by a police officer. That person is then under arrest.

■ ***Indictment*** The district or prosecuting attorney may believe there is enough evidence to make a case against a person suspected of a serious crime. She/he will then prepare a paper called a bill of indictment. This is a written statement accusing a person of a crime. The district attorney presents this paper to a grand jury. A grand jury is a body made up of from 12 to 23 citizens. Their names are taken from lists of voters. It is their job to decide whether the district attorney has given them enough legally acceptable evidence to justify bringing the accused person to trial. If the grand jury decides that there is enough, it issues a true bill, or an indictment. The accused person is now formally charged with the crime.

Grand jury hearings are held in secret. No visitors are allowed. The reason for this is that the grand jury may find that the evidence is not strong enough to support the accusation. In that case, it will not hand down an indictment. However, if the hearings were open to the public, innocent people might be unfairly incriminated.

In addition to its other duties, a grand jury has the power to conduct investigations of its own.

■ ***Information*** The Fifth Amendment says that "No person shall be held to answer for a capital or otherwise infamous crime, unless on a presentment or indictment of a grand jury." However, since 1884, this constitutional guarantee applies only to federal cases. Since that time, each state has been free to decide whether or not it wants to use a grand jury. In a state that does not use a grand jury, an information can be filed against a person thought to have committed a crime. An information is an accusation similar to a bill of indictment. It, also, follows a police investigation of a crime. It, also, accuses a person of a crime. However, it is not presented to a grand jury. Instead, it is presented under oath to a judge by the prosecuting attorney. An information, like a bill of indictment, must give enough facts about the crime and the accused person to justify issuing a warrant. A trial may then be held.

Hurtado *v.* California
110 U.S. 516, 4 S.Ct. 111, 28 L.Ed. 232 (1884)

TOPIC—Action for murder

FACTS—In 1879, California adopted a new article into its constitution. Article I, Section 8, reads as follows: "Offenses heretofore required to be prosecuted by indictment shall be prosecuted by information after examination and commitment by a magistrate."

Mr. Joseph Hurtado was prosecuted through means of an information. He was charged with murder and pleaded not guilty. A trial was held in 1882. There had been no investigation or indictment by a grand jury. The trial jury found Hurtado guilty of murder in the first degree. The court sentenced him to death. He appealed to the Supreme Court of California. This court agreed with the lower court.

The case was then appealed to the United States Supreme Court. The grounds for the appeal were that Hurtado had been tried in error because he had not been properly indicted by a grand jury. This, it was claimed, was in violation of the Fifth and Fourteenth Amendments of the Constitution of the United States. Therefore, Hurtado claimed, the decisions of both lower courts could not be legal. Hurtado said that he had been deprived of life or liberty without due process of law.

QUESTION—Under the Constitution of the United States, can a person be tried and convicted of first degree murder and sentenced to death without being indicted by a grand jury?

■ ***Arrest without warrant*** An arrest for a felony may be made by a police officer without a warrant in certain cases. Such an arrest may be made if the officer sees the crime being committed or attempted. It may also be made if the officer

has good reason (probable cause) to believe a person has committed or is about to commit a crime. Or an officer may make an arrest without a warrant if she/he has probable cause to believe a person has committed or is committing a crime and may hurt someone or escape if not arrested at once.

In the case of a misdemeanor, it is the general rule that an officer may make an arrest without a warrant only if he/she saw the act committed or attempted. However, this varies from state to state.

A citizen's arrest can also be made without a warrant. In the case of a felony, such an arrest can only be made if the crime has already been committed. The arresting citizen must have seen the crime committed. Or she/he must have probable cause to believe the person being arrested is the one who committed the crime.

In some states a citizen is also allowed to make an arrest for misdemeanors. In those states the same rules must be followed as when making an arrest for a felony.

■ ***Service of warrant*** An arrest warrant is good until the person named in it is arrested or until it is withdrawn. The arresting officer must show the warrant to the person being arrested if asked to do so. However, many state laws do not say that the arresting officer must have the warrant with him/her at the time of the arrest. If the accused person asks to see the warrant after the arrest, it must then be presented.

The warrant may be served, or presented, only in the state in which it was issued. Most states, however, follow a different policy in case of an interstate chase. An officer in *fresh pursuit* of a person may make an arrest outside the state in which the felony was committed. The person arrested is first turned over to the authorities of the state in which she/he was arrested. That person is then held there until extradicted, or handed over, to the state where the arrest warrant was issued. The request to hand over this person and the response to it are handled by officials of the two states.

Inside a state, a warrant issued in one county may be served by an officer in any county of that state. Some states allow a police officer from the county that issued the warrant to look for and arrest the accused anywhere in the state.

■ ***Rights of accused*** At the time of arrest, there are certain rights of which the accused must be told immediately. These rights have become known as the *Miranda Warnings* (page 270). The accused may waive these rights only if she/he understands what they are and gives them up knowingly and with full understanding.

In some states, a person who has been found innocent of the charges has the right to have the arrest record removed from the public files, destroyed, or turned over to him/her.

BETWEEN ARREST AND PROSECUTION

An arrested person, unless otherwise released, must be brought before an official of a court of law as soon as possible. The purpose of this is to tell such a person exactly what the charges against her/him are.

---

fresh pursuit The common-law right of a police officer chasing a suspected felon to cross a state line in order to make an arrest.

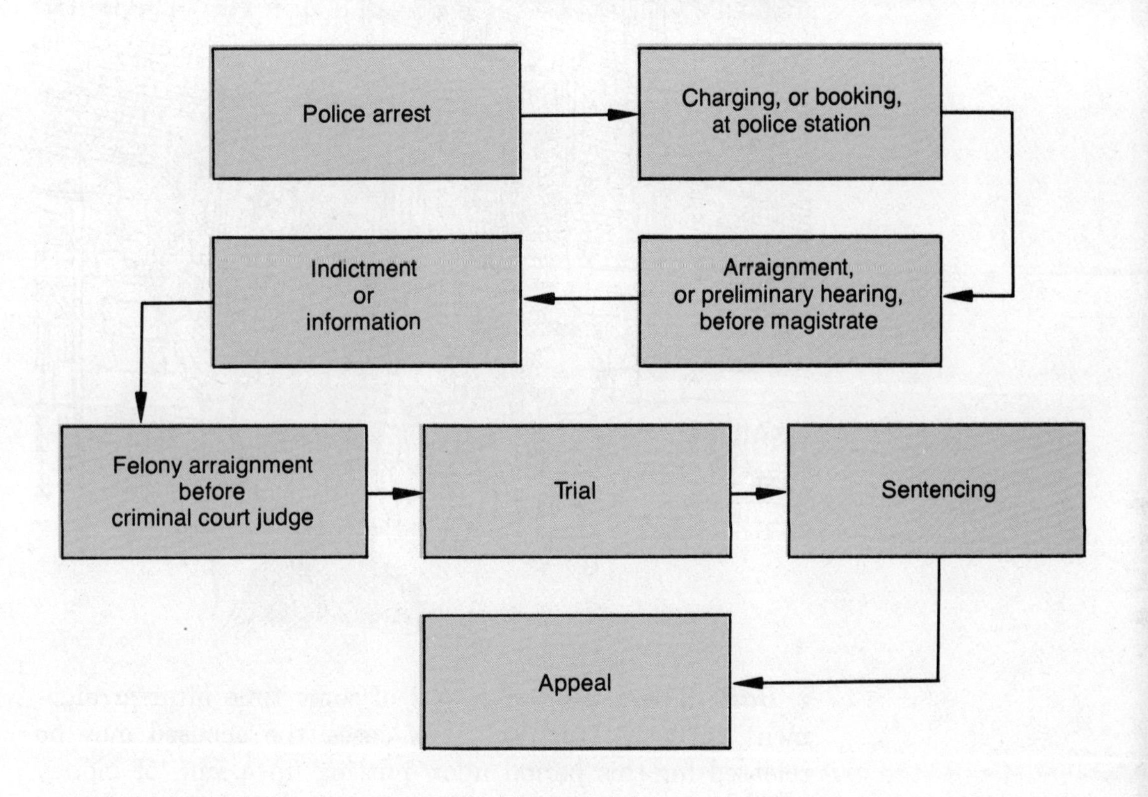

■ *Arraignment* The hearing at which the accused is told of the charge is called an arraignment. At that time the arrested person may enter a plea. That is, he/she may make a formal statement of "Guilty" or "Not guilty." If the charge is a misdemeanor, the arrested person *must* enter a plea at this hearing. In most felony cases, the accused need not enter a plea at once, but may do so at a later felony arraignment.

It is usually at the arraignment that a person who has pleaded not guilty is asked if she/he wants a trial with or without a jury. If the accused has pleaded guilty, there will be no trial. Instead, the judge will make sure that this person knows that he/she is giving up certain rights. The judge will also get all the important facts about why the person is being charged. Then the judge will pass sentence on the accused.

■ ***Bail*** There is often a wait of some time after arraignment until the trial. In many cases, the accused may be released for this period upon putting up a sum of money called bail (p. 115). In many states a person may be released on bail even before arraignment.

Bail is a security bond drawn up in a way that tries to ensure that the accused will appear at the trial. If such a person does appear, the bail money will be returned. If she/he does not appear, the money is not returned. If the offense is bailable, the judge sets the amount in line with the seriousness of the offense and whether it is felt the accused can be counted on to appear.

The idea of bail is rooted in the important American principle that a person is held innocent until proved guilty. Release allows the accused time to help prepare a defense. It also keeps a person from being punished before conviction.

Some people believe the bail system is unfair. They feel it discriminates against the poor. Poor people have little money to meet bail. Nor are they often able to get a bonding company to put the money up for them. A bonding company requires that the accused own something of enough value to act as security for the money it lends.

In some cases an accused person may be released without bail. This is mostly done in the case of misdemeanors by first offenders. The accused is released simply on a promise to appear for trial. This is known as releasing a person on personal recognizance (R.O.R.).

■ ***Plea bargaining*** Before the trial itself, plea bargaining might take place. This means that the accused is given a chance to plead guilty to a less serious charge than the one for which she/he was to be tried. In exchange the defendant agrees that she/he will not plead not guilty to the original charge. This kind of agreement avoids a trial.

Because of the great overcrowding of the criminal courts, prosecutors and judges are often willing to accept plea bargaining. Also, the defense may feel that the case against it is very strong. By pleading not guilty and going to trial, the accused runs the risk of receiving a heavier sentence. Even if she/he is innocent, a defendant might want to accept a sure, shorter sentence than take a chance of conviction at trial.

THE TRIAL

The American ideal that a person is innocent until proved guilty is at the heart of any trial. As you learned in the chapter on constitutional law, there are many safeguards in the Constitution for anyone accused of a crime. Such a person has certain constitutional rights. Here are a few of these rights.

1. A person has the right to a public trial.
2. A person has the right to be tried by an impartial jury.
3. A person has the right to face witnesses against him/her.
4. A person cannot be tried twice for the same offense.
5. A person has the right to be represented by a lawyer.
6. A person has the right to get her/his own witnesses.

UNITED STATES DISTRICT COURT
NORTHERN DISTRICT OF ILLINOIS
EASTERN DIVISION

UNITED STATES OF AMERICA	)	
	)	
-v-	)	No. 71 CR 368
	)	
MELVIN BAILEY, et al.	)	

WARRANT OF ARREST FOR WITNESS

TO: ANY U.S. MARSHAL or any other authorized officer:

You are hereby commanded to arrest FRED VALENTINE, and bring him forthwith before the United States District Court for the Northern District of Illinois, in the City of Chicago, State of Illinois, for the reason that he appears to be hiding to avoid appearing in the trial of Melvin Bailey, et al., in said District.

You are further commanded to detain him in your custody until he is discharged by the Court, pursuant to Rule 46(b) of the Federal Rules of Criminal Procedure, and Title 18, United States Code, Section 3149.

DATE: FEBRUARY 1972.

____
UNITED STATES MAGISTRATE

R E T U R N

Received __________, 19__ at ______________________________, and executed by arrest of FRED VALENTINE on ______________________, 1972 at ___________________________.

____

7. A person does not have to testify against herself/himself.
8. A person may not be deprived of life, liberty, or property without due process of law.

Proceedings Courtroom proceedings for criminal cases are very much like those for civil suits. If the defendant wants to be tried by a jury, possible jurors are gathered. A petit jury panel is selected. It is then sworn in, just as for a civil case. The charge against the defendant is read to the jury. The plea is given. The presenting of evidence begins.

The lawyer of the party that began the court action makes the opening statement. You will remember that in civil cases, that party is called the plaintiff. In criminal cases that party is called the prosecution. In criminal matters the offender is accused of breaking a law enacted by the people through their government. So the people's agent, the prosecutor, represents them and begins judicial action. As in civil cases, the accused is known as the defendant.

In the opening statement, the prosecution tells the court what it expects to prove. It also tells how it expects to do so. The defense has several choices. It, too, may make an opening statement. Or it may choose to make its statement when the prosecution has completed its case. Or it may choose to make none at all.

The presenting of each party's case and the order followed are much the same as in civil cases. The people (prosecution) present their case first. Witnesses are questioned in direct examination. *Real* or *documentary* evidence is presented to back the charge. Real evidence may be such a thing as the actual knife or gun that was used to commit a murder, for example. Documentary evidence may be in the form of letters, photographs, hotel guest registration, official records, etc.

Through cross-examination, the defense tries to shake the jury's belief in such evidence and in the testimony of prosecution witnesses.

At this point, the defense often moves that the case against the defendant be dismissed on grounds of insufficient evidence. If the judge refuses to do this, the defense presents its case. The pattern of direct examination and cross-examination is much the same as for the prosecution. It is very important to remember that the lawyer for the defense does not have to prove that the accused is innocent. She/he only has to place a reasonable doubt in the minds of the jury that the defendant committed the act in question.

Many factors are carefully weighed by the defense lawyer in deciding whether or not the defendant should testify. One of the rights given by the Constitution is that defendants cannot be made to incriminate themselves. In intense cross-examination this might happen. So the lawyer might decide not to allow the defendant to testify. On the other hand, the defense might believe it will have a stronger case if the defendant takes the witness stand. In that case, certainly she/he may do so. However, neither federal nor state courts allow a prosecutor to suggest to the jury that the accused is guilty if he/she decides not to testify.

When both parties have completed their cases, the lawyers make their closing arguments to the jury. The prosecution leads in making the closing statements. The defense follows. Then the prosecution is given a second opportunity to speak. In their closing statements the lawyers may only review evidence already presented. They may not introduce new evidence or ideas at this point.

Finally, the judge carefully instructs the jurors on the general principles of law that apply to the case. The judge also reminds them that a verdict of guilty can be made only if guilt has been proved beyond a reasonable doubt.

The jury then begins its deliberations. It gives its verdict just as it does in civil cases. However, for most criminal cases the decision must be unanimous.

---

beyond a reasonable doubt The degree of certainty that a juror must have in his/her own mind about the guilt of a criminal defendant. It means the evidence must be so complete and conclusive that all doubts are removed.

■ ***Sentencing*** When the jury finds a defendant guilty, it is the judge's duty to pass sentence. There are a great number of sentences that a judge might give. They range from fines, through different kinds and lengths of imprisonment, to death.

Passing sentence is a heavy responsibility. Most judges want time to consider as much information as possible about the crime and why it was committed. They want to consider what they know about the offender's character and past record. Judges also need time to think about which of all the possible sentences would be the wisest in each case. State laws generally give a time limit in which sentencing must be done. If needed, however, more time may be given. During the time between the verdict and the sentencing, the defendant may be placed in custody or continued on bail. This depends on the circumstances.

A judge cannot pass any sentence he/she might want to. Most often the laws against particular crimes also state the range of possible punishments for those crimes. For example, a certain crime may call for a jail sentence of from five to ten

years. That means the judge must decide on a jail sentence that is no less than five years, but no more than ten. The judge cannot select a sentence outside the limits set by law for a crime.

Sentencing itself is always done by the judge. But some states allow the jury to recommend the punishment for certain crimes. Before 1972 in some states, a judge could pass the death sentence in cases of capital crimes only if the jury recommended it.

Furman *v.* Georgia
408 U.S. 238, 92 S.Ct. 2726, 33 L.Ed. 346 (1972)

TOPIC—Action involving the death penalty as cruel and unusual punishment

FACTS—Mr. Furman was a young black man with only a sixth-grade education. One night he tried to enter another person's home. The owner of the home woke up and tried to stop him. Furman stated that when trying to escape he tripped and dropped his gun. He said the gun then went off. The bullet went through a closed door, killing the owner of the home.

Before Furman was brought to trial, he was given a mental examination. The medical report stated that he did have a "mild to moderate" mental problem. However, it also stated that he knew the difference between right and wrong and that he was able to work with his lawyer in preparing his defense.

The jury found Furman guilty of murder. A Georgia law allowed the jury to recommend either a sentence of death or life imprisonment. It recommended death, and the Georgia Supreme Court upheld the sentence. Furman appealed to the United States Supreme Court.

Two other men who had been sentenced to death also appealed to the United States Supreme Court. One had been sentenced in Georgia, the other in Texas. One of these men, like Furman, had very little education. He, too, had a mental problem. Both of these men were black. The United States Supreme Court joined all three cases for one hearing.

QUESTION—Does the death sentence constitute cruel and unusual punishment in violation of the Eighth Amendment?

The Supreme Court in its five-to-four *Furman* v. *Georgia* decision did not say that capital punishment in itself is unconstitutional. They declared it unconstitutional only as applied in the cases it was reviewing. Two of the judges did feel that the death penalty in any and all cases was unconstitutional. The other three judges who made the majority decision pointed out that the death penalty tended to fall almost entirely on the poor, on blacks, and on the uneducated. It was much less likely to be used in the case of other members of society even when the crimes committed were the same. These judges felt that the death penalty is "unusual" if it discriminates against people because of their "race, religion, wealth, social position, or class."

The decision of the court in *Furman* v. *Georgia* left the door open for states to pass capital punishment laws. But in order for these laws to be constitutional, they have to be very exact about just what crimes call for the death penalty. The death sentence *must* be passed in these cases. The laws must be so specific that neither the judge nor the jury can have any choice in the matter of a sentence. There must be no way in which these laws can be applied in a discriminatory way.

CORRECTIONS

The final part of the legal process is corrections. Corrections deals with people after a criminal court has found them guilty of breaking a law. The corrections system has several goals. One is to punish the criminal. Earlier in this book you looked at some examples of punishment that different societies have used through the centuries. Some were very cruel. Others appeared foolish. But they all serve to show that society has always acted against those who break its rules or laws.

An important goal of corrections has always been to protect and preserve society. Punishing an offender is one way in which society tries to protect itself against the same persons committing the same offenses over and over. It is also intended to deter, or discourage, others from committing such acts in the future. Today our society punishes people for crimes mostly by fines or imprisonment. As you have read, in a very few cases a serious crime is punished by death.

Another most important aim of corrections is to rehabilitate, or reform, offenders. This means finding ways to make such people become useful members of society.

What makes a criminal? Why does a person commit a crime? What is needed in order to become a crime-free society? There are no simple answers to those questions. But the search for the causes of crime is important. Good corrective treatment depends on an understanding of what caused a particular act in the first place. Today much thought is being given to what kind of correction the offender should receive. Should it be corrective measures that fit the criminal? Should it be punishment that fits the crime?

■ ***Capital punishment*** Much debate and difference of opinion center on the question of what is just punishment. This is particularly true in the case of capital punishment. Under the common law that English settlers brought to this country, many offenses could be punished by death. Today only such serious crimes as kidnapping, murder, rape, and armed robbery may be punished by death. And even in these cases there is much disagreement about whether this sentence is just. You have already learned from your study of *Furman* v. *Georgia* that there can be differences of opinion on the subject even among the Justices of the Supreme Court.

Those people who favor the death penalty reason as follows:

1. It helps to stop other people from committing the same crime.

2. The behavior of a person convicted of such a serious crime cannot be changed.
3. The police and the public should be protected.
4. A life imprisonment sentence allows an offender to be paroled, or released, after a number of years. That person may then repeat the criminal behavior.
5. Being in prison for a long time is cruel. It also presents a danger to prison officers.
6. It is very expensive to keep someone in prison for life. That money could be better spent for other things.

Those against the death penalty make the following points:

1. A person cannot imagine his/her own death. So the execution of an offender will not serve to discourage others.
2. Many capital offenses are committed suddenly, without thinking or planning. The death penalty in such cases is too extreme.
3. Not many of those who are convicted of capital crimes are people who have done such acts in the past. They are probably not habitual criminals.
4. Executing a person for any reason at all is immoral. No person or group of people should have the right to take life from any other person.
5. Capital punishment gives the offender no chance at all to reform. Such a sentence denies the idea that a person is able to change and improve.
6. In many cases where there has been a death sentence, the execution has been put off over and over again for years. This keeps the prisoner waiting to die and is in itself immoral.

■ ***Prison*** Most criminal cases are handled by state courts. This means that the greater part of the correction programs come under state laws. The differences in these laws are huge. Each state sets its own maximum and minimum sentences for different crimes. It also makes the rules that gov-

ern the correctional institutions. These places vary greatly. There are penal farms that use the labor of the prisoners to raise crops. There are forestry camps that may not even have guards or fences. There are minimum security prisons, where the prisoners' families may visit for certain periods. There are maximum security prisons, with high walls and guards armed with automatic rifles or machine guns. There are also special institutions for juvenile offenders.

The programs in the different prisons also vary greatly. In some there is much effort made to rehabilitate the prisoner. There are programs that include classes leading to a high school diploma. Some include college courses, skill development, and job training. The aim of these programs is to give the prisoner every possible chance to return to society as a law-abiding, useful citizen. On the other hand, many prisons have poor programs or none at all. These places do very little to prepare prisoners for a noncriminal life in society. They may, in fact, make it more likely that a prisoner will return to a life of crime when released.

■ ***Suspended sentence and probation*** A person found guilty of a crime may receive a suspended sentence. That means the judge has sentenced such a person to a term in prison and then allowed her/him to go free on certain conditions. Usually this person is placed under special court supervision for a definite length of time on good behavior. Such a person is on probation.

Massachusetts is credited with being the first state to make use of probation. John Augustus, a Boston shoemaker, offered his services to the Boston Police Court in August of 1841. He asked that a number of persons convicted of being drunk in public be released to his supervision. The prisoners were freed on bail in his custody and they went to work for him. He was the earliest known probation officer in the United States. His program was rated successful, and in 1878 Massachusetts passed the first probation law. By 1917 twenty-one states had passed such laws. In 1925 probation became part of the federal correctional program. At about the same time, probation for juveniles became available in all the states. It was not until 1956 that all states had probation laws for adults.

Even today not all offenders are allowed probation. It is used mostly with first offenders. Or it is used as a penalty for lesser offenses. Most state laws do not allow probation for serious crimes such as assault with a deadly weapon, selling drugs to juveniles, and armed robbery.

In order for a person to be considered for probation, he/she must appear to understand why the act committed was wrong and harmful. That person must show a real willingness to be law-abiding. And he/she must accept all the conditions and terms of probation. These terms include reporting to a probation officer at certain times for a period stated by the judge. This officer looks after the probationer and makes sure that the other terms of the probation are followed. The probationer must remain on good behavior and obey all laws. If the offender commits another crime while on probation, he/she will have to serve the original sentence. There will also be a sentence for the new crime. The probationer cannot move or change jobs without permission. He/she must work at a steady job or attend school regularly. Besides these terms, there may be other requirements. For example, if the crime had anything to do with drugs, the probationer might have to take part in a drug treatment program.

■ ***Parole*** Parole is the releasing of a convicted criminal before the whole sentence has been served. The parolee remains under the supervision of the paroling authority. Such a person can be returned to prison upon violation of any of the conditions set by that body. This means that although out in the community, a parolee is still under prison control. One important reason for parole is to make it less difficult for a person to make the change from living in prison to living in the community. It allows for a gradual return to a less controlled life.

Rules for granting parole vary from state to state. Some states will not allow parole at all in the case of certain crimes. Generally a prisoner is eligible for parole when some part of the maximum term has been served. The time must have been served with good behavior. Ideally, when a prisoner applies for parole a parole board makes a careful study of his/her character, history, and records. The board considers whether the prisoner is really ready for release. The members of the board discuss how much supervision would be needed. They consider how much and what kind of community assistance would be needed. They want to know such things as whether the prisoner has a home to go to. They want to know whether that person has had the promise of a job.

In most cases, when the prisoner appears before the parole board he/she is not represented by a lawyer. In most states the parole board does not have to tell the prisoner its reasons for not granting parole. Some courts, however, are setting up certain rules about this. The Supreme Court of New Jersey, for example, has ruled that a board must give reasons for not allowing parole. This court felt that knowing these reasons would be helpful in rehabilitating prisoners.

The parole board decides what the terms and conditions of the parole shall be. A parolee may not be allowed to leave a certain city or state. He/she may not be allowed to drink liquor or drive a car. A curfew may be set for such a person. He/she may need to get permission to change jobs or to get married. Parolees must not have guns. They must have nothing to do with known criminals.

When a prisoner has been granted parole, that person is assigned a supervisor called a parole officer. The parolee must report regularly to this officer. A good parole officer helps a parolee handle the many problems to be met in the community. Such help might be in the form of advice and counsel. Or it might be practical assistance in finding a new job. It is the job of the officer to help the parolee become a useful citizen.

---

curfew A regulation, issued by a public authority, ordering persons to keep off the streets between certain hours; also, sometimes a condition of parole or probation.

If a parolee does not live up to any one of the terms of the parole, he/she may be returned to prison. Most of those who go back to prison are sent there because they committed another offense while on parole. When this happens, a parolee may be returned to prison for the length of time that the parole was meant to cover. For example, if a person had a ten-year parole and committed an offense during the last year of that time, she/he could be returned to prison to serve a full ten years. Many states, however, give a returned prisoner credit for good "street time." In this case the person must stay in prison only for the time left on parole from the time of the violation.

■ ***Community programs*** Many states are studying the value of programs making use of community approaches to corrections. These programs include (1) pretrial intervention, (2) halfway houses, (3) work-release/study-release, and (4) home furloughs.

■ *Pretrial intervention* is meant to quickly rehabilitate the young first offender. The court puts off the trial for 90 days. During this time the young person is placed in a program of counseling, training, and job assistance. If the program is successful, the charges are dismissed. The case never comes to trial. In this way the young person avoids the damaging effects of having a criminal record.

■ *Halfway houses* are homelike residences found in many towns and cities. They are used as living quarters for those offenders whom the court does not want to send to, or keep in, prison. But at the same time the court feels that they need more supervision than probation allows. Halfway houses are also used to help people who have come from some kind of jail or prison. They provide the kind of situation that helps such people gradually become used to community life.

This is a program of supervised living that still allows for a certain amount of independence. People in such a program receive counseling services and other kinds of help. They can go out into the community for education, training, jobs, and recreation. They can visit their families and friends. But they must return to the halfway house at night.

■ *Work-release/study-release programs* make possible more control of an offender than does either probation or the halfway house. In this kind of program, carefully selected offenders are kept in jail or prison only at night or on weekends. The rest of the time they are allowed to follow a normal life. They can get a job or job training. They can go to high school or take college courses. They can visit their family or friends. They can enjoy entertainment or take part in sports. They can even do volunteer community work. This kind of program allows control over offenders without completely upsetting their family life, working life, or education.

■ *Home furloughs* allow offenders to leave prison for short visits home to their families and friends. As a rule these take place during holiday seasons or in the case of death or serious sickness in the family. The leaves are very short. Usually they can be no more than five days.

■ ***Pardons*** Pardons can be granted only by the President of the United States or the governor of a state. A pardon frees an offender from prison and from the sentence. In the eyes of the law, a person who has been pardoned is as innocent as if she/he had never committed the offense. Civil rights that have been lost because of the conviction are returned. Pardons have been granted in cases where it was felt that the need for mercy was more important than that the letter of the law be strictly followed. Pardons have also been granted in situations where innocent people had been wrongfully convicted.

Today gaining an understanding of what causes a person to commit a crime is a very important matter. Just as important is discovering the best ways to prevent crime. And finally there is the need to arrive at the best means of correction. Helping people who have committed a crime to return to the community as valuable members of society should be the most important goal of our correctional system.

THE LAW IS YOUR RESPONSIBILITY

From your study of *Our Legal Heritage,* it should be clear that the law is an important part of our way of life. It is vital to our democracy. We have a fine legal system. Is it perfect? Of course not. But in our form of government we are provided with the means to change and improve the system. Our legal system is hundreds of years old. It is constantly changing. Keeping what is good in the system and changing the things that need to be improved is a tremendous challenge. In order to achieve the ideal of equal justice for all, you must meet that challenge. That is your responsibility as Americans. It is part of "our legal heritage."

Reviewing the Chapter

Law-Related Terms

Statute of limitations *Pp. 223, 309*
Prosecution *P. 223*
Subpoena *Pp. 227–228, 309*
Arraignment *P. 245*
Parole *Pp. 259, 307*

Review Questions

1. Explain the differences between civil and criminal cases. *Pp. 219–220*
2. Use the case in the text to explain the steps in presenting a case. *Pp. 232–233*
3. List some sources of legal services in civil matters for people who cannot afford a lawyer. *P. 236*
4. **(a)** What is the difference between a felony and a misdemeanor? **(b)** What rights are lost by a convicted felon? *Pp. 236–238*
5. Explain three ways to obtain an arrest warrant. *Pp. 239–242, 303, 305, 306*
6. **(a)** Define bail and explain its purpose. **(b)** Why do judges, lawyers, and defendants sometimes accept plea bargaining? *Pp. 246–247, 302*
7. List the constitutional rights of a person accused of a crime. *Pp. 247–249*
8. What are some things a judge considers in sentencing a person convicted of a crime? *Pp. 251–252*
9. Explain the three goals of corrections. *Pp. 254–255*
10. What are the arguments for and against capital punishment? *Pp. 255–256*

Chapter Test

From the list below, select the answer that best completes each statement. Write your answers on a separate paper.

plea bargaining	arraignment
civil	indictment
statute of limitations	felony
subpoena	state
rehabilitate	parole

1. A ______ case usually involves a dispute between two private citizens.
2. In a criminal case, the charges are brought by the ______.
3. The ______ is the period of time within which charges must be brought.
4. A written order to appear in court to give testimony is a ______.
5. A ______ is a crime that is punishable by a fine and/or a prison sentence of over one year.
6. One way to initiate an arrest warrant is by ______.
7. The hearing at which an accused person is told the charge and may enter a plea is the ______.
8. The process by which the accused, the defense attorney, and the prosecutor bargain for the dismissal of some charge in exchange for a plea of guilty to another is called ______.
9. One of the goals of corrections is to ______.
10. A person released from prison earlier than the sentence date is on ______.

Decision of Court

1 Our Legal System

***p. 1 Garcia* v. *Allan and Iwasko (Iwasko* v. *Garcia)* YES.** In this case, the state court of appeals upheld the decision of the lower court. It decided that a person, such as Robert Iwasko, who takes part in a drag race on a public street is responsible for any accident that might happen even though he/she does not actually hit anyone. Drag racing is an illegal activity. Under the law, two or more persons who take part in an illegal activity are called joint tort-feasors. In this case, Allan and Iwasko were joint tort-feasors. Because they were drag racing, Allan and Iwasko both contributed to the cause of the accident. Both, then, would have to pay damages to Garcia.

3 Constitutional Law

***p. 59 Wisconsin* v. *Yoder* NO.** The United States Supreme Court found that in the case of Amish children, several years of high school would do little to serve their interest. It is one thing, the court felt, to say that there must be a year or two of compulsory education past the eighth grade when the goal is to prepare a child for life in modern society. But it is quite another thing to say that this education would prepare a child for life in a secluded Amish community. Amish religious beliefs play a most important part in their day-to-day lives. If the members of the Old Order Amish faith obeyed the state's school attendance law, they would be prevented from freely following their religious beliefs. To make Amish children attend public school past the eighth grade would violate their right to the free exercise of their religious beliefs.

DISSENT: Justice Douglas dissented in part. He said that religion is an individual experience. He had some questions about the religious liberty of some of the children in this case, but the children themselves were not given a chance to be heard by the Court.

***p. 67 Edwards* v. *California* NO.** The state court was wrong. The California law about persons coming into the state was a violation of the commerce clause of the Constitution. The movement of a person from state to state comes under the control of interstate commerce. This is regulated by Congress. The right to move freely from state to state is a right of every citizen of the United States. This right is guaranteed by the Fourteenth Amendment to the Constitution.

***p. 68 Heart of Atlanta Motel, Inc.* v. *United States* YES.** Congress has the power to regulate interstate commerce. The United States Supreme Court held that Congress could apply the laws of the Civil Rights Act of 1964, by way of the commerce clause, to motels serving interstate travelers. The Heart of Atlanta Motel had a legal duty to rent rooms to people regardless of race.

***p. 70 Toomer* v. *Witsell* NO.** The state law in question violated the privileges and immunities clause of Article IV of the Constitution and the equal protection clause of the Fourteenth Amendment. It threatened to exclude United States citizens from sharing in the fishing rights.

***p. 72 Gomillion* v. *Lightfoot* NO.** The United States Supreme Court found that the law for changing Tuskegee's boundaries was a violation of the equal protection clause of the Fourteenth Amendment. Laws passed to change electoral districts in order to keep blacks from voting are in violation of both the Fourteenth and the Fifteenth Amendments. A state cannot deny voting rights to its citizens in a discriminatory manner.

***p. 73 Green* v. *County School Board* NO.** The United States Supreme Court held that the plan had not put an end to segregation. The school system was told to integrate the two schools by other means in line with the Civil Rights Act and the equal protection clause of the Fourteenth Amendment.

***p. 76 Marsh* v. *Alabama* YES.** The United States Supreme Court held that a state law against handing out religious literature violates the First and Fourteenth Amendments to the Constitution. Most towns could not have barred this act. The fact that a "single company had legal title to all the town" does not close channels of communication between the people living there and the persons passing through.

DISSENT: Justice Reed, Chief Justice Stone, and Justice Burton did not agree with the rest of the Court. Justice Reed stated that it has never been held and is not now held that the freedoms of religion, speech, and the press are absolute and unlimited. What the decision in this case set up as a principle is that one may remain on private property against the will of the owner and against the law of the state. This would be true so long as the owner's objection is to the spreading of religious views.

***p. 77 United States* v. *O'Brien* NO.** The United States Supreme Court found that Congress may set up a system of registration for people that is meant to place them in the armed forces. It may require citizens to cooperate in this system. When O'Brien burned his card, he willfully did so against the interest of the government. Such acts would openly encourage others to destroy their cards. This would upset the smooth working of the Selective Service System.

DISSENT: Justice Douglas questioned whether the draft system is allowed when there has been no declaration of war.

***p. 78 Kovacs* v. *Cooper* NO.** Freedom of speech is guaranteed under the Constitution. But there are limits to this freedom. The United States Supreme Court held that the law against "loud and raucous noises" is under the control of town government. Citizens have a right not to hear these loud sounds and voices if they don't want to. The need to reasonably protect the privacy of homes or businesses from the distracting noises of cars or trucks with sound amplifiers is reason enough for the law.

DISSENT: Justices Murphy, Black, Douglas, and Rutledge felt that there was nothing at all to prove that the noise was either "loud" or "raucous" unless the words of the law meant any noise coming from an amplifier, however loud or soft it may be.

***p. 79 Wood* v. *Georgia* YES.** The United States Supreme Court found that an elected officer had the right to enter the field of political controversy. The part that elected officers play in our society makes it all the more important that they be allowed to freely state their ideas on matters of public interest. Having looked into the statements made in the news release and the circumstances under which they were made, the Court decided that these statements did not present a danger to the administration.

***p. 80 Adderly* v. *Florida* NO.** The United States Supreme Court held that for security reasons, jails are not as a rule open to the public. Demonstrations on jail grounds cannot be accepted.

DISSENT: Justices Douglas, Brennan, and Fortas and Chief Justice Warren dissented on the grounds that the students were being punished for exercising a constitutional right.

***p. 80 Edwards* v. *South Carolina* YES.** The United States Supreme Court found that in this case there was no threat of violence. There was plenty of police protection. The Capitol was an appropriate place to protest for change. A state does not have the right to make the peaceful expression of unpopular views a crime. These people were acting within their rights under the First Amendment.

DISSENT: Justice Clark felt that the chance of disorder was great and that the police had a right to keep order.

***p. 84 Lafayette Radio Electronics* v. *United States* YES.** The FCC has the power in the public interest to stop messages that serve no end other than the pure pleasure of sending them and receiving an answer or of talking about the equipment itself. It has been shown that those people who used CB for fun were taking up too much of the time available on the limited channels of the Citizens Band Radio Service. The company's petition was denied.

***p. 85 Gagliardo* v. *United States* YES.** Evidence was presented that under unusual atmospheric conditions or because the sender is near a state line, CB messages can be heard in other states. The appeals court felt that this is sufficient reason to say that such messages have enough effect on interstate commerce to give the federal government the power to regulate all citizens band radios. The fact that Gagliardo's messages may not have crossed state lines doesn't really make any difference. It is the total effect on interstate commerce of all citizens band radio messages that gives the federal government the power to make rules for all such radio sending. The appeal court decided that it was proper for the case to be tried in federal court because of the "commerce" clause.

The question of whether or not the words Gagliardo used were "indecent" was sent back to the lower court for a jury to decide in a new trial.

***p. 93 Mapp* v. *Ohio* NO.** The United States Supreme Court found that the security of one's privacy stands against forced entry by the police. The Court held that the evidence was gathered without a search warrant, in violation of Mapp's constitutional rights under the Fourth Amendment. These rights are enforceable against the states through the due process clause of the Fourteenth Amendment. The evidence could not be used against Mapp in a state court of law.

***p. 94 Stoner* v. *California* NO.** The United States Supreme Court found that to do so would be an invasion of constitutional rights under the Fourth Amendment. By renting a hotel room, the guest gives permission to maids, janitors, and clerks to enter that room. But these people may enter only in the performance of their regular duties. Any evidence gathered through an illegal entry cannot be used in court.

***p. 96 Terry* v. *Ohio* YES.** The United States Supreme Court stated that an officer of the law must have some power to make a reasonable search for weapons. This is in order to protect the officer if there is reason to believe he/she is dealing with an armed and dangerous person. This holds true whether or not the officer has good cause to arrest the person for a crime.

There is no exact rule in a case of this kind. Each case must stand upon its own facts. A police officer may notice unusual conduct and have reason to think the person with whom he/she is dealing might be armed and dangerous. In that case the officer is acting in the best interests of the law to go ahead with a reasonable search for the sake of safety. This has come to be known as the "stop and frisk" doctrine.

DISSENT: Justice Douglas dissented on the grounds that the stopping and frisking of the defendant was consititutional only if there was probable cause to believe a crime was about to be committed.

***p. 97 Chimel* v. *California* NO.** The United States Supreme Court found that such a search is unreasonable and therefore contrary to the meaning, intent, and scope of the Fourth Amendment. An arresting officer may search the person arrested in order to remove any weapons the prisoner might try to use in order to escape or resist arrest. A reasonable search of a place into which an arrested person might reach in order to get a weapon is in order. However, it is not in order for a routine search to be made of rooms other than the place in which the arrest is made. Such searches may be made only with a search warrant. This is a right guaranteed by the Fourth Amendment.

***p. 100 Green* v. *United States* NO.** The United States Supreme Court in a five-to-four decision held that the second degree charge at the first trial dismissed the chances for a first degree charge later. Green could not again be placed in jeopardy of being found guilty of first degree murder for the same offense.

***p. 102 United States* v. *Wade* NO.** The United States Supreme Court found that neither making a defendant appear in a lineup nor making such a person speak violates the right against self-incrimination. This right protects an accused person only from being made to testify against himself/herself.

***p. 103 Frontiero* v. *Richardson* YES.** The United States Supreme Court said that the different treatment complained about in Lt. Frontiero's case was unconstitutional discrimination against servicewomen in violation of the due process clause of the Fifth Amendment. The Court stated that "our nation has had a long and unfortunate history of sex discrimination . . . which in practical effect put women, not on a pedestal, but in a cage," making man "woman's protector and defender." As a result of those ideas, the Court noted that "our statute books gradually became laden with gross, stereotyped distinctions between the sexes." The Court also stated that through much of the nineteenth century, women could not hold elective office or serve on juries. They could not bring a lawsuit in their own names. Married women could not own or sell property. They could not serve as legal guardians of their own children. The Court found that these attitudes and practices have often resulted in placing women in an inferior legal position without regard to their abilities.

The Court further noted that Title VII of the Civil Rights Act of 1964 bans discrimination on the basis of "race, color, religion, sex or national origin." Applying this law and the constitutional provision of the Fifth Amendment's due process clause, the requirement that was challenged by Lt. Frontiero was declared unconstitutional.

***p. 106 Gideon* v. *Wainwright* YES.** The United States Supreme Court held that any person brought into court who is too poor to hire a lawyer cannot be sure of a fair trial unless a lawyer is appointed for him/her. The guarantee of counsel in the Sixth Amendment applies to all cases in the state as well as federal courts under the due process of law right of the Fourteenth Amendment (see page 71). The right to counsel must be maintained whether the crime is serious or minor.

***p. 107 Douglas* v. *California* YES.** When an appeal is decided without a lawyer being provided for an indigent party, an unconstitutional line has been drawn between the poor and the rich. This violates the principles of both the Sixth and the Fourteenth Amendments.

***p. 108 Escobedo* v. *Illinois* YES.** Where a police investigation is not being made into an unsolved crime but begins to focus on a person who has been taken into police custody, that person has a right to a lawyer. Escobedo had not been allowed to see his lawyer nor had he been warned by the police of his constitutional right to remain silent. The right to remain silent is guaranteed by the Fifth Amendment. The Sixth Amendment guarantees the right to counsel. His statements made during police questioning should not have been used against him at his trial because they were obtained unfairly. The United States Supreme Court ordered a new trial.

***p. 108 Estes* v. *Texas* NO.** The United States Supreme Court stated that the pretrial hearing had been made so public that it could only have impressed people with Estes' probable guilt. It is true that the public has a right to know what happens in its courts. But use of television, radio, and moving and still pictures in the court makes a setting that does not allow due process of law as guaranteed by the Fifth Amendment. It also destroys the Sixth Amendment right to an impartial jury. The Court ruled that the impact of television alone on the members of a jury is perhaps of the greatest importance.

Several of the judges also stated that it is against the Sixth Amendment for federal courts and against the Fourteenth Amendment for state courts to allow criminal trials to be televised to the public.

***p. 110 Miranda* v. *Arizona* NO.** By the provision of the Sixth Amendment a person held for questioning must be told clearly that he/she has the right to talk to a lawyer and to have the lawyer present during questioning. If a person is too poor to pay a lawyer, one must be provided for her/him. If a person does answer questions on his/her own and gives some facts before using the right to remain silent, this does not mean he/she has given up this right guaranteed by the Fifth Amendment.

The United States Supreme Court decided that Miranda had not really known of his right to remain silent. He also was not aware that he had the right to see a lawyer. The Court felt that although he had signed a typed statement saying that he did know his rights, this did not mean it was true. The police had kept Miranda from using his constitutional rights. Therefore, the statements he had made could not be accepted as evidence.

In this very important decision the United States Supreme Court set forth the rights (under the Fifth Amendment) of a person being arrested.

1. Before questioning begins, a person must be told by the police that he/she has the right to remain silent.
2. The person must be told by the police that anything he/she says may be used as evidence against him/her.

3. The person must be told by the police of his/her right to see a lawyer before being questioned and the right to have the lawyer present while being questioned.
4. If a person does agree to answer questions, he/she has the right to stop answering at any time.
5. The person may give up these rights only if it is done with free will, knowingly and intelligently.

DISSENT: Justices Harlan, Stewart, and White dissented on the grounds that the decision was not good constitutional law. Justice Clark dissented in part on the grounds that the accepting of a confession gotten by police questioning should depend on the circumstances under which it was received.

***p. 111 Sheppard* v. *Maxwell* YES.** The Supreme Court of the United States decided that the trial judge did not do his duty to protect Sheppard from the one-sided publicity. Neither did he handle the disruptive influences in the courtroom well enough. Sheppard had not received a fair trial as guaranteed by the Sixth Amendment.

***p. 112 Williams* v. *Florida* NO.** The United States Supreme Court stated that the Constitution does not say how many people should serve on a jury, and that therefore six were enough.

In writing its decision, the court traced the history of the size of juries under English law. It found that English juries have varied in size from 4 persons to 84. The reason that most have had 12 has never been discovered. In 1812, Lord Coke, an English lawyer and judge, explained that the "number of twelve is much respected in holy writ, as 12 apostles, 12 stones, 12 tribes, etc." However, no one really knows the reason for the 12-person jury. It is known, however, that some time in the fourteenth century, the size of the jury came to be fixed at 12.

In deciding this case the Supreme Court stated, "Consistent with this holding, we conclude that the petitioner's Sixth Amendment rights, as applied to the states through the Fourteenth Amendment, were not violated by Florida's decision to provide a 6-man rather than a 12-man jury. The judgment of the Florida District Court of Appeals is affirmed."

***p. 112 Baldwin* v. *New York* YES.** The United States Supreme Court reversed the decision of the lower courts. The Court stated that under the Sixth and Fourteenth Amendments, only "petty" offenses can be tried without a jury. No crime can be "petty" for purposes of the right to trial by jury when a sentence of more than six months in jail is possible.

***p. 113 Illinois* v. *Allen* NO.** The defendant can lose this right to be present at the trial if that person's acts upset trial procedure. Judges faced with upsetting acts must be given the right to meet the circumstances of each case. There are the following constitutional ways for a judge to handle a disorderly defendant such as Allen: (1) Bind and gag such a person, but keep him/her present. (2) Cite that person for contempt. (3) Take that person out of the court until a promise to act properly is given.

***p. 116 Carlson* v. *Landon* NO.** The United States Attorney General's act did not violate the Eighth Amendment. This amendment does not require the same reasonable bail for aliens under deportation charges that it does for citizens charged with bailable offenses.

***p. 116 Tate* v. *Short* YES.** The United States Supreme Court found that since Texas fines people for traffic violations, no one should be put in jail just for not having the money to pay. Prison in such a case would not be just. There are, however, other ways that the state can make a person pay a fine. It might allow the person, for example, to pay over a certain length of time.

***p. 118 Louisiana ex. rel. Francis* v. *Resweber* NO.** In a close vote, the United States Supreme Court decided that Francis's constitutional rights had not been violated. He had been represented by a lawyer according to due process of law. The court decided that failure of the machinery was no one's fault. Therefore a second attempt at carrying out the sentence should be made.

***p. 118 Powell* v. *State of Texas* YES.** The United States Supreme Court said that being drunk in public has been a crime all through our history. It was also true in early British history. The Court felt that in the best interest of our society, a person must not be excused from responsibility on account of drunkenness. He/she may, instead, be treated for alcoholism. However, in order to receive this treatment, such a person must first be removed from the streets. The court decided that the Texas law making it a crime to be drunk in public was not unconstitutional. Powell's conviction does not constitute cruel and unusual punishment under the Eighth Amendment.

4 Torts

***p. 123 Wire* v. *Williams* NO.** Jumping rope is not generally thought to be a dangerous act. The court found that the teacher could not have reasonably foreseen a danger that Diane would be hurt. The teacher did not have to pay damages.

***p. 126 Mohr* v. *Williams* YES.** Unless a doctor discovers a condition endangering the life of a patient during the operation, no other operation can be performed. Today many doctors solve this problem by having the patient give total consent to any operation the doctor thinks is in the best interest of the patient.

***p. 127 Lamb* v. *Woodry* NO.** Oregon law does not give the seller of goods the legal right to take back property by force. However, a seller may take back property if a duly named officer of the law is helping. In this case, Woodry used force to take back the stove. If, in doing so, he touched the resisting person, he is guilty of assault and battery. Lamb received $1,000 in damages.

***p. 128 Clayton* v. *New Dreamland Roller Skating Rink, Inc.* YES.** The evidence stated justifies a cause of action for battery. Brown may have acted with the best intentions. But the law holds him liable for any harm or injuries caused by his acts.

***p. 129 Fisher* v. *Carrousel Motor Hotel, Inc.* YES.** Actual physical hurt is not a requirement for a battery. Grabbing the plate from Fisher's hands was a wrong act amounting to a battery. The Supreme Court of the State of Texas agreed with what the trial court had decided.

***p. 129 Jones* v. *Fisher* NO.** In this case, the Fishers were not legally justified in forcing Jones to give up her personal property as security for the loan she owed them. The acts of the Fishers were an assault and battery upon the person of Jones. So the Fishers were liable to Jones for damages.

---

security Something of value left with someone as a guarantee of payment of a debt.

p. 131 Bird **v. *Jones*** **NO.** There is no false imprisonment unless one's freedom of movement is totally blocked. Bird was only kept from walking on the public footway. He was free to go across the bridge.

p. 132 Drabek **v. *Sabley*** **NO.** The court noted that when a child is taken into immediate custody, the child's parents "shall be notified as soon as possible." In this case Sabley's acts were reasonable up to the time he put Tom into the car. But then the restraint of Tom's liberty was total. Tom had been falsely imprisoned by Sabley. So Sabley had to pay damages.

p. 134 Harrison **v. *Wisdom*** **YES.** In cases such as this, where the danger is real and directly associated with the personal property involved, there is a legal right to protect the safety of the public.

p. 135 Ploof **v. *Putnam*** **YES.** The Vermont court upheld the right to enter land and make use of personal property belonging to another in times of emergency. There was a bad storm, and Ploof was faced with a choice of docking his boat or being drowned along with his family. The law gives this right to trespass in order to save life.

p. 136 Longenecker **v. *Zimmerman*** **YES.** In an action for trespass, the plaintiff is usually entitled to damages even though she/he may actually have benefited by the act of the defendant. In this case, Zimmerman trespassed when she ordered work done on the trees belonging to Longenecker. Zimmerman is legally liable for damage.

p. 138 State **v. *Preece*** **YES.** In this case, Preece was in his own home. If attacked there, he "was entitled to use the law of self-defense to kill another."

p. 140 Davies **v. *Mann*** **NO.** Davies recovered damages for the value of his donkey. Davies was negligent in letting his donkey graze close to the road. However, Mann did not use due care to avoid hitting the donkey. The law calls this the "last clear chance." Mann had the last clear chance to avoid an accident.

p. 141 King **v. *Smythe*** **YES.** Frank Smythe committed the negligent act. But Dr. Smythe was liable for the actions and damages caused while Frank was driving his car. In most states, when a car owner allows family members to drive the family auto for their own pleasure, the owner is responsible for negligent acts they may commit.

p. 142 Cohen **v. *Petty*** **NO.** If the loss of control is not foreseeable, there is no negligent act. It was an unavoidable accident that could not have been prevented by any type of reasonable care by Mr. Petty.

p. 142 Zelenko **v. *Gimbel Brothers, Inc.*** **YES.** A person has no legal duty to come to the aid of another person. But once aid is offered, there is a legal duty to act with due care.

p. 143 Kuhn **v. *Brugger*** **YES.** A twelve-year-old is not judged by adult standards of care. But a child's acts are expected to be as reasonable as that of a child or children of like age, mental ability, and experience. The decision of the trial court was upheld. Brugger was liable for his negligent acts. Damages were set in the amount of $116,604.40.

DISSENT: (Justice Bell): "The majority decision will require a parent and grandparent to keep under lock and key (and keep the key constantly in his or her pocket) every revolver, carving knife, butcher knife, and every possible dangerous household article... in order to be legally safe from suit.... If... a burglar or robber entered a man's home at night and he awoke, he would have to try to recall where he had hidden the key, get up in the dark, find it, unlock the drawer and finally get out the pistol, in order to defend himself or his property. By that time it would have been, in many instances, too late to defend himself or to capture the burglar. The present decision will also generate a tremendous number of lawsuits which will literally bankrupt young married couples who today have no maid or servant to aid them in tending the children, their home, the cooking, and everything connected with home life. A mother necessarily leaves carving knives, butcher knives, and other similar articles attractive to young children on the kitchen table or around their home where the children and their young friends constantly play, while she finishes cooking the meal, arranges, or waits on the table or answers the telephone or door. Inevitably a child will accidently or negligently or unwittingly injure a playmate. The law has never heretofore imposed such an unreasonable... standard of care on the owner of a home or the head of a family."

p. 145 Sheehan **v.** ***St. Paul & Duluth Railway Company*** **NO.** The property owner has no duty of care to an unknown trespasser. It is only after the property owner discovers the trespass that a duty of due care arises. The train crew did not discover the trespasser in time to use due care. Once the owner knows of the trespasser's presence, she/he must use reasonable care to avoid injury.

p. 146 Chicago B & Q Railroad Company **v.** ***Krayenbuhl*** **YES.** When the owner of dangerous equipment has reason to believe children trespass upon his/her property and would be attracted to a piece of equipment such as a railroad turntable, the property owner has a duty to protect them from any such danger.

p. 147 Kavafian **v.** ***Seattle Baseball Club Association*** **NO.** Kavafian's act is called assumption of risk. Kavafian had been to many baseball games before. He knew the risk in sitting in an unscreened spot. By doing so, he contributed to his accident and assumed all risks connected with it.

p. 148 Palsgraf **v.** ***Long Island Railroad Company*** **NO.** In this case, the danger could not have been expected. The dropping of the package of fireworks, the explosion, and the tipping of the scales were happenings that could not have been predicted. The railroad company was not negligent in this case.

p. 148 Laube **v.** ***Stevenson*** **YES.** There is a duty to warn a licensee of a dangerous condition on the property that the licensee might not know about or discover. This case is an example of the general rule of law that a property owner has a duty to warn licensees of dangerous conditions that the landowner knows about.

p. 149 King **v.** ***Lennen*** **YES.** Lennen knew that children trespassed and played near his pool. The state of the pool and the lack of adequate fencing made a serious danger. Due care on the part of the owner would have prevented the tragedy.

p. 150 Lemon **v.** ***Edwards*** **NO.** The owner of country land has no duty to look at trees to decide if they might possibly fall across a road. The falling of a tree is an act of nature. The landowner has no duty to use due care in such cases. The laws may be different in urban areas, where a property owner is liable for any damage done by a tree that falls on the property of another.

***p. 151 Filburn* v. *People's Palace & Aquarium Company, Ltd.* YES.** An elephant is in the class of animals known to be dangerous. Owners of such animals keep them at their own risk. Owners are strictly liable for any damages caused by the animals' acts.

***p. 152 Zarek* v. *Fredericks* YES.** Anyone who keeps a dangerous domestic animal is liable for any harm the animal causes. Some states have laws stating that a dog is "entitled to one bite" before it can be thought dangerous. Pennsylvania did not have such a law.

***p. 153 Luthringer* v. *Moore* YES.** In such an activity as exterminating, there is a high risk of serious harm to others. Moore knew or should have known that someone might be hurt by the gas.

***p. 153 Beck* v. *Bel Air Properties, Inc.* NO.** The construction and maintenance of new lots for building is not thought to be hazardous. Bulldozing in this case is not a hazardous act. Bel Air Properties, Inc. was not strictly liable for its acts.

***p. 154 Spano* v. *Perini Corporation* YES.** Blasting is a dangerous activity as recognized by law. Any person or company that engages in blasting activities is strictly liable for damages done to the property of others.

***p. 155 Rogers* v. *Elliott* NO.** If the ringing of the bell had affected the health or comfort of other persons in the community, this could have been held to be a nuisance. Only Rogers was disturbed by the ringing of the church bell, because of his nervous condition.

***p. 156 Bennett* v. *Norban* YES.** The angry statements and acts of the assistant manager were an unreasonable and serious interference with Bennett's person. This amounted to slander before the eyes of the public.

***p. 157 Fawcett Publications, Inc.* v. *Morris* YES.** The article was libelous of each member of the football team even though there was no reference to Morris personally. The judgment in favor of Morris and against Fawcett Publications, Inc. was upheld.

5 Property

***p. 161 Bridges* v. *Hawkesworth* YES.** The court decided that the money was lost property and that the finder of lost property has the right to it against all people except the true owner. The court decided that Bridges should have the money.

***p. 167 Belt* v. *Hamilton National Bank* YES.** A person may have an idea that is neither patentable nor subject to copyright. However, if that idea is more than just a thought and has been orally expressed in a concrete, detailed form, the law may allow a property right to exist. The court decided that Belt, as the owner of the idea, had a right to payment because his idea was used in the development of the program.

***p. 168 Erickson* v. *Sinykin* YES.** The court decided that the original owner of the money had given up ownership of his/her own free will. The fact that the money appeared to have been there for more than fifteen years lent support to the idea that it had been abandoned. Erickson had a right to get the money back from the hotel.

***p. 170 Commonwealth* v. *Polk* NO.** The court held that under a bailment the bailee must use utmost good faith and diligence in protecting the property trusted to him/her. The court decided that Polk did not prove he had done his best to protect the money. He would have to pay for the loss.

p. 171 Butler* v. *The Frontier Telephone Company. **YES.** The court ruled that Butler had been deprived of his property right to *reasonable* space above his land.

p. 172 Smith* v. *New England Aircraft Corporation **NO.** The court ruled that reasonable airspace over his land belonged to him. However, because of the need for airports, he could not keep the planes from flying over his land.

p. 172 Southwest Weather Research, Inc.* v. *Rounsaville **YES.** The court ruled that owners of land have the right to whatever rain, snow, or hail might fall on their land. The court ordered the weather company to stop seeding the clouds.

p. 174 Bove* v. *Donner-Hanna Coke Corporation **YES.** The city zoning laws allowed coke ovens to be run in that neighborhood. The court ruled that people who live in industrial neighborhoods must stand for a certain amount of discomfort.

p. 175 Cowling* v. *Colligan **YES.** The court ruled that Cowling was right and that the land owned by Colligan could not be used for commercial purposes.

p. 176 Berman* v. *Parker **NO.** The court decided that the rights of the Bermans would be satisfied when they received the just compensation called for in the Fifth Amendment.

6 Contracts

p. 183 Supt. and Trustees of Public Schools of City of Trenton* v. *Bennett **NO.** The court decided that the builder contracted to build and must do so in spite of the loss. The court said that a sudden tornado, a gale of wind, and the softness of the soil are all incidental. The builder had not shown that the performance of the contract was impossible. Bennett must build or suffer the loss.

p. 186 Broadnax* v. *Ledbetter **YES.** There must be an offer and an acceptance in order to have a true contract. In this case, the court found that there was an offer but that Broadnax had not accepted it, since he knew nothing about it.

p. 188 Owen* v. *Tunison **NO.** The court ruled that Tunison's statement was just an invitation to Owen to make further offers. $16,000 was a minimum price to Tunison. He was not offering to sell at that price.

p. 189 Craft* v. *Elder and Johnston Company **NO.** The court ruled there was no offer. There was only an invitation to the public to bargain. An advertisement is not an offer.

p. 190 Lefkowitz* v. *Great Minn. Surplus Store **YES.** The court ruled that this advertisement was an offer. Since Lefkowitz accepted by being the first person to come to the store, there was a contract. The store was held to the obligation made by formation of the contract. The court also ruled that the statement by the store that the sale was meant for women only was a change in the offer after it was accepted.

p. 191 Raffles* v. *Wichelhaus **NO.** It was shown that each man had meant a different ship. The court ruled that there was no meeting of the minds. So there was no binding contract.

p. 195 Whitman* v. *Anglum **NO.** The court ruled that even though it might be hard for Anglum to provide the milk, he could not be released from the contract because of a temporary disability. He must still perform his part of the agreement.

***p. 195 Surety Development Corp.* v. *Grevas* NO.** The court decided that even though there was bad timing on the part of the construction company in that the house was not finished until 5:30 P.M., there was honest and faithful performance of the contract on its part. There was not complete compliance with the agreement. But there was substantial compliance. Grevas must pay as agreed.

***p. 198 Keser* v. *Chagnon* YES.** The court ruled that Chagnon could break the contract. But it said that, because Chagnon misrepresented his age, damages could be awarded Keser. Those damages would be in the amount of the difference between the original purchase price and the value of the automobile when it was returned.

7 Family and Juvenile Law

***p. 201 Tyrrell's Estate* YES.** Every written will must be signed by the person who made it. The signature must be on the paper on which the will itself is written. In this case the signature on the outside of the envelope was not enough. The signature on a written will is a necessary part of the will. Without it, there is no will.

***p. 208 Balytat* v. *Morris* YES.** The court of appeals found that according to state law, in order for the will giving the entire estate to charity to be valid, it would have had to be made more than six months before death. Since the will was not made before that time, the estate must go to the granddaughter, who was next of kin.

***p. 211 Reed* v. *Reed* YES.** In a unanimous decision the United States Supreme Court declared that the arbitrary preference in favor of males in Section 15-314 of the Idaho Code could not legally stand because the Fourteenth Amendment commands that no state deny the equal protection of the law to any person. Because Section 15-314 provides different treatment on the basis of a person's sex, it is unconstitutional. The law was removed from Idaho's statutes.

***p. 213* In re *Gault* YES.** The United States Supreme Court decided that certain due process rights should be guaranteed in juvenile courts. The rights the Court decided must be guaranteed to juveniles included the following.

1. Notice of the charges made against the accused. This notice must be given in time to allow a defense to be prepared.
2. Representation by a lawyer. If the accused or her/his parents cannot afford to hire a lawyer, then the state must do so.
3. Confrontation and cross-examination of witnesses in court.
4. Right against self-incrimination. The accused must be told that she/he has

---

complete compliance The fulfilling of the terms of a contract in every respect or detail by a party to that contract.

substantial compliance The fulfilling of the essential terms of a contract in accomplishing the purpose of that contract although certain minor details may remain uncompleted.

next of kin Person or persons most closely related to another person by blood; also, in the distribution of an estate after an intestate owner's death, those with a legal right under state laws to share in that estate.

the right to remain silent. Also, the accused must be warned that anything she/he says may be used against her/him in court.

DISSENT: Justice Stewart dissented on the ground that standards for criminal trials should not be used in juvenile proceedings.

***p. 215* In re *Winship* YES.** The United States Supreme Court held that juveniles, like adults, have the constitutional right to proof beyond reasonable doubt when charged with an act that would be a crime when done by an adult. In prosecuting its case against any person accused of a crime, the state must prove "beyond a reasonable doubt" that the defendant is guilty. Without this absolute proof, no person can be convicted of a crime.

DISSENT: Chief Justice Burger and Justice Stewart dissented. They said that juvenile courts were set up in order to provide a less formal means for dealing with young offenders than the criminal courts offered.

8 Judicial Procedures

***p. 242 Hurtado* v. *California* YES.** The Supreme Court decided that the provisions of the Constitution of California's Article I, Section 8, were not unconstitutional. The Court felt that they did not deprive a person of the due process of law. The process of presentment of an information included an examination by a judge. This judge would have had to certify that the defendant was probably guilty. The defendant had a right to the services of a lawyer. She/he also had the right to cross-examine witnesses. Information presentment can result in no final judgment against a person. That person may choose a regular jury trial just as if she/he had been indicted by a grand jury. The decisions of the courts of California were affirmed.

p. 252 Furman* v. *Georgia The Court held that the carrying out of the death sentence *in the three cases before it* would be cruel and unusual punishment. It would be in violation of the Eighth and Fourteenth Amendments.

The Constitution of the United States of America

We the people of the United States, in order to form a more perfect union, establish justice, insure domestic tranquility, provide for the common defense, promote the general welfare, and secure the blessings of liberty to ourselves and our posterity, do ordain and establish this Constitution for the United States of America.

Preamble. This very important part of the Constitution names whom as the final authority? How does Art. VII reinforce this? Who authorized the Articles of Confederation?

ARTICLE I

LEGISLATIVE BRANCH

SECTION 1.

All legislative powers herein granted shall be vested in a Congress of the United States, which shall consist of a Senate and House of Representatives.

CONGRESS

Two houses. If Congress has all legislative power, how can such agencies as the Internal Revenue Service make rules?

SECTION 2.

The House of Representatives shall be composed of members chosen every second year by the people of the several States, and the electors in each State shall have the qualifications requisite for electors of the most numerous branch of the State legislature.

No person shall be a representative who shall not have attained to the age of twenty-five years, and been seven years a citizen of the United States, and who shall not, when elected, be an inhabitant of that State in which he shall be chosen.

Representatives and direct taxes shall be apportioned among the several States which may be included within this Union, according to their respective numbers, which shall be determined by adding to the whole number of free persons, including those bound to service for a term of years, and excluding Indians not taxed, three fifths of all other persons. The actual enumeration shall be made within three years after the first meeting of the Congress of the United States, and within every subsequent term of ten years, in such manner as they shall by law direct. The number of representatives shall not exceed one for every thirty thousand, but each State shall have at least one representative; and until such enumeration shall be made, the State of New Hampshire shall be entitled to choose three, Massachusetts eight, Rhode Island and Providence Plantations one,*

HOUSE OF REPRESENTATIVES

Membership; term; election. Electors = voters. How has this been affected by Amend. 15, 19, 24, and 26? Is two years long enough? too long?

Qualifications. Must a candidate live in the district he wants to represent? What chance of election would he probably have if he did not live there?

Apportionment. "Those bound to service" were indentured. Who were the "three fifths of all others"? Did they pay taxes? Should they have been represented? On what basis? How did Amend. 13 change this?

What is the "enumeration" called today? When was the most recent one taken?

No amendment has changed "one for every thirty thousand," but Congress limits the House to 435. Without that limit, how many members would there be? Each representative represents an average of how many people?

NOTE: Items that have been changed or replaced are underlined.

* Changed by the Fourteenth Amendment

Connecticut five, New York six, New Jersey four, Pennsylvania eight, Delaware one, Maryland six, Virginia ten, North Carolina five, South Carolina five, and Georgia three.

When vacancies happen in the representation from any State, the executive authority thereof shall issue writs of election to fill such vacancies.

The House of Representatives shall choose their speaker and other officers, and shall have the sole power of impeachment.

Vacancies. Why may a governor appoint a Senator but not a representative?

Officers; impeachment. Impeach = accuse of wrongdoing. Who may be impeached (Art. II–4)?

SECTION 3.

The Senate of the United States shall be composed of two senators from each State, chosen by the legislature thereof, for six years; and each senator shall have one vote.*

*Immediately after they shall be assembled in consequence of the first election, they shall be divided as equally as may be into three classes. The seats of the senators of the first class shall be vacated at the expiration of the second year, of the second class at the expiration of the fourth year, and of the third class at the expiration of the sixth year, so that one third may be chosen every second year; and if vacancies happen by resignation, or otherwise, during the recess of the legislature of any State, the executive thereof may make temporary appointments until the next meeting of the legislature, which shall then fill such vacancies.**

No person shall be a senator who shall not have attained to the age of thirty years, and been nine years a citizen of the United States, and who shall not, when elected, be an inhabitant of that State for which he shall be chosen.

The Vice President of the United States shall be president of the Senate, but shall have no vote, unless they be equally divided.

The Senate shall choose their other officers, and also a president pro tempore, in the absence of the Vice President, or when he shall exercise the office of President of the United States.

The Senate shall have the sole power to try all impeachments. When sitting for that purpose, they shall be on oath or affirmation. When the President of the United States is tried, the Chief Justice shall preside: and no person shall be convicted without the concurrence of two thirds of the members present.

* Changed by the Seventeenth Amendment

THE SENATE

Membership; term. Under Amend. 17, who chooses the senators? Since when?

Expiration of term; vacancies. Only one third of the Senate is replaced or re-elected at each election, but each Congress is "new." What are some benefits or drawbacks of not having a totally new Congress each time? A governor may fill a vacancy until his legislature directs a new election. See Amend. 17.

Qualifications. How do the qualifications for senator and representative differ? Why are they different?

Officers. As the Vice President may not be there, the president *pro tempore* acts as Senate president. Senators take daily turns presiding. Only the Vice President may break tie votes.

Impeachment. Note that the Senate acts as a court in impeachment; House appointees prosecute the case.

Judgment in cases of impeachment shall not extend further than to removal from office, and disqualification to hold any office of honor, trust or profit under the United States: but the party convicted shall nevertheless be liable and subject to indictment, trial, judgment and punishment, according to law.

Punishment. What is the only punishment the Senate can give in impeachments? What might the U.S. Attorney General do after a conviction in the Senate?

SECTION 4.

The times, places, and manner of holding elections for senators and representatives shall be prescribed in each State by the legislature thereof; but the Congress may at any time by law make or alter such regulations, except as to the places of choosing senators.

The Congress shall assemble at least once in every year, and such meeting shall be on the first Monday in December, unless they shall by law appoint a different day.*

ELECTIONS

Regulating elections. Remarkably, the first of many election laws was not passed until 1842. It set up election districts.

Assembly. This contrasted with the king's calling and dissolving Parliament at will.

SECTION 5.

Each house shall be the judge of the elections, returns and qualifications of its own members, and a majority of each shall constitute a quorum to do business; but a smaller number may adjourn from day to day, and may be authorized to compel the attendance of absent members, in such manner, and under such penalties as each house may provide.

Each house may determine the rules of its proceedings, punish its members for disorderly behavior, and, with the concurrence of two thirds, expel a member.

Each house shall keep a journal of its proceedings, and from time to time publish the same, excepting such parts as may in their judgment require secrecy; and the yeas and nays of the members of either house on any question shall, at the desire of one fifth of those present, be entered on the journal.

Neither house, during the session of Congress, shall, without the consent of the other, adjourn for more than three days, nor to any other place than that in which the two houses shall be sitting.

RULES AND PROCEDURES

Admitting members; quorum. The election winner must be accepted by the house he is elected to. Research: Sen. Hiram Revels, an interesting case of challenge. Since the power to punish is judicial, it cannot extend outside Congress. Explain.

Journals. The daily *Congressional Record* is the published journal. But since members can and do add to, change, or omit their remarks, no "reliable, accurate journal" exists.

Adjournments. This prevents one house from holding up the work of the other, as in Parliament under Charles II.

SECTION 6.

The senators and representatives shall receive a compensation for their services, to be ascertained by law, and paid out of the Treasury of the United States. They shall in all cases, except treason, felony and breach of the peace, be

PAY, PRIVILEGES, AND LIMITS

Pay; privileges. In 1969, Congress raised top-level salaries, including its own, by 42% to 100%. Research these in an al-

* Changed by the Twentieth Amendment

privileged from arrest during their attendance at the session of their respective houses, and in going to and returning from the same; and for any speech or debate in either house, they shall not be questioned in any other place.

No senator or representative shall, during the time for which he was elected, be appointed to any civil office under the authority of the United States, which shall have been created, or the emoluments thereof shall have been increased during such time; and no person holding any office under the United States shall be a member of either house during his continuance in office.

manac. Safeguarding members from arrest is based on English experience. How does this affect the people?

Limitations. In parliamentary republics, one person can run two or more executive departments. What must an American official do if he wishes to change jobs or get a raise?

SECTION 7.

All bills for raising revenue shall originate in the House of Representatives; but the Senate may propose or concur with amendments as on other bills.

Every bill which shall have passed the House of Representatives and the Senate, shall, before it become a law, be presented to the President of the United States; if he approve he shall sign it, but if not he shall return it, with his objections to that house in which it shall have originated, who shall enter the objections at large on their journal, and proceed to reconsider it. If after such reconsideration two thirds of that house shall agree to pass the bill, it shall be sent, together with the objections, to the other house, by which it shall likewise be reconsidered, and if approved by two thirds of that house, it shall become a law. But in all such cases the votes of both houses shall be determined by yeas and nays, and the names of the persons voting for and against the bill shall be entered on the journal of each house respectively. If any bill shall not be returned by the President within ten days (Sundays excepted) after it shall have been presented to him, the same shall be a law, in like manner as if he had signed it, unless the Congress by their adjournment prevent its return, in which case it shall not be a law.

Every order, resolution, or vote to which the concurrence of the Senate and House of Representatives may be necessary (except on a question of adjournment) shall be presented to the President of the United States; and before the same shall take effect, shall be approved by him, or being disapproved by him, shall be repassed by two thirds of the Senate and House of Representatives, according to the rules and limitations prescribed in the case of a bill.

LEGISLATION

Bills for raising money. In which house must tax bills originate? Why?

Bills into laws. Describe the ways in which the President may veto a bill. When Congress overrides a veto, how large a majority must there be in the House? in the Senate? Which part of this clause is best described as a "pocket veto."

Of what value is the taking and recording of a roll-call vote when Congress overrides a veto?

Veto power. This stops Congress from bypassing a possible veto under the pretense of passing a resolution. Why is a constitutional amendment the only legislation the President need not see?

SECTION 8.

The Congress shall have power to lay and collect taxes, duties, imposts and excises, to pay the debts and provide for the common defense and general welfare of the United States; but all duties, imposts and excises shall be uniform throughout the United States;

To borrow money on the credit of the United States;

To regulate commerce with foreign nations, and among the several States, and with the Indian tribes;

To establish a uniform rule of naturalization, and uniform laws on the subject of bankruptcies through the United States;

To coin money, regulate the value thereof, and of foreign coin, and fix the standard of weights and measures;

To provide for the punishment of counterfeiting the securities and current coin of the United States;

To establish post offices and post roads;

To promote the progress of science and useful arts by securing for limited times to authors and inventors the exclusive right to their respective writings and discoveries;

To constitute tribunals inferior to the Supreme Court;

To define and punish piracies and felonies committed on the high seas, and offenses against the law of nations;

To declare war, grant letters of marque and reprisal, and make rules concerning captures on land and water;

To raise and support armies, but no appropriation of money to that use shall be for a longer term than two years;

To provide and maintain a navy;

To make rules for the government and regulations of the land and naval forces;

To provide for calling forth the militia to execute the laws of the Union, suppress insurrections and repel invasions;

To provide for organizing, arming, and disciplining the militia, and for governing such part of them as may be employed in the service of the United States, reserving to the States respectively the appointment of the officers, and the authority of training the militia according to the discipline prescribed by Congress;

To exercise exclusive legislation in all cases whatsoever, over such district (not exceeding ten miles square) as may, by cession of particular States and the acceptance of Congress, become the seat of the government of the United States, and to exercise like authority over all places pur-

POWERS OF CONGRESS

Taxes; defense; welfare. Research: "pork barrel." **Borrowing.** Jefferson called bonds "taxation without representation." Explain. **Commerce.** The tribes are likened to foreign nations. What is their situation now?

Naturalization; bankruptcy. If states say who may vote, why not who may be a citizen?

Money; standards. How is the guarantee that your money is real a kind of freedom? There are no official U.S. standards of weights and measures.

Copyrights; patents. How do these promote progress? Are they fair? Explain.

Courts; law. Highjacking = piracy. What laws do you recommend to control it?

War; armed forces. The President can send troops into foreign action without a declaration of war by Congress. How can Congress' "power of the purse" curb such actions? **Navy.** Congress authorized a navy only when war with France was likely in 1798. **Militia** = National Guard, under command of governors until the President nationalizes them. **Captures.** In 1849 the Supreme Court ruled that the U.S. may not gain territory or property by right of conquest.

National capital. Maryland and Virginia both gave land for a national capital. Virginia took back its part in 1846.

chased by the consent of the legislature of the State in which the same shall be, for the erection of forts, magazines, arsenals, dockyards, and other needful buildings; and

To make all laws which shall be necessary and proper for carrying into execution the foregoing powers, and all other powers vested by this Constitution in the government of the United States, or in any department or officer thereof.

SECTION 9.

The migration or importation of such persons as any of the States now existing shall think proper to admit, shall not be prohibited by the Congress prior to the year one thousand eight hundred and eight, but a tax or duty may be imposed on such importation, not exceeding ten dollars for each person.

The privilege of the writ of habeas corpus *shall not be suspended, unless when in cases of rebellion or invasion the public safety may require it.*

No bill of attainder or ex post facto law shall be passed.

No capitation, or other direct, tax shall be laid, unless in proportion to the census or enumeration herein before directed to be taken.*

No tax or duty shall be laid on articles exported from any State.

No preference shall be given by any regulation of commerce or revenue to the ports of one State over those of another; nor shall vessels bound to, or from, one State be obliged to enter, clear, or pay duties in another.

No money shall be drawn from the Treasury, but in consequence of appropriations made by law; and a regular statement and account of the receipts and expenditures of all public money shall be published from time to time.

No title of nobility shall be granted by the United States: and no person holding any office of profit or trust under them, shall, without the consent of the Congress, accept of any present, emolument, office, or title of any kind whatever, from any king, prince, or foreign State.

SECTION 10.

No State shall enter into any treaty, alliance, or confederation; grant letters of marque and reprisal; coin money; emit bills of credit; make anything but gold and silver coin and tender in payment of debts, pass any bill of attainder,

* Changed by the Sixteenth Amendment

Elastic clause. This is the famous battleground for contenders over how strong the central government shall be.

FORBIDDEN POWERS

This was new! Kings were often curbed, but never a legislature. **Slavery.** In 1794 exports were banned; imports continued to 1865, despite the law of 1808.

Habeas corpus = you have the person; writ = written order. The writ's addressee must bring the prisoner promptly before the judge who issued the writ and who will decide if detention is legal. With right to counsel (Amend. 6), this clause ensures due process. Who can suspend this right? When? Why is it the most basic of civil rights? What others can be exercised without it? *Ex post facto* laws, passed after the act, make an innocent act a crime, make a lesser crime worse, increase the penalty, change rules of evidence to ensure conviction, and/or take away legal protections the accused would otherwise have had. Research: "due process of law."

POWERS FORBIDDEN STATES

With Secs. 8 and 9, this aims to help the States operate effectively without conflict among themselves or with the federal

ex post facto law, or law impairing the obligation of contracts, or grant any title of nobility.

No State shall, without the consent of the Congress, lay any imposts or duties on imports or exports, except what may be absolutely necessary for executing its inspection laws: and the net produce of all duties and imposts laid by any State on imports or exports, shall be for the use of the Treasury of the United States; and all such laws shall be subject to the revision and control of the Congress.

No State shall, without the consent of Congress, lay any duty of tonnage, keep troops, or ships of war in time of peace, enter into any agreement or compact with another State, or with a foreign power, or engage in war, unless actually invaded, or in such imminent danger as will not admit of delay.

government. Study these sections to understand which powers are granted to or withheld from Congress, the States, or both. **Prohibited actions.** The outstanding part of this clause is "impairing the obligation of contracts." Research: contract. In hard times, Confederation legislatures often postponed payments of any debts. How would this affect interstate commerce? How else might State action affect interstate commerce?

ARTICLE II

THE EXECUTIVE BRANCH

SECTION 1.

The executive power shall be vested in a President of the United States of America. He shall hold his office during the term of four years, and, together with the Vice President chosen for the same term, be elected as follows:

Each State shall appoint, in such manner as the legislature thereof may direct, a number of electors, equal to the whole number of senators and representatives to which the State may be entitled in the Congress: but no senator or representative, or person holding an office of trust or profit under the United States, shall be appointed an elector.

The electors shall meet in their respective States, and vote by ballot for two persons, of whom one at least shall not be an inhabitant of the same State with themselves. And they shall make a list of all the persons voted for, and of the number of votes for each; which they shall sign and certify, and transmit sealed to the seat of the government of the United States, directed to the president of the Senate. The president of the Senate shall, in the presence of the Senate and House of Representatives, open all the certificates, and the votes shall then be counted. The person having the greatest number of votes shall be the President, if such number be a majority of the whole number of electors appointed; and if there be more than one who have such

PRESIDENT, VICE PRESIDENT

Terms. There was no executive under the old Articles of Confederation. Should the President's term be longer? Explain. **Presidential electors.** Candidates for electors are chosen in various ways from State to State. All States determine electors by popular vote.

Electing executives. This entire paragraph was superseded by Amend. 12, ratified in 1804, which required electors to vote separately for President and Vice President. The amendment was seen to be necessary in 1800, when Thomas Jefferson and Aaron Burr were tied for first place, thus throwing the election into the House of Representatives. Only on the 36th ballot did Jefferson win. How-

*majority, and have an equal number of votes, then the House of Representatives shall immediately choose by ballot one of them for President; and if no person have a majority, then from the five highest on the list the said house shall in like manner choose the President. But in choosing the President, the votes shall be taken by States, the representation from each State having one vote; a quorum for this purpose shall consist of a member or members from two thirds of the States, and a majority of all the States shall be necessary to a choice. In every case, after the choice of the President, the person having the greatest number of votes of the electors shall be the Vice President. But if there should remain two or more who have equal votes, the Senate shall choose from them by ballot the Vice President.**

ever, Amend. 12 does not alter the fact that the people of the U.S. do not elect the President and Vice President but are required to elect others to do it for them.

The Congress may determine the time of choosing the electors, and the day on which they shall give their votes; which day shall be the same throughout the United States.

Election day. By law, the election is held on the Tuesday after the first Monday in November every fourth year from 1788. The day on which the electors (Electoral College) meet to vote is the Monday after the second Wednesday in December.

No person except a natural-born citizen, or a citizen of the United States, at the time of the adoption of this Constitution, shall be eligible to the office of President; neither shall any person be eligible to that office who shall not have attained to the age of thirty-five years, and been fourteen years a resident within the United States.

Presidential qualifications. Except for the first (why?), the President must be a native. Washington was a native, but many well-qualified men of his era were not. Research: which signers of the Constitution were not natives? **Disability.** Amend. 25, ratified in 1967, enlarges upon this clause.

In case of the removal of the President from office, or of his death, resignation, or inability to discharge the powers and duties of the said office, the same shall devolve on the Vice President, and the Congress may by law provide for the case of removal, death, resignation, or inability, both of the President and Vice President, declaring what officer shall then act as President, and such offer shall act accordingly, until the disability be removed, or a President shall be elected.

The President shall, at stated times, receive for his services a compensation, which shall neither be increased nor diminished during the period for which he shall have been elected, and he shall not receive within that period any other emolument from the United States, or any of them.

Salary. The intent is to avoid his catering to Congress or to the state governments for a raise or gifts.

Before he enter on the execution of his office, he shall take the following oath or affirmation:—"I do solemnly swear (or affirm) that I will faithfully execute the office of President of the United States, and will to the best of my

Oath of office. "Or affirm respects Moses' commandment and Jesus' words in Matthew: "Swear not at all [say only] Yea

* Changed by the Twelfth Amendment

ability, preserve, protect and defend the Constitution of the United States."

. . . Nay . . . more than these come of the evil one."

SECTION 2.

The President shall be commander in chief of the army and navy of the United States, and of the militia of the several States, when called into the actual service of the United States; he may require the opinion, in writing, of the principal officer in each of the executive departments, upon any subject relating to the duties of their respective offices, and he shall have power to grant reprieves and pardons for offenses against the United States, except in cases of impeachment.

PRESIDENTIAL POWERS

Military powers; reprieves, pardons. Executive departments accounted for 95% of the 3 million federal civilian employees in the early 1970's. How is the restriction on pardons part of checks and balances? How can Congress control the commander in chief?

He shall have power, by and with the advice and consent of the Senate, to make treaties, provided two thirds of the senators present concur; and he shall nominate, and by and with the advice and consent of the Senate, shall appoint ambassadors, other public ministers and consuls, judges of the Supreme Court, and all other officers of the United States, whose appointments are not herein otherwise provided for, and which shall be established by law: but the Congress may by law vest the appointment of such inferior officers, as they think proper, in the President alone, in the courts of law, or in the heads of departments.

Treaties; appointments. Who are some appointed officers not named in the Constitution? Research: some instances when the Senate refused its consent. How are checks and balances built into this clause?

The President shall have power to fill up all vacancies that may happen during the recess of the Senate, by granting commissions which shall expire at the end of their next session.

Filling vacancies; interim appointments. How does this clause exemplify checks and balances?

SECTION 3.

He shall from time to time give to the Congress information of the state of the Union, and recommend to their consideration such measures as he shall judge necessary and expedient; he may, on extraordinary occasions, convene both houses, or either of them, and in case of disagreement between them with respect to the time of adjournment, he may adjourn them to such time as he shall think proper; he shall receive ambassadors and other public ministers; he shall take care that the laws be faithfully executed, and shall commission all the officers of the United States.

PRESIDENT AND CONGRESS

Other duties. The President makes one or more reports to Congress soon after it meets each year. Usually he gives a State of the Union message to a meeting of both houses.

SECTION 4.

The President, Vice President, and all civil officers of the United States, shall be removed from office on impeach-

IMPEACHMENT

Removal of officers. Which elected officers may not be im-

ment for, and conviction of, treason, bribery, or other high crimes and misdemeanors.

peached? Why? Which appointed officers?

ARTICLE III

JUDICIAL BRANCH

SECTION 1.

The judicial power of the United States shall be vested in one Supreme Court, and in such inferior courts as the Congress may from time to time ordain and establish. The judges, both of the Supreme and inferior courts, shall hold their offices during good behavior, and shall, at stated times, receive for their services, a compensation which shall not be diminished during their continuance in office.

FEDERAL COURTS

Judicial power; federal judges. These judges are the only U.S. officers to hold lifetime jobs; their salaries cannot be reduced. How do these two facts help the parties in a lawsuit?

SECTION 2.

The judicial power shall extend to all cases, in law and equity, arising under this Constitution, the laws of the United States, and treaties made, or which shall be made, under their authority;—to all cases affecting ambassadors, other public ministers and consuls;—to all cases of admiralty and maritime jurisdiction;—to controversies to which the United States shall be a party;—to controversies between two or more States;—between a State and citizens of another State;—between citizens of different States,—between citizens of the same State claiming lands under grants of different States, and between a State, or the citizens thereof, and foreign States, citizens or subjects.

In all cases affecting ambassadors, other public ministers and consuls, and those in which a State shall be party, the Supreme Court shall have original jurisdiction. In all the other cases before mentioned, the Supreme Court shall have appellate jurisdiction, both as to law and fact, with such exceptions, and under such regulations as the Congress shall make.

The trial of all crimes, except in cases of impeachment, shall be by jury; and such trial shall be held in the State where the said crimes shall have been committed; but when not committed within any State, the trial shall be at such place or places as the Congress may by law have directed.

FEDERAL JURISDICTION

Federal cases. How do federal court cases differ from State court cases? In 1798, Amend. 11 stopped anyone from suing a State in federal court. Equity, a judicial method of seeing that justice is done when a law causes specific injustice or hardship, is found only where Anglo-American law prevails—Americans traveling or residing in other countries, beware!

Supreme Court jurisdiction. If a defendant objects to a court verdict, he may appeal to the next higher court. The Supreme Court is the highest U.S. court of appeals.

Jury trials. Amend. 5, 6, and 7 add further detail to the right of trial by jury in the State where the crime occurred.

SECTION 3.

Treason against the United States shall consist only in levying war against them, or in adhering to their enemies,

TREASON

Definition. A professor said he hoped the Communists would

giving them aid and comfort. No person shall be convicted of treason unless on the testimony of two witnesses to the same overt act, or on confession in open court.

The Congress shall have power to declare the punishment of treason, but no attainder of treason shall work corruption of blood, or forfeiture except during the life of the person attainted.

ARTICLE IV

SECTION 1.

Full faith and credit shall be given in each State to the public acts, records, and judicial proceedings of every other State. And the Congress may by general laws prescribe the manner in which such acts, records, and proceedings shall be proved, and the effect thereof.

SECTION 2.

The citizens of each State shall be entitled to all privileges and immunities of citizens in the several States.

A person charged in any State with treason, felony, or other crime, who shall flee from justice, and be found in another State, shall on demand of the executive authority of the State from which he fled, be delivered up to be removed to the State having jurisdiction of the crime.

*No person held to service or labor in the State, under the laws thereof, escaping into another, shall, in consequence of any law or regulation therein, be discharged from such service or labor, but shall be delivered up on claim of the party to whom such service or labor may be due.**

SECTION 3.

New States may be admitted by the Congress into this Union; but no new State shall be formed or erected within the jurisdiction of any other State; nor any State be formed by the junction of two or more States, or parts of States, without the consent of the legislatures of the States concerned as well as of the Congress.

The Congress shall have power to dispose of and make all needful rules and regulations respecting the territory or other property belonging to the United States; and nothing in this Constitution shall be so construed as to prejudice any claims of the United States, or of any particular State.

* Changed by the Thirteenth Amendment

win the Vietnam war. Was he a traitor? What about war protesters? spies?

Punishment. Treason penalties include fines, prison, and death. In old times, the State took a traitor's property.

THE STATES

RELATIONS OF THE STATES

Full faith and credit. Will an Iowa marriage be legal in Utah? If Idaho acquits a man of a specific crime, can Oregon try him for it?

DUTIES OF STATE TO STATE

Citizens' privileges. A State may not discriminate unreasonably against nonresidents. **Fugitives.** Returning fugitives is extradition. Why might a governor refuse extradition?

Persons held to service. This provision refers to runaway slaves. How does this clause show that strong disagreements already existed over slavery?

ADMISSION OF NEW STATES

Formation; admission. Can New York City become a new State, as many wish? How? Which States were formed from others?

Territories; federal property. Congress can either govern a territory directly or authorize it to set up a legislature and a court system.

SECTION 4.

The United States shall guarantee to every State in this Union a republican form of government, and shall protect each of them against invasion; and on application of the legislature, or of the executive (when the legislature cannot be convened) against domestic violence.

PROTECTION OF THE STATES

Guarantees. What does "republic" tell about how representatives are chosen or whom they represent? Explain the phrase *democratic republic*.

ARTICLE V

The Congress, whenever two thirds of both houses shall deem it necessary, shall propose amendments to this Constitution, or, on the application of the legislatures of two thirds of the several States, shall call a convention for proposing amendments, which, in either case, shall be valid to all intents and purposes, as part of this Constitution, when ratified by the legislatures of three fourths of the several States, or by conventions in three fourths thereof, as the one or the other mode of ratification may be proposed by the Congress; provided [*that no amendment which may be made prior to the year one thousand eight hundred and eight shall in any manner affect the first and fourth clauses in the ninth section of the first article, and*] *that no State, without its consent, shall be deprived of its equal suffrage in the Senate.*

AMENDMENTS

Amending the Constitution. In another world's first, a government set up ways in which it could be changed without violence. Describe two ways in which the Constitution may be amended. (*Note:* The Supreme Court says that "two thirds of both houses" means only members present, not entire membership.) What parts could not be changed before 1808? When were these parts changed? How?

ARTICLE VI

All debts contracted and engagements entered into, before the adoption of this Constitution, shall be as valid against the United States under this Constitution, as under the Confederation.

This Constitution, and the laws of the United States which shall be made in pursuance thereof; and all treaties made, or which shall be made, under the authority of the United States, shall be the supreme law of the land; and the judges in every State shall be bound thereby, anything in the Constitution or laws of any State to the contrary notwithstanding.

The senators and representatives before mentioned, and the members of the several State legislatures, and all executive and judicial officers, both of the United States, and of the several States, shall be bound by oath or affirmation to support this Constitution; but no religious test shall ever be

GENERAL PROVISIONS

Confederation debts. The Constitution guarantees payment of all debts contracted under the Articles of Confederation.

Supreme law. Why are treaties part of the supreme law of the land? How has the U.S. kept its treaties with the Indians? Research: what those treaties promised the Indians.

Oath; religious test. How does State officials' support of the Constitution protect everyone? Banning religious tests was a first in world law. Was that a

required as a qualification to any office or public trust under the United States.

good idea? Why were religious tests banned?

ARTICLE VII

The ratification of the conventions of nine States shall be sufficient for the establishment of this Constitution between the States so ratifying the same.

Done in Convention by the unanimous consent of the States present the seventeenth day of September in the year of our Lord one thousand seven hundred and eighty-seven, and of the independence of the United States of America the twelfth. In witness whereof we have hereunto subscribed our names.

George Washington, President
(VIRGINIA)

MASSACHUSETTS
Nathaniel Gorham
Rufus King

NEW YORK
Alexander Hamilton

GEORGIA
William Few
Abraham Baldwin

DELAWARE
George Read
Gunning Bedford
John Dickinson
Richard Bassett
Jacob Broom

VIRGINIA
John Blair
James Madison

PENNSYLVANIA
Benjamin Franklin
Thomas Mifflin
Robert Morris
George Clymer
Thomas FitzSimons
Jared Ingersoll
James Wilson
Gouvernor Morris

NEW HAMPSHIRE
John Langdon
Nicholas Gilman

NEW JERSEY
William Livingston
David Brearley
William Paterson
Jonathan Dayton

CONNECTICUT
William Samuel Johnson
Roger Sherman

NORTH CAROLINA
William Blount
Richard Dobbs Spaight
Hugh Williamson

SOUTH CAROLINA
John Rutledge
Charles Cotesworth Pinckney
Charles Pinckney
Pierce Butler

MARYLAND
James McHenry
Daniel of St. Thomas Jenifer
Daniel Carroll

RATIFICATION

Conventions, 1787–1790

Del.	7 Dec 87	Unanimous
Pa.	12 Dec 87	46–23
N.J.	18 Dec 87	Unanimous
Ga.	2 Jan 88	Unanimous
Conn.	9 Jan 88	128–40
Mass.	6 Feb 88	187–168 *
Md.	28 Apr 88	63–11
S.C.	27 May 88	149–73
N.H.	21 Jun 88	57–46 *
Va.	25 Jun 88	87–76 *
N.Y.	26 Jul 88	30–27 *
N.C.	21 Nov 89	187–77
R.I.	29 May 90	34–22

* Strongly urged Bill of Rights

FIRST AMENDMENT—1791

Congress shall make no law respecting an establishment of religion, or prohibiting the free exercise thereof; or

Religion; speech; assembly. Some other democracies tax everyone to support religion. Why doesn't the U.S.?

abridging the freedom of speech, or of the press; or the right of the people peaceably to assemble, and to petition the government for a redress of grievances.

SECOND AMENDMENT—1791

A well-regulated militia, being necessary to the security of a free State, the right of the people to keep and bear arms, shall not be infringed.

Right to bear arms. Are handguns or rifles of greater value to a militia? If you were a dictator, what would you do about privately owned firearms? Why?

THIRD AMENDMENT—1791

No soldier shall, in time of peace, be quartered in any house, without the consent of the owner, nor in time of war, but in a manner to be prescribed by law.

Housing troops. Explain how quartering soldiers in private homes could be a method of controlling the nation's civilian population.

FOURTH AMENDMENT—1791

The right of the people to be secure in their persons, houses, papers, and effects, against unreasonable searches and seizures, shall not be violated, and no warrants shall issue, but upon probable cause, supported by oath or affirmation, and particularly describing the place to be searched, and the persons or things to be seized.

Unlawful search. Do you think that the use of electronic "snooping" devices, including wiretapping, by the police violates a person's right to be "secure . . . against unreasonable searches"? Explain your answer.

FIFTH AMENDMENT—1791

No person shall be held to answer for a capital or otherwise infamous crime, unless on a presentment or indictment of a grand jury, except in cases arising in the land or naval forces, or in the militia, when in actual service in time of war or public danger; nor shall any person be subject for the same offense to be twice put in jeopardy of life or limb; nor shall be compelled in any criminal case to be a witness against himself, nor be deprived of life, liberty, or property, without due process of law; nor shall private property be taken for public use without just compensation.

Rights of accused. Jeopardy begins as a jury is sworn, and ends on acquittal; if jury can't agree, if a mistrial occurs, or if conviction is reversed on appeal, **due process** (= legal fair play) begins anew. Only Anglo-American law assumes accused is not guilty until so proved and stops anyone's being forced to witness against oneself. Each step of proof must protect accused's rights.

SIXTH AMENDMENT—1791

In all criminal prosecutions, the accused shall enjoy the right to a speedy and public trial, by an impartial jury of the State and district wherein the crime shall have been committed, which district shall have been previously ascertained by law, and to be informed of the nature and cause

Criminal procedure. There are so many cases that years may elapse between indictment and trial. Should there be a cut-off time when, if there has been no trial, the indictment is dismissed and the accused is free?

of the accusation; to be confronted with the witnesses against him; to have compulsory process for obtaining witnesses in his favor, and to have the assistance of counsel for his defense.

Why should the accused have the aid of counsel? Explain the proverb: He who is his own lawyer has a fool for a client.

SEVENTH AMENDMENT—1791

In suits at common law, where the value in controversy shall exceed twenty dollars, the right of trial by jury shall be preserved, and no fact tried by a jury shall be otherwise reexamined in any court of the United States, than according to the rules of the common law.

EIGHTH AMENDMENT—1791

Excessive bail shall not be required, nor excessive fines imposed, nor cruel and unusual punishments inflicted.

Bail, penalties. England forbade bails and fines so high as to deprive one of one's home or means of livelihood. Is death a "cruel punishment"?

NINTH AMENDMENT—1791

The enumeration in the Constitution of certain rights shall not be construed to deny or disparage others retained by the people.

People's rights retained. This amendment answers those who were against aiding a bill of rights. What must their arguments have been?

TENTH AMENDMENT—1791

The powers not delegated to the United States by the Constitution, nor prohibited by it to the States are reserved to the States respectively, or to the people.

Reserved powers. This guarantees the pre-Constitutional sovereignty of the States. Why was this important to the early Republicans?

ELEVENTH AMENDMENT—1795

The judicial power of the United States shall not be construed to extend to any suit in law or equity, commenced or prosecuted against one of the United States, by citizens of another State, or by citizens or subjects of any foreign State.

Suing States. This amends Art. III–2. Any nonresident must sue a State in that State's own courts, not in federal or other out-of-state courts.

TWELFTH AMENDMENT—1804

The electors shall meet in their respective States, and vote by ballot for President and Vice President, one of whom, at least, shall not be an inhabitant of the same State with themselves; they shall name in their ballots the person voted for as Vice President, and they shall make distinct lists of all persons voted for as President and of all persons voted for as Vice President, and of the number of votes for

Separate election of President and Vice President. Must an elector vote for the candidates who win the popular election in his district? This amends Art. II–1–c. Amend. 20 changes March 4 to January 20, and tells what to do if neither a President nor a Vice President has

each, which lists they shall sign and certify, and transmit sealed to the seat of government of the United States, directed to the president of the Senate;—The president of the Senate shall, in the presence of the Senate and House of Representatives, open all the certificates and the votes shall then be counted;—The person having the greatest number of votes for President shall be the President, if such number be a majority of the whole number of electors appointed; and if no person have such majority, then from the persons having the highest numbers not exceeding three on the list of those voted for as President, the House of Representatives shall choose immediately, by ballot, the President. But in choosing the President, the votes shall be taken by States, the representation from each State having one vote; a quorum for this purpose shall consist of a member or members from two thirds of the States, and a majority of all the States shall be necessary to a choice. And if the House of Representatives shall not choose a President whenever the right of choice shall devolve upon them, before the fourth day of March next following, then the Vice President shall act as President, as in the case of the death or other constitutional disability of the President. The person having the greatest number of votes as Vice President shall be the Vice President, if such number be a majority of the whole number of electors appointed, and if the person have a majority, then from the two highest numbers on the list, the Senate shall choose the Vice President; a quorum for the purpose shall consist of two thirds of the whole number of senators and a majority of the whole number shall be necessary to a choice. But no person constitutionally ineligible to the office of President shall be eligible to that of Vice President of the United States.*

been chosen by inauguration day.

THIRTEENTH AMENDMENT—1865

SECTION 1.

Neither slavery nor involuntary servitude, except as a punishment for crime whereof the party shall have been duly convicted, shall exist within the United States, or any place subject to their jurisdiction.

SECTION 2.

Congress shall have power to enforce this article by appropriate legislation.

Slavery prohibited. Some laws passed to enforce this amendment deal with peonage, under which a person in debt to another must work without pay until the debt is "worked out." Isn't this an old-fashioned idea that no longer applies to anyone? If you don't think so, explain.

* Changed by the Twentieth Amendment

FOURTEENTH AMENDMENT—1868

SECTION 1.

All persons born or naturalized in the United States, and subject to the jurisdiction thereof, are citizens of the United States and of the State wherein they reside. No State shall make or enforce any law which shall abridge the privileges or immunities of citizens of the United States; nor shall any State deprive any person of life, liberty, or property, without due process of law; nor deny to any person within its jurisdiction the equal protection of the laws.

Citizens and the States. This, with the Preamble and Art. VII, reinforces the idea that the foremost political relationship is between the people and the federal government, which the people authorize. Before the Civil War, all States, not just southern ones, restricted citizenship to whites. How would States' Righters feel about this amendment?

SECTION 2.

Representatives shall be apportioned among the several States according to their respective numbers, counting the whole number of persons in each State, excluding Indians not taxed. But when the right to vote at any election for the choice of electors for President and Vice President of the United States, representatives in Congress, the executive and judicial officers of a State, or the members of the legislature thereof, is denied to any of the male inhabitants of such State, being twenty-one years of age, and citizens of the United States, or in any way abridged, except for participation in rebellion, or other crime, the basis of representation therein shall be reduced in the proportion which the number of such male citizens shall bear to the whole number of male citizens twenty-one years of age in such State.

Apportionment. This amendment adds to Art. I–2–c by saying that if a State denies the vote to any group, that State's delegation in Congress shall be reduced. If such reduction never took place in a State that denied blacks the vote for a hundred years, were the senators and representatives of that State legally present in Congress? (*Note:* Courts refuse to make decisions on this "political" question. Congress has never challenged a member for being elected under discriminatory laws or situations.)

SECTION 3.

No person shall be a senator or representative in Congress, or elector of President and Vice President, or hold any office, civil or military, under the United States, or under any State, who, having previously taken an oath, as a member of Congress, or as an officer of the United States, or as a member of any State legislature, or as an executive or judicial officer of any State, to support the Constitution of the United States, shall have engaged in insurrection or rebellion against the same, or given aid or comfort to the enemies thereof. But Congress may by a vote of two thirds of each house, remove such disability.

Dealing with rebels. This section denies the privilege of serving in any public office to any former officeholder who took part in the rebellion of the 1860's (See Art. VII.) Congress removed the disability in 1898 so that former Confederate officers could serve in the Spanish-American War.

SECTION 4.

The validity of the public debt of the United States, authorized by law, including debts incurred for payment of

Civil War debt. The Confederate states sold bonds and issued paper money. Can any of those

pensions and bounties for services in suppressing insurrection or rebellion, shall not be questioned. But neither the United States nor any State shall assume or pay any debt or obligation incurred in aid of insurrection or rebellion against the United States, or any claim for the loss or emancipation of any slave; but all such debts, obligations and claims shall be held illegal and void.

former Confederate states pay off those bonds or redeem that money today? Explain your answer. (*Note:* In this section is the only use of the word *slave* in the Constitution.)

SECTION 5.

The Congress shall have power to enforce, by appropriate legislation, the provisions of this article.

FIFTEENTH AMENDMENT—1870

Right to vote. This third and last Reconstruction amendment was meant to guard the people against the misuse of State power. Look up "Jim Crow laws" and "Grandfather clause" to see how some States tried to evade this amendment.

SECTION 1.

The right of citizens of the United States to vote shall not be denied or abridged by the United States or by any State on account of race, color, or previous condition of servitude.

SECTION 2.

The Congress shall have power to enforce this article by appropriate legislation.

SIXTEENTH AMENDMENT—1913

Income taxes. This amendment gets around Art. I and its requirement for equal apportionment of taxes.

The Congress shall have power to lay and collect taxes on incomes, from whatever source derived, without apportionment among the several States, and without regard to any census or enumeration.

SEVENTEENTH AMENDMENT—1913

Direct election of senators. Corruption in state legislatures and deadlocked votes often allowed seats to remain vacant for long periods. How was this harmful to the people of the State?

The Senate of the United States shall be composed of two senators from each State, elected by the people thereof, for six years; and each senator shall have one vote. The electors in each State shall have the qualifications requisite for electors of the most numerous branch of the State legislatures.

When vacancies happen in the representation of any State in the Senate, the executive authority of such State shall issue writs of election to fill such vacancies: Provided, that the legislature of any State may empower the executive thereof to make temporary appointments until the people fill the vacancies by election as the legislature may direct.

EIGHTEENTH AMENDMENT *—1919

SECTION 1.

After one year from the ratification of this article the manufacture, sale, or transportation of intoxicating liquors within, the importation thereof into, or the exportation thereof from the United States and all territory subject to the jurisdiction thereof for beverage purposes is hereby prohibited.

SECTION 2.

The Congress and the several States shall have concurrent power to enforce this article by appropriate legislation.

SECTION 3.

This article shall be inoperative unless it shall have been ratified as an amendment to the Constitution by the legislatures of the several States, as provided in the Constitution, within seven years from the date of the submission hereof to the States by the Congress.

Prohibition. Forbidding the sale of intoxicating liquors was first proposed in the mid-nineteenth century. The Prohibition party was organized in 1869. By 1906, 18 states had at one time or another adopted prohibition, though only a few still retained it. The amendment resulted from the efforts of temperance organizations such as the Woman's Christian Temperance Union and the Anti-Saloon League.

This was the first amendment to include a time limit for ratification. Up to this time, about 1,500 proposed amendments had been sent to the States. How many had been approved?

NINETEENTH AMENDMENT—1920

SECTION 1.

The right of citizens of the United States to vote shall not be denied or abridged by the United States or by any State on account of sex.

SECTION 2.

Congress shall have power, by appropriate legislation, to enforce the provisions of this article.

Women's suffrage. Suffrage = right to vote. Women's votes were not new in the U.S. Women had voted in Wyoming since 1869; Colorado, 1893; Utah and Idaho, 1896; Washington, 1910. Montana sent Jeannette Rankin to the House in 1916, four years before this amendment went into effect.

TWENTIETH AMENDMENT—1933

SECTION 1.

The terms of the President and Vice President shall end at noon on the 20th day of January, and the terms of sena-

Terms of President, Congress. One big change made by this amendment was that Congress was already in session when the President took office. Thus, the

* Repealed by the Twenty-first Amendment

tors and representatives at noon on the 3d day of January, of the years in which such terms would have ended if this article had not been ratified; and the terms of their successors shall then begin.

SECTION 2.

The Congress shall assemble at least once in every year, and such meeting shall begin at noon on the 3d day in January, unless they shall by law appoint a different day.

SECTION 3.

If, at the time fixed for the beginning of the term of the President, the President-elect shall have died, the Vice President-elect shall become President. If a President shall not have been chosen before the time fixed for the beginning of his term, or if the President-elect shall have failed to qualify, then the Vice President-elect shall act as President until a President shall have qualified; and the Congress may by law provide for the case wherein neither a President-elect nor a Vice President-elect shall have qualified, declaring who shall then act as President, or the manner in which one who is to act shall be selected, and such persons shall act accordingly until a President or Vice President shall have qualified.

SECTION 4.

The Congress may by law provide for the case of the death of any of the persons from whom the House of Representatives may choose a President whenever the right of choice shall have devolved upon them, and for the case of the death of any of the persons from whom the Senate may choose a Vice President whenever the right of choice shall have devolved upon them.

SECTION 5.

Sections 1 and 2 shall take effect on the 15th day of October following the ratification of this article.

SECTION 6.

This article shall be inoperative unless it shall have been ratified as an amendment to the Constitution by the legislatures of three fourths of the several States within seven years from the date of its submission.

outgoing President would no longer have to call a special session for the Senate to confirm new Cabinet appointments. The time between election and the beginning of terms was shortened by about one fourth of a year. What developments had made this possible as well as desirable?

This amends Amend. 12 by providing for the failure of both the President-elect and the Vice President-elect to qualify and for the possibility of deaths among candidates when the Electoral College has failed to elect a President and Vice President.

TWENTY-FIRST AMENDMENT—1933

SECTION 1.

The eighteenth article of amendment to the Constitution of the United States is hereby repealed.

SECTION 2.

The transportation or importation into any State, territory, or possession of the United States for delivery or use therein of intoxicating liquors, in violation of the laws thereof, is hereby prohibited.

SECTION 3.

This article shall be inoperative unless it shall have been ratified as an amendment to the Constitution by conventions in the several States, as provided in the Constitution, within seven years from the date of submission hereof to the States by the Congress.

Prohibition repealed; local option guaranteed. The Prohibition Amendment, passed 13 years earlier, had been widely violated. It had resulted in bootlegging—the illegal manufacture and sale of intoxicating beverages. Organized gangs had taken over the business of supplying illegal liquor, with a great rise in crime. The amendment repealing prohibition was swiftly ratified. But states and communities still have the option to prohibit the sale of alcoholic beverages within their boundaries.

TWENTY-SECOND AMENDMENT—1951

No person shall be elected to the office of the President more than twice, and no person who has held the office of President, or acted as President, for more than two years of a term to which some other person was elected President shall be elected to the office of the President more than once.

But this Article shall not apply to any person holding the office of President when this Article was proposed by the Congress, and shall not prevent any person who may be holding the office of President, or acting as President, during the term within which this Article becomes operative from holding the office of President or acting as President during the remainder of such term.

Two-term limit for Presidents. No President sought a third term until Franklin D. Roosevelt did so in 1940. Amend. 22 came about largely because Roosevelt broke this unwritten tradition. Roosevelt, a Democrat, was elected not only to a third term but to a fourth. When the Republicans gained control of Congress a few years later, they introduced this amendment. Note that it was worded so as not to apply to Harry S. Truman, the President at the time that it was proposed and adopted.

TWENTY-THIRD AMENDMENT—1961

SECTION 1.

The District constituting the seat of government of the United States shall appoint in such manner as the Congress may direct:

A number of electors of President and Vice President equal to the whole number of senators and representatives in Congress to which the District would be entitled if it

Presidential vote for D.C. When the Constitution was drawn up, there was no District of Columbia. The right to choose electors for President and Vice President was granted only to the states. Amend. 23 finally gave the citizens of the District of Columbia the same

were a State, but in no event more than the least populous State; they shall be in addition to those appointed by the States, but they shall be considered, for the purposes of the election of President and Vice President, to be electors appointed by a State; and they shall meet in the District and perform such duties as provided by the twelfth article of amendment.

SECTION 2.

The Congress shall have power to enforce this article by appropriate legislation.

rights in presidential elections that the citizens of the states had always possessed.

TWENTY-FOURTH AMENDMENT—1964

Poll tax. *Poll* is an old German word for head. A poll tax is one an individual pays just for existing.

SECTION 1.

The right of citizens of the United States to vote in any primary or other election for President or Vice President, for electors for President or Vice President, or for senator or representative in Congress, shall not be denied or abridged by the United States or any state by reason of failure to pay any poll tax or other tax.

SECTION 2.

The Congress shall have power to enforce this article by appropriate legislation.

TWENTY-FIFTH AMENDMENT—1967

Presidential succession. When the Vice President should take over the President's duties in case of disability had never been defined. Some Presidents have had private agreements; others have not. But the numerous illnesses of Dwight Eisenhower in the 1950's and the tragic death of J. F. Kennedy in 1963 were behind the movement that resulted in this amendment.

SECTION 1.

In case of the removal of the President from office or his death or resignation, the Vice President shall become President.

SECTION 2.

Whenever there is a vacancy in the office of the Vice President, the President shall nominate a Vice President who shall take the office upon confirmation by a majority vote of both houses of Congress.

SECTION 3.

Whenever the President transmits to the president pro tempore of the Senate and the speaker of the House of Representatives his written declaration that he is unable to discharge the powers and duties of his office, and until he transmits to them a written declaration to the contrary, such powers and duties shall be discharged by the Vice President as Acting President.

SECTION 4.

Whenever the Vice President and a majority of either the principal officers of the executive departments or of such other body as Congress may by law provide, transmit to the president pro tempore of the Senate and the speaker of the House of Representatives their written declaration that the President is unable to discharge the powers and duties of his office, the Vice President shall immediately assume the powers and duties of the office as Acting President.

Thereafter, when the President transmits to the president pro tempore of the Senate and the speaker of the House of Representatives his written declaration that no inability exists, he shall resume the powers and duties of his office unless the Vice President and a majority of either the principal officers of the executive department or of such other body as Congress may by law provide, transmit within four days to the president pro tempore of the Senate and the speaker of the House of Representatives their written declaration that the President is unable to discharge the powers and duties of his office. Thereupon Congress shall decide the issue, assembling within 48 hours for that purpose if not in session. If the Congress, within 21 days after receipt of the latter written declaration, or, if Congress is not in session, within 21 days after Congress is required to assemble, determines by two-thirds vote of both houses that the President is unable to discharge the powers and duties of his office, the Vice President shall continue to discharge the same as Acting President; otherwise, the President shall resume the powers and duties of his office.

TWENTY-SIXTH AMENDMENT—1971

SECTION 1.

The right of citizens of the United States, who are eighteen years of age or older, to vote shall not be denied or abridged by the United States or by any State on account of age.

SECTION 2.

The Congress shall have power to enforce this article by appropriate legislation.

Eighteen made voting age. For the past 30 years the nation had been drafting young men below the age of twenty-one and sending them to war. Rarely were they allowed to vote. That, in addition to the fact that modern communications have resulted in a more knowledgeable and better educated group of under-21's, brought strong support for Amend. 26.

Glossary

abandoned property Property that has been given up by an owner who has no intention of ever claiming it again.

abandonment In divorce law, the purposeful leaving of one's husband or wife without intending to return.

acceptance Voluntary agreement to the offer and terms of a contract that makes that contract binding.

acquittal The setting free by court decision of someone from a charge or an accusation of an offense.

administrative law Rules, regulations, and policies carrying the force of law and made by a commission or agency established by legislation.

administrator A person who has the legal authority to manage, settle, or dispose of the estate of a dead person, a minor, an insane person, or any legally incompetent person.

adverse possession The use of property for a certain length of time by someone who is not the true owner but behaves as if he/she is. In such cases, if the true owner does not exercise his/her ownership rights within that period, the law allows the user, or adverse possessor, to become the true owner.

agent Someone authorized by another person to act for him/her.

aggressor One who starts an attack or a quarrel.

alien A foreign-born person who is not a citizen of the country in which he/she lives.

alternate juror A person selected to replace a juror who cannot continue to serve on a particular jury.

answer In a pleading, a response to a plaintiff's complaint. All allegations, or charges, must have a response.

appeal A legal proceeding by which a case is brought from a lower to a higher court for rehearing.

appellant A person who appeals the decision of a lower court to a higher court for review.

appellate court A court that does not hear the original trying of a case; cases are appealed to it from a lower court.

appellee The party who argues in an appealed case against the setting aside of the decisions of the lower court; the party at whom the attack or appeal is aimed.

arraign To call a person into court to answer an indictment.

arrest warrant A written order by a court or other proper authority directing the arrest of a certain person or persons.

arson The malicious burning of a house or building.

assault An unlawful, deliberate threat to use force or attempt to physically harm someone.

bail A sum of money or a bond given to a court to guarantee the appearance of a prisoner at his/her trial in order to obtain that prisoner's release from jail.

bailee A person who holds the goods of another for a specific purpose agreed upon by the two persons.

bailment The act of placing goods in trust by one person with another for a specified purpose upon the understanding that the goods will be returned when that purpose is accomplished.

battery The actual and unlawful use of force by one person on another.

beyond a reasonable doubt The degree of certainty that a juror must have in his/her own mind about the guilt of a criminal defendant. It means the evidence must be so complete and conclusive that all doubts are removed.

bilateral contract An agreement in which mutual promises have been exchanged, creating a legally binding contract between the parties.

bill of indictment A formal written accusation placed before the grand jury by the public prosecuting attorney. The purpose of the indictment is to allow the grand jury to decide if someone should be tried for a crime.

binding agreement The strict legal responsibility of the parties to a contract to keep the terms of that contract or agreement.

breach of contract The failure by a party to an agreement to perform any or all of the terms of the agreement for which he/she is legally responsible.

breach of the peace Unlawful disturbance of the public peace and quiet.

brief A written argument or summary of a case.

building code Laws passed by local legislatures that place restrictions on the way in which a building may be constructed and set standards for the quality of materials used.

burden of proof The obligation to prove the truth of disputed fact(s) related to a case being tried before a court.

burgess An elected representative of the legislature of colonial Virginia.

capital crime A criminal offense punishable by death.

challenge To dispute, to question the legality, to defy.

churchman Historically, a church official or member of a religious order.

citation A reference to a source of (legal) authority.

cite To refer to, mention, name, or quote.

citizen's arrest In certain circumstances, the legally acceptable arrest of another person by someone other than a duly sworn peace officer.

civil government A political body formed with the power to make laws and regulations to ensure the orderly functioning of society.

civil law The system of law based on written statutes or codes rather than on court decisions. The term is also used to show that no criminal act or law is involved.

civil suit A lawsuit brought by a private individual or group to recover money or property or to enforce or protect a civil right.

clerk of the court A person employed by a court to keep records, schedule hearings and notify the parties, and perform many other duties depending on the activities of the court.

code book of law A book that contains an organized statement of laws, rules, or principles.

commercial zoning Local laws allowing business offices, stores, and apartment buildings to be built in certain areas of a town or city.

commissioner A representative of some level or unit of government. This person has both judicial and administrative powers.

common law The system of law based on court decisions instead of laws passed by a legislature or similar body.

compensation Amends made through payment of money to someone for loss or injury suffered by him/her.

complaint A formal accusation or charge brought against a person.

complete compliance The fulfilling of the terms of a contract in every respect or detail by a party to that contract.

condemnation of property The declaring by government that certain buildings are unfit for use in their present state and should be torn down. The owners deprived of their property as a result are to be compensated by the government.

confront witness To challenge the testimony of a witness.

congressional committees Members of Congress formed into temporary groups to investigate matters of national concern; also, permanent committees to pass on legislation that will be presented to the House or Senate.

consideration Something of value given in return for a performance or promise of performance by another for the purpose of forming a contract.

consumer goods Commercial products or things that satisfy people's wants.

contempt of court Lack of respect for the dignity or authority of the court or interference with its orderly administration of justice.

contract A promise or set of promises for which one is legally responsible.

copyright The legal protection of the works of artists and authors giving them the exclusive right to publish their works or to decide who may publish them.

corrections Whatever punishment or treatment the court imposes on convicted persons.

counsel Lawyer employed or appointed to represent and advise someone in legal matters.

counterclaim A claim by a defendant in response to a complaint; the purpose is to defeat that complaint.

county clerk An elected official of the county government who may be in charge of keeping property records, overseeing elections, and issuing certain licenses.

court action A legal proceeding brought by someone seeking judgment against another for a claimed wrong or injury.

court costs The amount of money spent by a party to a law suit for such things as filing fees or jury fee.

court reporter A person who is authorized to record court proceedings as they occur.

credit card A card, issued by a bank, special company, or store, that entitles the holder to buy goods on credit rather than by paying cash.

criminal law The aspect of law dealing with an act that a government has determined to be injurious to the public and for which the offender should be prosecuted.

cross-examination The questioning of a witness by the party against whom the witness was called, to test the truthfulness of that witness's testimony.

curfew A regulation, issued by a public authority, ordering persons to keep off the streets between certain hours; also, sometimes a condition of parole or probation.

customary law A body of unwritten, longstanding practices that regulated social life among early peoples.

damages Loss or harm resulting from injury; money awarded by the courts to someone who has suffered loss or harm.

default The failure to perform a duty that one is legally bound to perform.

defendant The party being sued or charged in a court of law.

deport To send an alien back to the country from which he/she came when the presence of that person is considered undesirable.

deposition A written record of the testimony of a witness given under oath.

deputy A person appointed as a substitute with power to act; an assistant who takes charge when his/her superior is absent.

descent and distribution The inheritance of property from a person who has died without leaving a will. The manner of distributing the property is fixed by state law.

desertion In divorce law, leaving one's husband or wife without that person's consent and giving up all responsibilities and duties toward that person.

determination A court decision settling or ending a legal dispute.

directed verdict Where the evidence is so much in favor of one person that the judge directs the jury to make a certain decision or verdict.

discovery A method by which opposing parties in a legal proceeding obtain information from one another by asking questions, examining documents, etc. The purpose is to establish before going to trial what issues or points are in dispute.

disqualify To make unfit; to take away a power, right, or privilege.

dissenting opinion Formal opinion, by one or more judges of an appeals court, that disagrees with the disposition made of a case by the court, with the facts or law on the basis of which the court arrived at its decision, and/or with the principles of law announced by the court in deciding the case.

district attorney The prosecuting officer of a judicial district.

double jeopardy Trial of a person for a second time for the same crime in the same jurisdiction. The Fifth and Fourteenth Amendments make such a trial unlawful unless there is an appeal from a conviction.

due care Standard or acceptable amount of care or legal duty one reasonable person owes another person.

due process of law The constitutional procedures and rights granted to an accused that must be followed before his/her life, liberty, or property can be taken away.

ealdorman In Anglo-Saxon England, chief officer in shire, or county, appointed by the king.

eminent domain The right of Congress to take private property for public use without the owner's consent. The Fifth Amendment requires that "just compensation" be made in such cases.

English Parliament The lawmaking body of England (the United Kingdom).

escheat The reverting of property to the state when there is no one else to legally inherit it.

evidence Anything submitted to a court—testimony of witnesses, documents, objects, etc.—by which the truth of the matter at issue may be determined.

express contract A directly and clearly stated agreement containing all the elements necessary for a good contract.

extradite To deliver from one state a person accused or convicted of a crime to the government of the state in which the crime was committed.

false imprisonment The unlawful use of threat or force by one person to restrain or detain another.

fee simple In the feudal system, the holding of land in exchange for a fixed yearly rent and an oath of loyalty to the person from whom the land was held. Today, fee simple in the United States is the most complete kind of land ownership.

felony A serious crime punishable by a fine and a prison sentence of over one year or by such a prison sentence alone.

feudalism Political system, existing in Europe between the ninth and fifteenth centuries, in which service and loyalty were given in exchange for land and protection. Vassals, or servants, were under the protection of feudal lords, or nobles.

fief A feudal estate given by the king to a lord and over which the lord had certain rights.

franchise Freedom, right, or privilege.

fraud Cheating.

freeholder At the breaking up of the feudal system, a person who held land in return for a yearly rent paid to the landlord.

fresh pursuit The common-law right of a police officer chasing a suspected felon to cross a state line in order to make an arrest.

fundamental maxim A basic and accepted general truth or principle.

goodwill In business, the favor or good reputation a store has established that is beyond the mere value of what it sells.

grand jury A group of persons legally chosen to hear the charges and evidence against someone accused of a crime and to decide whether or not that person should stand trial.

grounds The basis, or cause, for a legal action.

guild An association of people with similar interests or jobs.

hazardous act A dangerous act that may result in harm or damage to person or property.

heir One who inherits or is entitled to inherit a title or property.

hung jury A jury that cannot reach a verdict.

immunity Freedom from, or protection against, penalty.

impartial Not showing favor of one above another.

implied contract A contract in which the parties by their acts or conduct indicate an agreement; a contract that is not directly expressed.

importation tax A charge imposed by the government for bringing certain goods into this country from another country.

incriminate To hold someone responsible for a crime; to imply guilt; to expose someone else to a charge of crime.

indictment by grand jury A formal or written charge, presented by a grand jury to the court, on the basis of which an accused person is brought to trial.

indigent A person without money or property.

industrial zoning Local laws allowing factories and plants to be built in certain areas of a town or city.

infidelity In divorce law, the unfaithfulness of a man to his wife or of a woman to her husband.

information Evidence gathered by the police or prosecutor that is the basis for formally accusing someone of a crime. The grand jury is not involved in the matter.

inherit To receive something by right or legal title from an ancestor at his/her death.

intentional torts Acts of willful or deliberate aggression, committed with intent to injure someone, to damage his/her property, or to cause emotional distress.

interstate commerce Business or trade between two or more states or their citizens.

intestate The state or condition of dying without leaving a will.

invitation A request made by one person to another to become a party to a contract; it does not constitute a formal offer and cannot be part of a valid contract.

invitee A person who has been invited to another's property for business purposes.

irrelevant Not directly connected or related to the matter, topic, or issue being discussed.

issue In a trial, a matter that is in dispute between two parties.

joint tort-feasors Two or more persons legally responsible for a single injury to another.

judicial procedures The methods or rules by which justice is carried out within the legal system.

judicial system The established and organized process and procedures that deal with the administration of justice.

jurisdiction The legal authority of a court to try a case; power of those in authority.

jury In a trial, a group of people legally chosen and sworn to inquire into the facts of a case and to give their decision according to the evidence.

jury commission A group of persons responsible for keeping an up-to-date list of prospective jurors.

jury panel A group of persons, qualified to be jurors, from which a petit jury is selected.

jury roll The list of names of persons eligible to serve on a jury.

justice of the peace A judge who has limited powers and duties and presides over a court with limited jurisdiction.

juvenile court A court that handles charges against children under a certain age only, usually in an informal and nonpublic manner.

kinship A relationship based on blood ties rather than on marriage.

lawsuit A case before a court of law in which someone seeks justice for a claimed wrong or injury.

lease A legal agreement giving one person (lessee) the right to use the property of another (lessor, or landlord) for a certain period of time and for a consideration commonly called rent.

lessor A landlord; the person who owns and leases property to a tenant, or lessee.

liable Legally responsible.

libel A written statement or picture that damages a person's reputation.

licensee A person permitted to go onto another's property merely for his/her interest, pleasure, or convenience; a person whose presence is not invited, but tolerated. Also, a person who possesses a license.

lobby A group of persons who try to influence legislators, usually to pass certain laws.

lobbying Conducting activities aimed at influencing legislators.

lord A man of high position or rank.

lost property Property that the owner has given up without intending to do so.

magistrate The judge of a court that has limited authority.

majority decision A judgment or decision arrived at by a majority of the judges reviewing a particular case.

manor In the Middle Ages, a large piece of land, held by a lord who had a number of rights over the land and the people who lived on it.

manslaughter The unlawful taking of a life without malice, voluntarily or involuntarily. Examples are crimes of passion and accidents that result from criminal carelessness.

meeting of the minds A clear understanding by both parties to a contract of exactly what exchange is meant in the agreement.

mental anguish Injury that includes all forms of mental pain for which a person may be legally compensated. Examples are deep grief, distress, anxiety, and fright.

minor A person who is under the age at which he/she may exercise certain civil and personal rights.

misdemeanor An offense, less serious than a felony, that is punishable by a fine and/or imprisonment of less than a year.

moral obligation A debt or responsibility that one feels bound to honor because of conscience or duty.

murder in the first degree The deliberate, planned killing of someone; the killing of someone during the commission of a serious offense.

murder in the second degree The malicious killing of someone, without deliberate planning.

naturalize To admit to citizenship.

neglect In divorce law, the ignoring of responsibilities and duties.

negligent act An action in which there is failure to use reasonable care to avoid injury to oneself or others.

next of kin Person or persons most closely related to another person by blood; also, in the distribution of an estate after an intestate owner's death, those with a legal right under state laws to share in that estate.

notary public A public official who has the authority to administer oaths and certify contracts and other documents.

nuisance act An act that endangers the general welfare, offends the senses, violates the laws of decency, or interferes with the comfortable use of another person's property. A public nuisance offends the general public or a large section of it. A private nuisance offends only a particular person or persons.

offer A statement of intention to make a contract expressed by one party to another.

ordinance An order or a law of a city or town.

parole Under certain conditions, the releasing of a convicted criminal before the entire sentence has been served, the parolee to remain under supervision of the parole authority.

parole officer An officer appointed to supervise and report on a convicted criminal who is released on parole from prison.

patent A grant of exclusive right to an inventor, for a certain period of time, to make, use, and sell his/her invention.

peasant One of an independent class of farmers, farm laborers, or small landowners.

penalty The punishment set by law for the commission of some offense; the sum of money fixed by law to be paid as a punishment for the nonperformance of a contract.

personal property A person's movable possessions; examples are furniture and clothes. Also, trademarks, copyrights, patents, and goodwill of a business.

petit jury A group of persons, usually twelve in number, sworn to decide on the facts of a case being tried.

petition A written request for action or relief.

plaintiff A person who brings a lawsuit.

plea The answer of the accused, to the charge made against him/her, as "Guilty" or "Not guilty".

plea bargaining The process by which the accused, the defense attorney, and the prosecutor bargain for the dismissal of some charge in exchange for a plea of guilty to another (usually lesser) charge.

pleadings Written documents filed by a plaintiff or a defendant in a legal action. The plaintiff's complaint and the defendant's answer are called pleadings.

pleas of the Crown Certain crimes that English kings claimed had to be tried in the royal courts. Some examples would be breaking the king's peace, treason, harboring outlaws, and housebreaking.

precedent A court decision that sets an example to be followed in deciding similar cases.

prejudice To injure or damage by some opinion or action; to make someone turn against another.

presenting jury In Norman England, the group of accusers who brought charges against a person.

probable cause Reasonable cause; the existence of sufficient facts and circumstances to cause a reasonable person to believe a crime has been committed.

probate court A special court that reviews the will of a dead person to make sure it is legally acceptable and supervises the handling of the estates of persons who died with or without leaving a will.

probation The suspension of the sentence of a convicted offender, giving him/her freedom on the promise of good behavior and under the supervision of a probation officer.

probation officer An officer appointed to aid, supervise, and report on a convicted offender who is on probation.

prosecution The act or process of bringing a suit against, seeking to enforce by legal process; the act of beginning and carrying on a legal proceeding.

quarantine To prevent the movement of people, animals, plants, or goods in order to keep them from spreading disease or pests.

quiet enjoyment The right of a person who leases property to use and enjoy it without being disturbed or troubled.

quit rent After the breaking up of the feudal system, the fixed yearly rent paid by landholders in fee simple.

real estate agent A person who buys, sells, or rents property in behalf of another person for a fee.

real property Land, and generally whatever is permanently attached to it. Examples are buildings, trees, minerals, water, and oil. Real property is also called real estate.

reformatory school A penal institution to which young offenders may be sent for training and rehabilitation.

rehabilitate To improve the behavior of a convicted offender in order to return him/her to useful and constructive activity in the community.

relevant Having direct connection to a particular matter, topic, or issue–usually a court case.

remand To send a case back to a lower court for further action.

residential zoning Local laws allowing single and/or double family dwellings to be built in certain parts of a town or city.

restrict To limit or place under special rules.

right of curtesy The legal right of a man to a share of his dead wife's real property during his lifetime.

right of dower The legal right of a wife to use and financially benefit from her dead husband's real property for her lifetime.

search warrant A written order by a judge directing that certain places or persons be searched in order to seize particular items for use as evidence in a court trial.

security Something of value left with someone as a guarantee of payment of a debt.

seditious libel In English law, the publishing of statements with the intent of causing antigovernment feeling.

self-defense The protection of oneself or one's family or property from assault or destructive violence.

self-incrimination Implying the guilt or wrongdoing of oneself.

serf In the Middle Ages, a member of a farming or laboring class of servant or slave status subject to the will of a lord.

shares of stock Shares in the ownership of a corporation.

shilling Unit of money long used in England.

shire In Anglon-Saxon and Norman England, a division of land; a county.

shire reeve In Anglo Saxon and Norman England, a person appointed by the king to assist the ealdorman, or chief officer, of a county.

slander Spoken words of a false nature, tending to damage another's reputation.

small claims court A court in which civil suits involving relatively small sums of money are tried by a judge, usually without a jury. It is not necessary for either the party who is suing or the party being sued to have a lawyer in such a court.

smattering Superficial, or shallow, knowledge.

statute A law passed by a legislature.

statute of limitations A law that fixes the amount of time during which legal proceedings can be begun. The amount of time will vary with the type of action, the jurisdiction, and the circumstances of the case.

strict liability Legal responsibility for the injury or damage to person or property resulting from an activity that is by its very nature extremely dangerous. Examples are injuries caused by blasting, drilling, or tearing down buildings.

subpoena A written notice ordering a certain person to appear before the court to give testimony.

substantial compliance The fulfilling of the essential terms of a contract in accomplishing the purpose of that contract although certain minor details may remain uncompleted.

sue To seek judgment against someone by taking legal action against him/her in a court of law.

summons A written notice to a person that he/she must appear in court on a specified day.

suspended sentence A jail sentence that does not have to be served in jail if certain conditions are met.

temporary restraining order A court order whereby an action or a law will not be enforced or permitted until a full court hearing on the subject is held.

tenancy The temporary occupying or possessing of land or buildings owned by another person.

tenant A person who rents a house, an apartment, or an office and pays an agreed-upon sum of money to a landlord, or lessor.

tenant farmer In a feudal system, a farm laborer who held land owned by a lord in exchange for certain services.

testate The state or condition of leaving a will at one's death.

testator A person who makes a will.

testimony Spoken statements made under oath in a legal proceeding. For example, a witness *testifies* under oath.

tort A private or civil wrong done by one person against another. Some torts, such as assault, may also be crimes, which are offenses against the public at large or the state.

trademark A design or symbol that identifies the exclusive owner or manufacturer of an article.

trespass The unlawful act of entering another person's property without permission.

trespasser A person who comes onto the property of another without the owner's permission.

truancy Unreasonable absence from school.

unauthorized Not having legal or official approval.

unilateral contract A one-sided agreement in which only one of the parties makes a promise to do or not to do something in return for something performed by the other party.

valid contract A legally binding agreement that will be upheld by the courts.

violate To break a law, an oath, or an agreement; to badly offend or outrage.

violation The breaking or ignoring of rules, laws, oaths, or contracts.

voting districts Divisions of state, city, or county set up for purposes of voting.

witness A person called to testify under oath in a legal proceeding.

zoning laws Laws passed by local legislatures that determine what types of buildings (houses, stores, offices, factories) may be built in certain parts of a town or city.

Index

Photo Credits

PAGE	CREDIT
29	Culver Pictures, Inc.
30	Brown Brothers
33, 38	Culver Pictures, Inc.
42	Courtesy, The Essex Institute, Salem, Massachusetts
50	Library of Congress
53	Independence National Historical Park
60	Everett C. Johnson from DeWys, Inc.
184	Culver Pictures, Inc.
212	Historical Picture Service, Chicago

3 4 5 6 7 8 9 10—VH—90 89 88 87 86 85 84 83